History of Ideas on Woman

A Source Book

ROSEMARY AGONITO

A PERIGEE BOOK

A Perigee Book
Published by The Berkley Publishing Group
A division of Penguin Putnam Inc.
375 Hudson Street
New York, NY 10014

First edition: November 1978
ISBN: 0-399-11964-7 (hardcover)
ISBN: 0-399-50379-X (trade paperback)

The Penguin Putnam Inc. World Wide Web site address is
http://www.penguinputnam.com

Library of Congress Cataloging
Card Number: 77-087122

Printed in the United States of America

15   16   17   18   19   20   21   22   23   24

To my mother
Filomena Giambattista

Acknowledgments

Selections from Aristotle's "De Generatione Animalium," translated by Arthur Platt, and "Historia Animalium," translated by D'Arcy Thompson, are reprinted by permission of the Oxford University Press.

Selection from Thomas Aquinas' *Summa Theologica*, translated by the Fathers of the English Dominican Province, is reprinted by permission of Benziger Bruce & Glencoe, Inc.

Selection from Jean Jacques Rousseau's "Discourse on Political Economy," translated by G. D. H. Cole, in *The Social Contract and Discourses*, Everyman's Library Edition, is reprinted by permission of J. M. Dent & Sons, Ltd. and E. P. Dutton & Co., Inc.

Selection from Immanuel Kant's *Observations on the Feeling of the Beautiful and the Sublime*, translated by John T. Goldthwait, Copyright © 1960 by the Regents of the University of California, is reprinted by permission of the University of California Press.

Selection from Georg Hegel's *The Philosophy of Right*, translated by S. W. Dyde, is reprinted by permission of George Bell & Sons, Ltd.

Preface

Despite a burgeoning body of materials in virtually all areas of Women's Studies, there continues to exist no single collection of primary sources in the history of ideas on Woman. This book is designed to fill that gap by presenting the most significant and representative thinking in the history of Western civilization on all aspects of the Woman Question. By providing ready access to materials from different historical periods, the book will meet the needs of a variety of disciplines concerned with Women's Studies. The selections provide primary source readings not only for a wide range of courses within Women's Studies programs as such, but also for courses in history, philosophy, political theory, and psychology that deal with the Woman Question. In addition, this collection of writings by many of the most important thinkers in the Western tradition may serve as a supplementary text for more generalized courses in Western civilization, intellectual history, humanities, history of philosophy, political theory, and social sciences, among others. For persons doing research in Women's

Studies the book offers access to much-needed primary sources that have been, up to this point, widely scattered and difficult to come by.

The order of the readings is roughly chronological, although minor liberties have been taken with the sequence in order to preserve the connections within periods such as the Greek and the early Christian periods. The particular selections have been chosen not only because of their influence in the developing history of thought on woman, but because they reflect the issues and thinking that are representative of their various periods.

I am indebted to my colleagues in the Society for Women in Philosophy for many stimulating and rigorous discussions on the conceptual aspects of Women's Studies. I am especially grateful to Professor Sandra Harding for her advice concerning the book and to Professor James Campbell, my colleague at Eisenhower College, for his active interest in the area. For their help in preparing the manuscript, my thanks to Ms. Jeanne Coleates, Ms. Edna Estrachan, and Ms. Lavonne Calabrese. Finally, I owe much to my husband, Joseph, for his continuing assistance and to Gian Carlo and Mae Lee.

Rosemary Agonito
Eisenhower College

Contents

13 / Contents

Genesis

The Judaic biblical account of the origin of the human race preserves its ancient oral sources in two conflicting stories, one written down during the tenth century B.C., the other during the sixth century B.C. The later story, which appears first in the text, makes no distinction between man and woman: both are created in the divine image and both are subject to the same injunctions regarding their functions in life. However, the other creation story, with its account of man's downfall, is better-known and has historically been more influential. Consistent with the well-entrenched Hebrew patriarchal culture, it originally provided the etiological prop for a tradition in which the father was the undisputed head of the household and the women lived rigidly circumscribed lives. In biblical times a Jewish wife, who was sometimes one of many, could be put away at the wish of her husband. Virginity upon marriage was strictly required, and she might be stoned if found to be adulterous. Confined to domestic chores, which afforded her little rest, she was expected to work hard. At the same time woman was associated with religious taboos, was considered ceremonially unclean, and had no standing before the law. By virtue of her secondary creation, that is, of the merely derivative character of her existence described in the earlier Genesis account, woman could justifiably be considered naturally inferior and subordinate to man. Created out of man and for man, to relieve his loneliness and to help him, woman is shown to be responsible also for man's troubles, not the least of which is his loss of immortality. In the male-oriented religion of the Jews and later of the Christians, these concepts of woman's inferiority and troublesomeness became entrenched in Western tradition, remaining virtually impregnable into the twentieth century.

THE CREATION AND FALL
OF MAN AND WOMAN*

And God said, Let us make man in our image, after our likeness: and let them have dominion over the fish of the sea, and over the fowl of the air, and over the cattle, and over all the earth, and over every creeping thing that creepeth upon the earth.

So God created man in his own image, in the image of God created he him; male and female created he them.

And God blessed them, and God said unto them, Be fruitful and multiply, and replenish the earth, and subdue it: and have dominion over the fish of the sea, and over the fowl of the air, and over every living thing that moveth upon the earth. . . .

And the Lord God formed man out of the dust of the ground, and breathed into his nostrils the breath of life; and man became a living soul.

And the Lord God planted a garden eastward in Eden; and there he put man whom he had formed.

* From Genesis 1:26-27; 2:7-9, 15-25; 3:1-20, King James Version.

And out of the ground made the Lord God to grow every tree that is pleasant to the sight, and good for food; the tree of life also in the midst of the garden and the tree of knowledge of good and evil. . . .

And the Lord God took the man, and put him into the garden of Eden to dress it and to keep it.

And the Lord God commanded the man, saying, Of every tree of the garden thou mayest freely eat:

But of the tree of the knowledge of good and evil, thou shalt not eat of it: for in the day that thou eatest thereof thou shalt surely die.

And the Lord God said, It is not good that the man should be alone; I will make an help meet for him.

And out of the ground the Lord God formed every beast of the field, and every fowl of the air; and brought them unto Adam to see what he would call them: and whatsoever Adam called every living creature, that was the name thereof.

And Adam gave names to all cattle, and to the fowl of the air, and to every beast of the field; but for Adam there was not found an help meet for him.

And the Lord God caused a deep sleep to fall upon Adam, and he slept: and he took one of his ribs, and closed up the flesh instead thereof;

And the rib, which the Lord God had taken from man, made he a woman, and brought her unto the man.

And Adam said, This is now bone of my bones, and flesh of my flesh: she shall be called Woman, because she was taken out of Man.

Therefore shall a man leave his father and his mother, and shall cleave unto his wife: and they shall be one flesh.

And they were both naked, the man and his wife, and were not ashamed.

Now the serpent was more subtil than any beast of the field which the Lord God had made. And he said unto the woman, Yea, hath God said, Ye shall not eat of every tree of the garden?

And the woman said unto the serpent, We may eat of the fruit of the trees of the garden:

But of the fruit of the tree which is in the midst of the garden, God hath said, Ye shall not eat of it, neither shall ye touch it, lest ye die.

And the serpent said unto the woman, Ye shall not surely die:

For God doth know that in the day ye eat thereof, then your eyes shall be opened, and ye shall be as gods, knowing good and evil.

And when the woman saw that the tree was good for food, and that it was pleasant to the eyes, and a tree to be desired to make one wise, she took of the fruit thereof, and did eat, and gave also unto her husband with her; and he did eat.

And the eyes of them both were opened and they knew that they were naked; and they sewed fig leaves together, and made themselves aprons.

And they heard the voice of the Lord God walking in the garden in the cool of the day: and Adam and his wife hid themselves from the presence of the Lord God amongst the trees of the garden.

And the Lord God called unto Adam, and said unto him, Where art thou?

And he said, I heard thy voice in the garden, and I was afraid, because I was naked; and I hid myself.

And he said, Who told thee that thou wast naked? Hast thou eaten of the tree, whereof I commanded thee that thou shouldest not eat?

And the man said, The woman whom thou gavest to be with me, she gave me of the tree, and I did eat.

And the Lord God said unto the woman, What is this that thou hast done? And the woman said, The serpent beguiled me, and I did eat.

And the Lord God said unto the serpent, Because thou hast done this, thou art cursed above all cattle, and above every beast of the field: upon thy belly shalt thou go, and dust shalt thou eat all the days of thy life:

And I will put enmity between thee and the woman, and between thy seed and her seed; it shall bruise thy head, and thou shalt bruise his heel.

Unto the woman he said, I will greatly multiply thy sorrow and thy conception; in sorrow thou shalt bring forth children; and thy desire shall be to thy husband, and he shall rule over thee.

And unto Adam he said, Because thou hast hearkened unto the voice of thy wife, and hast eaten of the tree, of which I commanded thee, saying, Thou shalt not eat of it: cursed is the ground for thy sake; in sorrow shalt thou eat of it all the days of thy life;

Thorns also and thistles shall it bring forth to thee; and thou shalt eat the herb of the field;

In the sweat of thy face shalt thou eat bread, till thou return unto the ground; for out of it wast thou taken: for dust thou art, and unto dust shalt thou return.

And Adam called his wife's name Eve; because she was the mother of all living.

Plato

The status of women in Athens during the fourth and fifth centuries B.C. was little better than that of its slaves. Cut off from the duties and rewards of citizenship and confined to the home, a respectable woman led a life consisting of an endless round of domestic trivia periodically interrupted by the birth of children. A girl was raised for marriage, an institution designed to ensure legitimate heirs for men. She could look forward to spending her life serving a man for whom she seldom had any genuine affection, since her father had arranged the marriage, and with whom she could not be truly a friend, since her inferior status and lack of education rendered her servile and uninteresting. In this context Plato wrote his revolutionary proposal for the best possible state, *The Republic*. His views on women were startlingly unconventional and, ironically, are still so over 2,500 years later. In *The Republic* Socrates, whom we assume represents Plato's viewpoints, expresses the astonishing belief that the present status of women is a perversion of nature and a waste of the resources of half the population. He argues that there is nothing inherent in woman's nature to prevent her engaging in the social functions of the citizen, including those of the Philosopher King, who is equipped to rule by virtue of wisdom. Wanting to bring women fully into the life of the state for the ultimate benefit of society, Socrates recognizes that this will never happen if women are continually burdened by domestic chores. Thus emerges his most radical proposal calling for the abolition of the nuclear family among certain groups and the promotion of society itself as a family in which divisive interests are eliminated. Socrates, who begins the discussion here, is arguing with his student Glaucon.

WOMEN AS EQUAL TO MEN
IN THE STATE *

Well, I replied, I suppose that I must retrace my steps and say what I perhaps ought to have said before in the proper place. The part of the men has been played out, and now properly enough comes the turn of the women. Of them I will proceed to speak, and the more readily since I am invited by you.

For men born and educated like our citizens, the only way, in my opinion, of arriving at a right conclusion about the possession and use of women and children is to follow the path on which we originally started, when we said that the men were to be the guardians and watchdogs of the herd.

True.

Let us further suppose the birth and education of our women to be subject to similar or nearly similar regulations; then we shall see whether the result accords with our design.

* From Plato, *The Republic,* in *The Dialogues of Plato,* trans. Benjamin Jowett, 3rd ed. (Oxford: Clarendon Press, 1892), Vol. 3, B. 5.

What do you mean?

What I mean may be put into the form of a question, I said: Are dogs divided into hes and shes, or do they both share equally in hunting and in keeping watch and in the other duties of dogs? or do we entrust to the males the entire and exclusive care of the flocks, while we leave the females at homes, under the idea that the bearing and suckling their puppies is labour enough for them?

No, he said, they share alike; the only difference between them is that the males are stronger and the females weaker.

But can you use different animals for the same purpose, unless they are bred and fed in the same way?

You cannot.

Then, if women are to have the same duties as men, they must have the same nurture and education?

Yes.

The education which was assigned to the men was music and gymnastic.

Yes.

Then women must be taught music and gymnastic and also the art of war, which they must practise like the men?

That is the inference, I suppose.

I should rather expect, I said, that several of our proposals, if they are carried out, being unusual, may appear ridiculous.

No doubt of it.

Yes, and the most ridiculous thing of all will be the sight of women naked in the palaestra, exercising with the men, especially when they are no longer young; they certainly will not be a vision of beauty, any more than the enthusiastic old men who in spite of wrinkles and ugliness continue to frequent the gymnasia.

Yes, indeed, he said: according to present notions the proposal would be thought ridiculous.

But then, I said, as we have determined to speak our minds, we must not fear the jests of the wits which will be directed against this sort of innovation; how they will talk of women's attainments both in music and gymnastic, and above all about their wearing armour and riding upon horseback!

Very true, he replied.

Yet having begun we must go forward to the rough places of the law; at the same time begging of these gentlemen for once in their life to be serious. Not long ago, as we shall remind them, the Hellenes were of the opinion, which is still generally received among the barbarians, that the sight of a naked man was ridiculous and improper; and when first the Cretans and then the Lacedaemonians introduced the custom, the wits of that day might equally have ridiculed the innovation.

No doubt.

But when experience showed that to let all things be uncovered was far better than to cover them up, and the ludicrous effect to the outward eye vanished before the better principle which reason asserted, then the man was perceived to be a fool who directs the shafts of his ridicule at any other sight but that of folly and vice, or seriously inclines to weigh the beautiful by any other standard but that of the good.

Very true, he replied.

First, then, whether the question is to be put in jest or in earnest, let us come to an understanding about the nature of woman: Is she capable of sharing either wholly or partially in the actions of men, or not at all? And is the art of war one of those arts in which she can or can not share? That will be the best way of commencing the enquiry, and will probably lead to the fairest conclusion.

That will be much the best way.

Shall we take the other side first and begin by arguing against ourselves; in this manner the adversary's position will not be undefended.

Why not? he said.

Then let us put a speech into the mouths of our opponents. They will say: "Socrates and Glaucon, no adversary need convict you, for you yourselves, at the first foundation of the State, admitted the principle that everybody was to do the work suited to his own nature." And certainly, if I am not mistaken, such an admission was made by us. "And do not the natures of men and women differ very much indeed?" And we shall reply: Of course they do. Then we shall be asked, "Whether the tasks assigned to men and to women should not be different, and such as are agreeable to their different natures?" Certainly they should. "But if so, have you not fallen into a serious inconsistency in saying that men and women, whose natures are so entirely different, ought to perform the same actions?"—What defence will you make for us, my good Sir, against any one who offers these objections?

That is not an easy question to answer when asked suddenly; and I shall and I do beg of you to draw out the case on our side.

These are the objections, Glaucon, and there are many others of a like kind, which I foresaw long ago; they made me afraid and reluctant to take in hand any law about the possession and nurture of women and children.

By Zeus, he said, the problem to be solved is anything but easy.

Why yes, I said, but the fact is that when a man is out of his depth, whether he has fallen into a little swimming bath or into mid-ocean, he has to swim all the same.

Very true.

And must not we swim and try to reach the shore: we will hope that Arion's dolphin or some other miraculous help may save us?

I suppose so, he said.

Well then, let us see if any way of escape can be found. We acknowledged—did we not? that different natures ought to have different pursuits, and that men's and women's natures are different. And now what are we saying?—that different natures ought to have the same pursuits,—this is the inconsistency which is charged upon us.

Precisely.

Verily, Glaucon, I said, glorious is the power of the art of contradiction!

Why do you say so?

Because I think that many a man falls into the practice against his will. When he thinks that he is reasoning he is really disputing, just because he cannot define and divide, and so know that of what he is speaking; and he will pursue a merely verbal opposition in the spirit of contention and not of fair discussion.

Yes, he replied, such is very often the case; but what has that to do with us and our argument?

A great deal; for there is certainly a danger of our getting unintentionally into a verbal opposition.

In what way?

Why, we valiantly and pugnaciously insist upon the verbal truth, that different natures ought to have different pursuits, but we never considered at all what was the meaning of sameness or difference of nature, or why we distinguished them when we assigned different pursuits to different natures and the same to the same natures.

Why, no, he said, that was never considered by us.

I said: Suppose that by way of illustration we were to ask the question whether there is not an opposition in nature between bald men and hairy men; and if this is admitted by us, then, if bald men are cobblers, we should forbid the hairy men to be cobblers, and conversely?

That would be a jest, he said.

Yes, I said, a jest; and why? because we never meant when we constructed the State, that the opposition of natures should extend to every difference, but only to those differences which affected the pursuit in which the individual is engaged; we should have argued, for example, that a physician and one who is in mind a physician may be said to have the same nature.

True.

Whereas the physician and the carpenter have different natures?

Certainly.

And if, I said, the male and female sex appear to differ in their fitness for any art or pursuit, we should say that such pursuit or art ought to be assigned to one or the other of them; but if the difference consists only in women bearing and men begetting children, this does not amount to a proof that a woman differs from a man in respect of the sort of education she should receive; and we shall therefore continue to maintain that our guardians and their wives ought to have the same pursuits.

Very true, he said.

Next, we shall ask our opponent how, in reference to any of the pursuits or arts of civic life, the nature of a woman differs from that of a man?

That will be quite fair.

And perhaps he, like yourself, will reply that to give a sufficient answer on the instant is not easy; but after a little reflection there is no difficulty.

Yes, perhaps.

Suppose then that we invite him to accompany us in the argument, and then we may hope to show him that there is nothing peculiar in the constitution of women which would affect them in the administration of the State.

By all means.

Let us say to him: Come now, and we will ask you a question:— when you spoke of a nature gifted or not gifted in any respect, did you mean to say that one man will acquire a thing easily, another with difficulty; a little learning will lead the one to discover a great deal; whereas the other, after much study and application, no sooner learns than he forgets; or again, did you mean, that the one has a body which is a good servant to his mind, while the body of the other is a hindrance to him?—would not these be the sort of differences which distinguish the man gifted by nature from the one who is ungifted?

No one will deny that.

And can you mention any pursuit of mankind in which the male sex has not all these gifts and qualities in a higher degree than the female? Need I waste time in speaking of the art of weaving, and the management of pancakes and preserves, in which womenkind does really appear to be great, and in which for her to be beaten by a man is of all things the most absurd?

You are quite right, he replied, in maintaining the general

inferiority of the female sex: although many women are in many things superior to many men, yet on the whole what you say is true.

And if so, my friend, I said, there is no special faculty of administration in a state which a woman has because she is a woman, or which a man has by virtue of his sex, but the gifts of nature are alike diffused in both; all the pursuits of men are the pursuits of women also, but in all of them a woman is inferior to a man.

Very true.

Then are we to impose all our enactments on men and none of them on women?

That will never do.

One woman has a gift of healing, another not; one is a musician, and another has no music in her nature?

Very true.

And one woman has a turn for gymnastic and military exercises, and another is unwarlike and hates gymnastic?

Certainly.

And one woman is a philosopher, and another is an enemy of philosophy; one has spirit, and another is without spirit?

That is also true.

Then one woman will have the temper of a guardian, and another not. Was not the selection of the male guardians determined by differences of this sort?

Yes.

Men and women alike possess the qualities which make a guardian; they differ only in their comparative strength or weakness.

Obviously.

And those women who have such qualities are to be selected as the companions and colleagues of men who have similar qualities and whom they resemble in capacity and in character?

Very true.

And ought not the same natures to have the same pursuits?

They ought.

Then as we were saying before, there is nothing unnatural in assigning music and gymnastic to the wives of the guardians—to that point we come round again.

Certainly not.

The law which we then enacted was agreeable to nature, and therefore not an impossibility or mere aspiration; and the contrary practice, which prevails at present, is in reality a violation of nature.

That appears to be true.

We had to consider, first, whether our proposals were possible, and secondly whether they were the most beneficial?

Yes.

And the possibility has been acknowledged?

Yes.

The very great benefit has next to be established?

Quite so.

You will admit that the same education which makes a man a good guardian will make a woman a good guardian; for their original nature is the same?

Yes.

I should like to ask you a question.

What is it?

Would you say that all men are equal in excellence, or is one man better than another?

The latter.

And in the commonwealth which we were founding do you conceive the guardians who have been brought up on our model system to be more perfect men, or the cobblers whose education has been cobbling?

What a ridiculous question!

You have answered me, I replied: Well, and may we not further say that our guardians are the best of our citizens?

By far the best.

And will not their wives be the best women?

Yes, by far the best.

And can there be anything better for the interests of the State than that the men and women of a State should be as good as possible?

There can be nothing better.

And this is what the arts of music and gymnastic, when present in such manner as we have described, will accomplish?

Certainly.

Then we have made an enactment not only possible but in the highest degree beneficial to the State?

True.

Then let the wives of our guardians strip, for their virtue will be their robe, and let them share in the toils of war and the defence of their country; only in the distribution of labours the lighter are to be assigned to the women, who are the weaker natures, but in other respects their duties are to be the same. And as for the man who laughs at naked women exercising their bodies from the best of motives, in his laughter he is plucking "A fruit of unripe wisdom" and he himself is ignorant of what he is laughing at, or what he is about;—for that is, and ever will be, the best of sayings. *That the useful is the noble and the hurtful is the base.*

Very true.

Here, then, is one difficulty in our law about women, which we may say that we have now escaped; the wave has not swallowed us up alive for enacting that the guardians of either sex should have all their pursuits in common; to the utility and also to the possibility of this arrangement the consistency of the argument with itself bears witness.

Yes, that was a mighty wave which you have escaped.

Yes, I said, but a greater is coming; you will not think much of this when you see the next.

Go on; let me see.

The law, I said, which is the sequel of this and of all that has preceded, is to the following effect,—"that the wives of our guardians are to be common, and their children are to be common, and no parent is to know his own child, nor any child his parent."

Yes, he said, that is a much greater wave than the other; and the possibility as well as the utility of such a law are far more questionable.

I do not think, I said, that there can be any dispute about the very great utility of having wives and children in common; the possibility is quite another matter and will be very much disputed.

I think that a good many doubts may be raised about both.

You imply that the two questions must be combined, I replied. Now I meant that you should admit the utility; and in this way, as I thought, I should escape from one of them, and then there would remain only the possibility.

But that little attempt is detected, and therefore, you will please to give a defence of both.

Well, I said, I submit to my fate. Yet grant me a little favour: let me feast my mind with the dream as day dreamers are in the habit of feasting themselves when they are walking alone; for before they have discovered any means of effecting their wishes—that is a matter which never troubles them—they would rather not tire themselves by thinking about possibilities; but assuming that what they desire is already granted to them, they proceed with their plan, and delight in detailing what they mean to do when their wish has come true—that is a way which they have of not doing much good to a capacity which was never good for much. Now I myself am beginning to lose heart, and I should like, with your permission to pass over the question of possibility at present. Assuming therefore the possibility of the proposal, I shall now proceed to enquire how the rulers will carry out these arrangements, and I shall demonstrate that our plan, if executed, will be of the greatest benefit to the State and to the guardians. First of all, then, if you have no objection, I will endeavour with your help to consider the advantages of the measure; and hereafter the question of possibility.

I have no objection; proceed.

First, I think that if our rulers and their auxiliaries are to be worthy of the name which they bear, there must be willingness to obey in the one and the power of command in the other; the guardians must themselves obey the laws, and they must also imitate the spirit of them in any details which are entrusted to their care.

That is right, he said.

You, I said, who are their legislator, having selected the men, will now select the women and give them to them;—they must be as far as possible of like natures with them; and they must live in common houses and meet at common meals. None of them will have anything specially his or her own; they will be together, and will be brought up together, and will associate at gymnastic exercises. And so they will be drawn by a necessity of their natures to have intercourse with each other—necessity is not too strong a word, I think?

Yes, he said;—necessity, not geometrical, but another sort of necessity which lovers know, and which is far more convincing and constraining to the mass of mankind.

True, I said; and this, Glaucon, like all the rest, must proceed after an orderly fashion; in a city of the blessed, licentiousness is an unholy thing which the rulers will forbid.

Yes, he said, and it ought not to be permitted.

Then clearly the next thing will be to make matrimony sacred in the highest degree, and what is most beneficial will be deemed sacred?

Exactly.

And how can marriages be made most beneficial?—that is a question which I put to you, because I see in your house dogs for hunting, and of the nobler sort of birds not a few. Now, I beseech you, do tell me, have you ever attended to their pairing and breeding?

In what particulars?

Why, in the first place, although they are all of a good sort, are not some better than others?

True.

And do you breed from them all indifferently, or do you take care to breed from the best only?

From the best.

And do you take the oldest or the youngest, or only those of ripe age?

I choose only those of ripe age.

And if care was not taken in the breeding, your dogs and birds would greatly deteriorate?

Certainly.

And the same of horses and animals in general?

Undoubtedly.

Good heavens! my dear friend, I said, what consummate skill will our rulers need if the same principle holds of the human species!

Certainly, the same principle holds; but why does this involve any particular skill?

Because, I said, our rulers will often have to practise upon the body corporate with medicines. Now you know that when patients do not require medicines, but have only to be put under a regime, the inferior sort of practitioner is deemed to be good enough; but when medicine has to be given, then the doctor should be more of a man.

That is quite true, he said; but to what are you alluding?

I mean, I replied, that our rulers will find a considerable dose of falsehood and deceit necessary for the good of their subjects; we were saying that the use of all these things regarded as medicines might be of advantage.

And we were very right.

And this lawful use of them seems likely to be often needed in the regulations of marriages and births.

How so?

Why, I said, the principle has been already laid down that the best of either sex should be united with the best as often, and the inferior with the inferior, as seldom as possible; and that they should rear the offspring of the one sort of union, but not of the other, if the flock is to be maintained in first-rate condition. Now these goings on must be a secret which the rulers only know, or there will be a further danger of our herd, as the guardians may be termed, breaking out into rebellion.

Very true.

Had we not better appoint certain festivals at which we will bring together the brides and bridegrooms, and sacrifices will be offered and suitable hymeneal songs composed by our poets: the number of weddings is a matter which must be left to the discretion of the rulers, whose aim will be to preserve the average of population? There are many other things which they will have to consider, such as the effects of wars and diseases and any similar agencies, in order as far as this is possible to prevent the State from becoming either too large or too small.

Certainly, he replied.

We shall have to invent some ingenious kind of lots which the less worthy may draw on each occasion of our bringing them together, and then they will accuse their own ill-luck and not the rulers.

To be sure, he said.

And I think that our braver and better youth, besides their other honours and rewards, might have greater facilities of intercourse with women given them; their bravery will be a reason, and such fathers ought to have as many sons as possible.

True.

And the proper officers, whether male or female or both, for offices are to be held by women as well as by men—

Yes—

The proper officers will take the offspring of the good parents to the pen or fold, and there they will deposit them with certain nurses who dwell in a separate quarter; but the offspring of the inferior, or of the better when they chance to be deformed, will be put away in some mysterious, unknown place, as they should be.

Yes, he said, that must be done if the breed of the guardians is to be kept pure.

They will provide for their nurture, and will bring the mothers to the fold when they are full of milk, taking the greatest possible care that no mother recognizes her own child: and other wet-nurses may be engaged if more are required. Care will also be taken that the process of suckling shall not be protracted too long; and the mothers will have no getting up at night or other trouble, but will hand over all this sort of thing to the nurses and attendants.

You suppose the wives of our guardians to have a fine easy time of it when they are having children.

Why, said I, and so they ought. Let us, however, proceed with our scheme. We were saying that the parents should be in the prime of life?

Very true.

And what is the prime of life? May it not be defined as a period of about twenty years in a woman's life, and thirty in a man's?

Which years do you mean to include?

A woman, I said, at twenty years of age may begin to bear children to the State, and continue to bear them until forty; a man may begin at five-and-twenty, when he has passed the point at which the pulse of life beats quickest, and continue to beget children until he be fifty-five.

Certainly, he said, both in men and women those years are the prime of physical as well as of intellectual vigour. . . .

But would any of your guardians think or speak of any other guardian as a stranger?

Certainly he would not; for every one whom they meet will be regarded by them either as a brother or sister, or father or mother, or son or daughter, or as the child or parent of those who are thus connected with him.

Capital, I said; but let me ask you once more: Shall they be a family in name only; or shall they in all their actions be true to the name? For example, in the use of the word "father," would the care of a father be implied and the filial reverence and duty and obedience to him which the law commands; and is the violator of these duties to be regarded as an impious and unrighteous person who is not likely to receive much good either at the hands of God or of man? Are these to be or not to be the strains which the children will hear repeated in their ears by all the citizens about those who are intimated to them to be their parents and the rest of their kinsfolk?

These, he said, and none other; for what can be more ridiculous than for them to utter the names of family ties with the lips only and not to act in the spirit of them? . . .

Both the community of property and the community of families, as I am saying, tend to make them more truly guardians: they will not tear the city in pieces by differing about "mine" and "not mine"; each man dragging any acquisition which he has made into a separate house of his own, where he has a separate wife and children and private pleasures and pains; but all will be affected as far as may be by the same pleasures and pains because they are all of one opinion about what is near and dear to them, and therefore they all tend towards a common end.

Certainly, he replied. . . .

You agree then, I said, that men and women are to have a common way of life such as we have described—common education, common children; and they are to watch over the citizens in common whether abiding in the city or going out to war; they are to keep watch together, and to hunt together like dogs; and always and in all things, as far as they are able, women are to share with the men? And in so doing they will do what is best, and will not violate, but preserve the natural relation of the sexes.

Aristotle

Although a devoted student of Plato, Aristotle did not accept his teacher's views on women. He instead represented the orthodox Greek position, which he sought to justify by various means in his philosophical works. Of particular interest are his biological writings, especially "The Generation of Animals," which investigates the reproduction of life and the female's role in this, and his political work, *Politics,* which discusses woman's status in society. Although the dates of these works are disputed, they are believed to have been composed between 347 and 322 B.C. In essence Aristotle maintains that woman is a mutilated or incomplete man, a thesis that has enjoyed a long and persistent history culminating in Freud's theories about woman. Aristotle accepts the pre-Socratic notion that women are colder than men. Since he associates heat with life or soul, he therefore supposes women to have less soul than men. Moreover, because woman is deficient in vital heat, she is unable to "cook" to the point of purity her secretion (menstrual blood), which unites with a male's secretion (semen) to form a new human being. The male's contribution to generation is pure and hence more valuable than woman's, although both, of course, are necessary. Specifically, man contributes the form or essence of the embryo while woman merely provides the nutrition necessary to maintain it; that is, the male, not the female, creates human life. Ultimately, woman's deficiency, or lack of the male principle—sentient and rational soul—affect the bodily, intellectual, and social status of women for the worse. She is physically weaker, less capable of rational thought, and subordinate to the rule of men.

THE DIFFERENCES BETWEEN
MEN AND WOMEN*

Thus we shall make it clear (1) whether the female also produces semen like the male and the foetus is a single mixture of two semens, or whether no semen is secreted by the female, and, (2) if not, whether she contributes nothing else either to generation but only provides a receptacle, or whether she does contribute something, and, if so, how and in what manner she does so. . . .

On this subject, then, so much may be laid down. But since it is necessary (1) that the weaker animal also should have a secretion greater in quantity and less concocted, and (2) that being of such a nature it should be a mass of sanguineous liquid, and (3) since that which Nature endows with a smaller portion of heat is weaker, and (4) since it has already been stated that such is the character of the

* From Aristotle, "De Generatione Animalium," trans. Arthur Platt, in *The Oxford Translation of Aristotle*, ed. W.D. Ross (Oxford: Clarendon Press, 1912), Vol. 5, Bks. I, II; "Historia Animalium," trans. D'Arcy W. Thompson, in *O.T.A.* (1910), Vol. 4, Bk. IX; *Politics*, trans. Benjamin Jowett (Oxford: Clarendon Press, 1885), Bk. I.

sanguineous - containing blood

female—putting all these considerations together we see that the sanguineous matter discharged by the female is also a secretion. And such is the discharge of the so-called catamenia.   — menses

It is plain, then, that the catamenia are a secretion, and that they are analogous in females to the semen in males. . . .

Now a boy is like a woman in form, and the woman is as it were an impotent male, for it is through a certain incapacity that the female is female, being incapable of concocting the nutriment in its last stage into semen (and this is either blood or that which is analogous to it in animals which are bloodless owing to the coldness of their nature). As then diarrhoea is caused in the bowels by the insufficient concoction of the blood, so are caused in the blood-vessels all discharges of blood, including that of the catamenia, for this also is such a discharge, only it is natural whereas the others are morbid.   — caused by pertaining to disease - menses in normal in ♀

Thus it is clear that it is reasonable to suppose that generation comes from this. For the catamenia are semen not in a pure state but in need of working up, just as in the formation of fruits the nutriment is present, when it is not yet sifted thoroughly, but needs working up to purify it. Thus the catamenia cause generation by mixture with the semen. . . .

In all products of Nature or art, a thing is made by something actually existing out of that which is potentially such as the finished product. Now the semen is of such a nature, and has in it such a principle of motion, that when the motion is ceasing each of the parts comes into being, and that as a part having life or soul. . . .

Has the semen soul, or not? The same argument applies here as in the question concerning the parts. As no part, if it participate not in soul, will be a part except in an equivocal sense (as the eye of a dead man is still called an "eye"), so no soul will exist in anything except that of which it is soul; it is plain therefore that semen both has soul, and is soul, potentially. . . .

The next question to raise and to answer is this. If, in the case of those animals which emit semen into the female, that which enters makes no part of the resulting embryo, where is the material part of it diverted if (as we have seen) it acts by means of the power residing in it? It is not only necessary to decide whether what is forming in the female receives anything material, or not, from that which has entered her, but also concerning the soul in virtue of which an animal is so called (and this is in virtue of the sensitive part of the soul)—does this exist originally in the semen and in the unfertilized embryo or not, and if it does whence does it come? For nobody would put down the unfertilized embryo as soulless or in every sense bereft of life (since both the semen and the embryo of an animal have every bit as much life as a plant), and it is productive up to a certain point. That then they possess the nutritive soul is plain (and plain is it from the discussions elsewhere about soul why this soul must be acquired first). As they develop they also acquire the sensitive soul in virtue of which an animal is an animal. For e.g. an animal does not become at the same time an animal and a man or a horse or any other particular animal. For the end is developed last, and the peculiar character of the species is the end of the generation in each individual. Hence arises a question of the greatest difficulty, which we must strive to solve to the best of our ability and as far as possible. When and how and whence is a share in reason acquired by those animals that participate in this principle? It is plain that the semen and the unfertilized embryo, while still separate from each other, must be assumed to have the nutritive soul potentially, but not actually, except that (like those unfertilized embryos that are separated from the mother) it absorbs nourishment and performs the function of the nutritive soul. For at first all such embryos seem to live the life of a plant. And it is clear that we must be guided by this in speaking of the sensitive and the rational soul. For all three kinds of soul, not only the nutritive, must be possessed potentially before they are possessed in actuality. And it is necessary either (1) that they should all come into being in the embryo without existing previously outside it, or (2) that they should all exist previously, or (3) that some should so exist and others not. Again, it is necessary that they should either (1) come into being in the material supplied by the female without entering with the semen of the male, or (2) come from the male and be imparted to the material in the female. If the latter, then either all of them, or none, or some must come into being in the male from outside.

Now that it is impossible for them all to pre-exist is clear from this consideration. Plainly those principles whose activity is bodily cannot exist without a body, e.g., walking cannot exist without feet. For the same reason also they cannot enter from outside. For neither is it possible for them to enter by themselves, being inseparable from a body, nor yet in a body, for the semen is only a secretion of the nutriment in process of change. It remains, then, for the reason alone so to enter and alone to be divine, for no bodily activity has any connexion with the activity of reason. . . .

Let us return to the material of the semen in and with which comes away from the male the spiritus conveying the principle of soul. Of this principle there are two kinds; the one is not connected with matter, and belongs to those animals in which is included something divine (to wit, what is called the reason), while the other is inseparable from matter. . . .

Now semen is a secretion and is moved with the same movement as that in virtue of which the body increases (this increase being due to subdivision of the nutriment in its last stage). When it has entered the uterus it puts into form the corresponding secretion of the female and moves it with the same movement wherewith it is moved itself. For the female's contribution also is a secretion, and has all the parts in it potentially though none of them actually; it has in it potentially even those parts which differentiate the female from the male, for just as the young of mutilated parents are sometimes born mutilated and sometimes not, so also the young born of a female are sometimes female and sometimes male instead. For the female is, as it were, a mutilated male, and the catamenia are semen, only not pure; for there is only one thing they have not in them, the principle of soul. For this reason, whenever a wind-egg is produced by any animal, the egg so forming has in it the parts of both sexes potentially, but has not the principle in question, so that it does not develop into a living creature, for this is introduced by the semen of the male. When such a principle has been imparted to the secretion of the female it becomes an embryo. . . .

To consider now the region of the uterus in the female—the two blood-vessels, the great vessel and the aorta, divide higher up, and many fine vessels from them terminate in the uterus. These become over-filled from the nourishment they convey, nor is the female nature able to concoct it, because it is colder than man's; so the blood is excreted through very fine vessels into the uterus, these being unable on account of their narrowness to receive the excessive quantity and the result is a sort of haemorrhage. The period is not accurately defined in women, but tends to return during the waning of the moon. . . .

In all females, then, there must necessarily be such a secretion, more indeed in those that have blood and of these most of all in man, but in the others also some matter must be collected in the uterine region. The reason why there is more in those that have blood and most in man has been already given, but why, if all females have such a secretion, have not all males one to correspond? . . .

Now the reason why it is not all males that have a generative secretion, while all females do, is that the animal is a body with soul or life; the female always provides the material, the male that which fashions it, for this is the power that we say each possess, and this is what is meant by calling them male and female. Thus while it is necessary for the female to provide a body and a material mass, it is not necessary for the male, because it is not within the work of art or the embryo that the tools or the maker must exist. While the body is from the female, it is the soul that is from the male, for the soul is the reality of a particular body. . . .

The embryo, then, grows by means of the umbilicus in the same way as a plant by its root, or as animals themselves when separated from the nutriment within the mother, of which we must speak later at the time appropriate for discussing them. But the parts are not differentiated, as some suppose, because like is naturally carried to like. Besides many other difficulties involved in this theory, it results from it that the homogeneous parts ought to come into being each one separate from the rest, as bones and sinews by themselves, and flesh by itself, if one should accept this cause. The real cause why each of them comes into being is that the secretion of the female is potentially such as the animal is naturally, and all the parts are potentially present in it, but none actually. It is also because when the active and the passive come in contact with each other in that way in which the one is active and the other passive (I mean in the right manner, in the right place, and at the right time), straightway the one acts and the other is acted upon. The female, then, provides matter, the male the principle of motion. . . .

Of the animals that are comparatively obscure and short-lived the characters or dispositions are not so obvious to recognition as are those of animals that are longer-lived. These latter animals appear to have a natural capacity corresponding to each of the passions: to cunning or simplicity, courage or timidity, to good temper or to bad, and to other similar dispositions of mind. . . .

In all genera in which the distinction of male and female is found, Nature makes a similar differentiation in the mental characteristics of the two sexes. This differentiation is the most obvious in the case of human kind and in that of the larger animals and the viviparous quadrupeds. In the case of these latter the female is softer in character, is the sooner tamed, admits more readily of caressing, is more apt in the way of learning. . . .

In all cases, excepting those of the bear and leopard, the female is less spirited than the male; in regard to the two exceptional cases, the superiority in courage rests with the female. With all other animals the female is softer in disposition than the male, is more mischievous, less simple, more impulsive, and more attentive to the nurture of the young; the male, on the other hand, is more spirited than the female, more savage, more simple and less cunning. The traces of these differentiated characteristics are more or less visible everywhere, but they are especially visible where character is the more developed, and most of all in man.

The fact is, the nature of man is the most rounded off and complete, and consequently in man the qualities or capacities above referred to are found in their perfection. Hence woman is more compassionate than man, more easily moved to tears, at the same time is more jealous, more querulous, more apt to scold and to strike. She is, furthermore, more prone to despondency and less hopeful than the man, more void of shame or self respect, more false of speech, more deceptive, and of more retentive memory. She is also more wakeful, more shrinking, more difficult to rouse to action, and requires a smaller quantity of nutriment.

He who thus considers things in their first growth and origin, whether a state or anything else, will obtain the clearest view of them. In the first place (1) there must be a union of those who cannot exist without each other; for example, of male and female, that the race may continue; and this is a union which is formed, not of deliberate purpose, but because, in common with other animals and with plants, mankind have a natural desire to leave behind them an image of themselves. And (2) there must be a union of natural ruler and subject, that both may be preserved. For he who can foresee with his mind is by nature intended to be lord and master, and he who can work with his body is a subject, and by nature a slave; hence master and slave have the same interest. Nature, however, has distinguished between the female and the slave. For she is not niggardly, like the smith who fashions the Delphian knife for many uses; she makes each thing for a single use, and every instrument is best made when intended for one and not for many uses. But among barbarians no distinction is made between women and slaves, because there is no natural ruler among them: they are a community of slaves, male and female. Wherefore the poets say,—"It is meet that Hellenes should rule over barbarians"; as if they thought that the barbarian and the slave were by nature one.

Out of these two relationships between man and woman, master and slave, the family first arises, and Hesiod is right where he says,—"First house and wife and an ox for the plough," for the ox is the poor man's slave. The family is the association established by nature for the supply of men's every day wants, and the members of it are called by Charondas "companions of the cupboard," and by Epimenides the Cretan, "companions of the manger." But when several families are united, and the association aims at something more than the supply of daily needs, then comes into existence the village. . . .

When several villages are united in a single community, perfect and large enough to be nearly or quite self-sufficing, the state comes into existence, originating in the bare needs of life, and continuing in existence for the sake of a good life. And therefore, if the earlier forms of society are natural, so is the state, for it is the end of them, and the [completed] nature is the end. For what each thing is when fully developed, we call its nature, whether we are speaking of a man, a horse, or a family. Besides, the final cause and end of a thing is the best, and to be self-sufficing is the end and the best.

Hence it is evident that the state is a creation of nature, and that man is by nature a political animal. . . .

Seeing then that the state is made up of households, before speaking of the state, we must speak of the management of the household. The parts of the household are the persons who compose it, and a complete household consists of slaves and freemen. Now we should begin by examining everything in its least elements; and the first and least parts of a family are master and slave, husband and wife, father and children. We have therefore to consider what each of these three relations is and ought to be:—I mean the relation of master and servant, of husband and wife, and thirdly of parent and child.

But is there any one thus intended by nature to be a slave, and for whom such a condition is expedient and right, or rather is not all slavery a violation of nature?

There is no difficulty in answering this question, on grounds both of reason and of fact. For that some should rule, and others be ruled is a thing, not only necessary, but expedient; from the hour of their birth, some are marked out for subjection, others for rule.

And whereas there are many kinds both of rulers and subjects, that rule is the better which is exercised over better subjects—for example, to rule over men is better than to rule over wild beasts. The work is better which is executed by better workmen; and where one man rules and another is ruled, they may be said to have a work. In all things which form a composite whole and which are made up of parts, whether continuous or discrete, a distinction between the ruling and the subject element comes to light. Such a duality exists in living creatures, but not in them only; it originates in the constitution of the universe; even in things which have no life, there is a ruling principle, as in musical harmony. But we are wandering from the subject. We will, therefore, restrict ourselves to the living creature which, in the first place, consists of soul and body: and of these two, the one is by nature the ruler, and the other the subject. But then we must look for the intentions of nature in things which retain their nature, and not in things which are corrupted. And therefore we must study the man who is in the most perfect state both of body and soul, for in him we shall see the true relation of the two; although in bad or corrupted natures the body will often appear to rule over the soul, because they are in an evil and unnatural condition. First then we may observe in living creatures both a despotical and a constitutional rule; for the soul rules the body with a despotical rule, whereas the intellect rules the appetites with a constitutional and royal rule. And it is clear that the rule of the soul over the body, and of the mind and the rational element over the passionate is natural and expedient; whereas the equality of the two or the rule of the inferior is always hurtful. The same holds good of animals as well as of men; for tame animals have a better nature than wild, and all tame animals are better off when they are ruled by man; for then they are preserved. Again, the male is by nature superior, and the female inferior; and the one rules, and the other is ruled; this principle, of necessity, extends to all mankind. Where then there is such a difference as that between soul and body, or between men and animals (as in the case of those whose business is to use their body, and who can do nothing better), the lower sort are by nature slaves, and it is better for them as for all inferiors that they should be under the rule of a master. For he who can be, and therefore is another's, and he who participates in reason enough to apprehend, but not to have, reason, is a slave by nature. Whereas the lower animals cannot even apprehend reason; they obey their instincts. And indeed the use made of slaves and of tame animals is not very different; for both with their bodies minister to the needs of life. Nature would like to distinguish between the bodies of freemen and slaves, making the one strong for servile labour, the other upright, and although useless for such services, useful for political life in the arts both of war and peace. But this does not hold universally: for some slaves have the souls and others have the bodies of freemen. And doubtless if men differed from one another in the mere forms of their bodies as much as the statues of the Gods do from men, all would acknowledge that the inferior class should be slaves of the superior. And if there is a difference in the body, how much more in the soul? but the beauty of the body is seen, whereas the beauty of the soul is not seen. It is clear, then, that some men are by nature free, and others slaves, and that for these latter slavery is both expedient and right. . . .

Of household management we have seen that there are three parts—one is the rule of a master over slaves, which has been discussed already, another of a father, and the third of a husband. A husband and father rules over wife and children, both free, but the rule differs, the rule over his children being a royal, over his wife a constitutional rule. For although there may be exceptions to the order of nature, the male is by nature fitter for command than the female, just as the elder and full-grown is superior to the younger and more immature. But in most constitutional states the citizens rule and are ruled by turns, for the idea of a constitutional state implies that the natures of the citizens are equal, and do not differ at all. Nevertheless, when one rules and the other is ruled we endeavour to create a difference of outward forms and names and titles of respect, which may be illustrated by the saying of Amasis about his foot-pan. The relation of the male to the female is of this kind, but there the inequality is permanent. The rule of a father over his children is royal, for he receives both love and the respect due to age, exercising a kind of royal power. And therefore Homer has appropriately called Zeus "father of Gods and men," because he is the king of them all. For a king is the natural superior of his subjects, but he should be of the same kin or kind with them, and such is the relation of elder and younger, of father and son.

Thus it is clear that household management attends more to men than to the acquisition of inanimate things, and to human excellence more than to the excellence of property which we call wealth, and to the virtue of freemen more than to the virtue of slaves. A question may indeed be raised, whether there is any excellence at all in a slave beyond merely instrumental and ministerial qualities— whether he can have the virtues of temperance, courage, justice, and the like; or whether slaves possess only bodily and ministerial qualities. And, whichever way we answer the question, a difficulty arises; for, if they have virtue, in what will they differ from freemen? On the other hand, since they are men and share in reason, it seems absurd to say that they have no virtue. A similar question may be raised about women and children, whether they too have virtues: ought a woman to be temperate and brave and just, and is a child to be called temperate, and intemperate, or not? So in general we may ask about the natural ruler, and the natural subject, whether they have the same or different virtues. For a noble nature is equally required in both, but if so, why should one of them always rule, and the other always be ruled? Nor can we say that this is a question of degree, for the difference between ruler and subject is a difference of kind, and therefore not of degree; yet how strange is the supposition that the one ought, and that the other ought not, to have virtue! For if the ruler is intemperate and unjust, how can he rule well? If the subject, how can he obey well? If he be licentious and cowardly, he will certainly not do his duty. It is evident therefore, that both of them must have a share of virtue, but varying according to their various natures. And this is at once indicated by the soul, in which one part naturally rules, and the other is subject, and the virtue of the ruler we maintain to be different from that of the subject; the one being the virtue of the rational, and the other of the irrational part. Now, it is obvious that the same principle applies generally, and therefore almost all things rule and are ruled according to nature. But the kind of rule differs;—the freeman rules over the slave after another manner from that in which the male rules over the female, or the man over the child; although the parts of the soul are present in all of them, they are present in different degrees. For the slave has no deliberative faculty at all; the woman has, but it is without authority, and the child has, but it is immature. So it must necessarily be with the moral virtues also; all may be supposed to partake of them, but only in such manner and degree as is required by each for the fulfilment of his duty. Hence the ruler ought to have moral virtue in perfection, for his duty is entirely that of a master artificer, and the master artificer is reason; the subjects, on the other hand, require only that measure of virtue which is proper to each of them. Clearly, then, moral virtue belongs to all of them; but the temperance of a man and of a woman, or the courage and justice of a man and of a woman, are not, as Socrates maintained, the same; the courage of a man is shown in commanding, of a woman in obeying. And this holds of all other virtues, as will be more clearly seen if we look at them in detail, for those who say generally that virtue consists in a good disposition of the soul, or in doing rightly, or the like, only deceive themselves. Far better than such definitions is their mode of speaking, who, like Gorgias, enumerate the virtues. All classes must be deemed to have their special attributes; as the poet says of women, "Silence is a woman's glory," but this is not equally the glory of man. . . .

Inasmuch as every family is a part of a state, and these relationships are the parts of a family, the virtue of the part must have regard to the virtue of the whole. And therefore, women and children must be trained by education with an eye to the state, if the virtues of either of them are supposed to make any difference in the virtues of the state. And they must make a difference: for the children grow up to be citizens, and half the free persons in a state are women.

Plutarch

During the first century A.D. attitudes towards women in Greece and Rome softened somewhat, although old assumptions and practices remained essentially intact. This softening appears to have resulted from increased control over property by women, greater access to certain kinds of education for girls, and what may hesitantly be called a fledgling women's rights movement, especially in Rome. Plutarch, a Greek who spent considerable time in Rome, reflects the continuation of the restrictive, patriarchal practices of the past in a form mellowed by the passage of time and events. In "Conjugal Precepts," a letter written to a couple on the occasion of their marriage, Plutarch specifies the ideal of wedded life and thereby presents us with a conceptual "picture" of the status that women, still bred for the sole purpose of marriage, could hope to achieve. Although Plutarch accepts the subordinate status of women, a wife is ideally the moral and intellectual equal of her husband, and a well-ordered home depends on the consent of both husband and wife. While it is still unseemly for a woman to have likes and dislikes of her own, and while she must conform in all things to the temper of her husband, yet she is to share in her husband's business, recreation, cares, and joys—she is no longer totally cut off from her husband's world. Plutarch believed that friendship and reciprocal affection are possible between husband and wife. Although property is still owned by the husband, even if his wife brought the largest share to the marriage, Plutarch urges that the "mine" and "not mine" attitude be abolished in a spirit of common enjoyment. Finally, instruction in mathematics, philosophy, and astronomy are recommended for women, although its purpose is limited to developing moral virtue. In the end, however, paternalism still predominates—woman is still like a child—a wife's husband is both her father and her mother.

THE ROLES AND VIRTUES
OF MEN AND WOMEN*

PLUTARCH TO POLLIANUS AND EURYDICE
SENDETH GREETING

Now that the nuptial ceremonies are over, and that the priestess of Ceres has joined you both together in the bands of matrimony according to the custom of the country, I thought a short discourse of this nature might not be either unacceptable or unseasonable, but rather serve as a kind epithalamium to congratulate your happy conjunction; more especially, since there can be nothing more useful in conjugal society than the observance of wise and wholesome precepts, suitable to the harmony of matrimonial converse. . . .

---

* From Plutarch, "Conjugal Precepts," in *Moralia,* translation revised by William H. Goodwin (Boston: Little, Brown and Company, 1906), Vol. 2: Introduction, 3, 6, 8, 9, 11-12, 14, 16-20, 26, 31-33, 36, 42, 46, 48. Renumbered here.

1. It especially behooves those people who are newly married to avoid the first occasions of discord and dissension; considering that vessels newly formed are subject to be bruised and put out of shape by many slight accidents, but when the materials come once to be settled and hardened by time, nor fire nor sword will hardly prejudice the solid substance. . . .

2. They who rather choose to be the mistresses of senseless fools than the obedient wives of wise and sober husbands are like those people that prefer misguidance of the blind before the conduct of them that can see and know the way.

3. Some men, either unable or unwilling to mount themselves into their saddles through infirmity or laziness, teach their horses to fall upon their knees, and in that posture to receive their riders. In like manner there are some persons who, have married young ladies not less considerable for the nobility of their birth than their wealthy dowries, take little care themselves to improve the advantages of such a splendid conjunction, but with a severe moroseness labor to depress and degrade their wives, proud of the mastery and vaunting in domestic tyranny. Whereas in this case it becomes a man to use the reins of government with as equal regard to the quality and dignity of the woman as to the stature of the horse.

4. We behold the moon then shining with a full and glorious orb, when farthest distant from the sun; but, as she warps back again to meet her illustrious mate, the nearer she makes her approach, the more she is eclipsed until no longer seen. Quite otherwise, a woman ought to display the charms of her virtue and the sweetness of her disposition in her husband's presence, but in his absence to retire to silence and reservedness at home.

5. As in musical concords, when the upper strings are so tuned as exactly to accord, the base always gives the tone; so in well-regulated and well-ordered families, all things are carried on with the harmonious consent and agreement of both parties, but the conduct and contrivance chiefly redounds to the reputation and management of the husband.

6. It is a common proverb, that the sun is too strong for the

north wind; for the more the wind ruffles and strives to force a man's upper garment from his back, the faster he holds it, and the closer he wraps it about his shoulders. But he who so briskly defended himself from being plundered by the wind, when once the sun begins to scald the air, all in a dropping sweat is then constrained to throw away not only his flowing garment but his tunic also. This puts us in mind of the practice of most women, who, being limited by their husbands in their extravagances of feasting and superfluities of habit, presently fill the house with noise and uproar; whereas, if they would but suffer themselves to be convinced by reason and soft persuasion, they would of themselves acknowledge their vanity and submit to moderation.

7. As there is little or no use to be made of a mirror, though in a frame of gold enchased with all the sparkling variety of the richest gems, unless it render back the true similitude of the image it receives; so is there nothing of profit in a wealthy dowry, unless the conditions, the temper, the humor of the wife be conformable to the natural disposition and inclination of the husband, and he sees the virtues of his own mind exactly represented in hers. Or, if a fair and beautiful mirror that makes a sad and pensive visage look jocund and gay, or a wanton or smiling countenance show pensive and mournful, is therefore presently rejected as of no value; thus may not she be thought an angry, peevish, and importunate woman, that louts and lowers upon the caresses of a husband, and when he courts the pastime of her affections, entertains him with frumps and taunts, but when she finds him serious in business, allures him then with her unseasonable toyings to pleasure and enjoyment? For the one is an offence of impertinency, the other a contempt of her husband's kindness. But, as geometricians affirm that lines and surfaces are not moved of themselves, but according to the motions of the bodies to which they belong, so it behooves a woman to challenge no peculiar passion or affection as her own, but to share with her husband in business, in his recreations, in his cares, and in his mirth.

8. The Persian kings, when they contain themselves within the

limits of their usual banquets, suffer their married wives to sit down at their tables; but when they once design to indulge the provocations of amorous heats and wine, then they send away their wives, and call for their concubines, their gypsies, and their songstresses, with their lascivious tunes and wanton galliards. Wherein they do well, not thinking it proper to debauch their wives with the tipsy frolics and dissolute extravagances of their intemperance.

If therefore any private person, swayed by the unruly motions of his incontinency, happen at any time to make a trip with a kind she-friend or his wife's chambermaid, it becomes not the wife presently to lower and take pepper in the nose, but rather to believe that it was his respect to her which made him unwilling she should behold the follies of ebriety and foul intemperance.

9. Princes that be addicted to music increase the number of excellent musicians; if they be lovers of learning, all men strive to excel in reading and in eloquence; if given to martial exercises, a military ardor rouses straight the drowsy sloth of all their subjects. Thus husbands effeminately finical only teach their wives to paint and polish themselves with borrowed lustre. The studious of pleasure render them immodest and whorish. On the other side, men of serious, honest, and virtuous conversations make sober, chaste, and prudent wives.

10. A young Lacedaemonian lass, being asked by an acquaintance of hers whether she had yet embraced her husband, made answer, No; but that he had embraced her. And after this manner, in my opinion, it behooves an honest woman to behave herself toward her husband, never to shun nor to disdain the caresses and dalliances of his amorous inclinations, when he himself begins; but never herself to offer the first occasion of provocation. For the one savors of impudent harlotry, the other displays a female pride and imperiousness void of conjugal affection.

11. It behooves a woman not to make peculiar and private friendships of her own, but to esteem only her husband's acquaintance and familiars as hers. Now as the Gods are our chiefest and most beneficials friends, it behooves her to worship and adore only

those Deities which her husband reputes and reverences for such. But as for quaint opinions and superstitious innovations, let them be exterminated from her outermost threshold. For no sacrifices or services can be acceptable to the Gods, performed by women, as it were, by stealth and in secret, without the knowledge of the husband.

12. Plato asserts those cities to be the most happy and best regulated where these expressions, "This is mine," "This is not mine," are seldomest made use of. For that then the citizens enjoy in common, so far as is convenient, those things that are of greatest importance. But in wedlock those expressions are utterly to be abolished. For as the physicians say that the right side being bruised or beaten communicates its pain to the left; so indeed the husband ought to sympathize in the sorrows and afflictions of the woman, and much more does it become the wife to be sensible of the miseries and calamities of the husband; to the intent that, as knots are made fast by knitting the bows of a thread one within another, so the ligaments of conjugal society may be strengthened by the mutual interchange of kindness and affection. This Nature herself instructs us, by mixing us in our bodies; while she takes a part from each, and then blending the whole together produces a being common to both, to the end that neither may be able to discern or distinguish what was belonging to another, or lay claim to assured propriety. Therefore is community of estate and purses chiefly requisite among married couples, whose principal aim it ought to be to mix and incorporate their purchases and disbursements into one substance, neither pretending to call this hers or that his, but accounting all inseparably peculiar to both. However, as in a goblet where the proportion of water exceeds the juice of the grape, yet still we call the mixture wine; in like manner the house and estate must be reputed the possession of the husband, although the woman brought the chiefest part.

13. The question being put by some of his friends to a certain Roman why he had put away his wife, both sober, beautiful, chaste, and rich, the gentleman, putting forth his foot and showing his

buskin, said: Is not this a new, handsome, complete shoe?—yet no man but myself knows where it pinches me. Therefore ought not a woman to boast either of her dower, her parentage, or beauty; but in such things as most delight a husband, pleasantness of converse, sweetness of disposition, and briskness of humor, there to show nothing of harshness, nothing distasteful, nothing offensive, but from day to day to study behavior jocund, blithe, and conformable to his temper. . . .

14. Dionysius, the tyrant of Sicily, sent several costly presents of rich apparel, necklaces, and bracelets to the daughters of Lysander, which however the father would never permit the virgins to accept, saying: These gaudy presents will procure more infamy than honor to my daughters. And indeed, before Lysander, Sophocles in one of his tragedies had uttered the following sentence to the same effect:

> Mistake not, silly wretch; this pompous trim
> Rather disgraces than proclaims thee great,
> And shows the rage of thy lascivious heat.

For, as Crates said, that is ornament which adorns; and that adorns a woman which renders her more comely and decent. This is an honor conferred upon her, not by the lustre of gold, the sparkling of emeralds and diamonds, nor splendor of the purple tincture, but by the real embellishments of gravity, discretion, humility, and modesty.

15. Theano, as she was dressing herself one morning in her chamber, by chance discovered some part of her naked arm. Upon which, one of the company crying out, Oh, what a lovely arm is there!—'Tis very true, said she, but yet not common. Thus ought a chaste and virtuous woman not only to keep her naked arms from open view, but to lock up her very words and set a guard upon her lips, especially in the company of strangers, since there is nothing which sooner discovers the qualities and conditions of a woman than her discourse.

16. Phidias made the statue of Venus at Elis with one foot upon

the shell of a tortoise, to signify two great duties of a virtuous woman, which are to keep at home and be silent. For she is only to speak to her husband, or by her husband. Nor is she to take amiss the uttering her mind in that manner, through another more proper organ.

17. Princes and kings honor themselves in giving honor to philosophers and learned men. On the other side, great personages admired and courted by philosophers are no way honored by their flatteries, which are rather a prejudice and stain to the reputation of those that use them. Thus it is with women, who in honoring and submitting to their husbands win for themselves honor and respect, but when they strive to get the mastery, they become a greater reproach to themselves than to those that are so ignominiously henpecked. But then again, it behooves a husband to control his wife, not as a master does his vassal, but as the soul governs the body, with the gentle hand of mutual friendship and reciprocal affection. For as the soul commands the body, without being subject to its pleasures and inordinate desires, in like manner should a man so exercise his authority over his wife, as to soften it with complaisance and kind requital of her loving submission.

18. It is generally observed that mothers are fondest of their sons, as expecting from them their future assistance when they grow into years, and that fathers are kindest to their daughters, as standing most in need of their paternal succor. And perhaps, out of that mutual respect which the man and his wife bear one to another, either of them would seem to carry greater affection for that which is proper and familiar to the other. But this pleasing controversy is easily reconciled. For it becomes a woman to show the choicest of her respects and to be more complaisant to the kindred of her husband than to her own to make her complaints to them, and conceal her discontents from her own relations. For the trust which she reposes in them causes them to confide in her, and her esteem of them increases their respects to her.

19. The Athenians yearly solemnized three sacred seedtimes. . . . But more scared than all these is the nuptial ploughing and sowing,

in order to the procreation of children. And therefore Sophocles rightly calls Venus the fruitful Cytherea. For which reason it highly imports both the man and the woman, when bound together by the holy tie of wedlock, to abstain from all unlawful and forbidden copulation, and from ploughing and sowing where they never desire to reap any fruit of their labor, or, if the harvest come to perfection, they conceal and are ashamed to own it.

20. What said a woman to King Philip, that pulled and hauled her to him by violence against her will? Let me go, said she, for when the candles are out, all women are alike. This is aptly applied to men addicted to adultery and lust. But a virtuous wife, when the candle is taken away, ought then chiefly to differ from all other women. For when her body is not to be seen, her chastity, her modesty, and her peculiar affection to her husband ought then to shine with their brighest lustre.

21. As to what remains, in reference to superfluity of habit and decent household furniture, dear Eurydice, what Timoxenas has written to Aristylla.

And do you, Pollianus, never believe that women will be weaned from those toys and curiosities wherein they take a kind of pride, and which serve for an alleviation of their domestic solitude, while you yourself admire the same things in other women, and are taken with the gayety of golden beakers, magnificent pictures for your houses, and rich trappings for your mules and horses. For it were a strange moroseness to debar a woman those ornamental vanities which naturally her sex admire, nor will it easily be endured without regret, where she sees the man much more indulgent to his own humor.

Since then thou art arrived at those years which are proper for the study of such sciences as are attained by reason and demonstration, endeavor to complete this knowledge by conversing with persons that may be serviceable to thee in such a generous design. And as for thy wife, like the industrious bee, gather everywhere from the fragrant flowers of good instruction, replenish thyself with whatever may be of advantage to her, and impart the same to her again in loving and familiar discourse, both for thy own and her improvement.

> For father thou and mother art to her;
> She now is thine, and not the parent's care.

Nor is it less to thy commendation to hear what she returns:

> And you, my honored husband, are my guide
> And tutor in philosophy beside,
> From whose instructions I at once improve
> The fruits of knowledge and the sweets of love.

For such studies as these fix the contemplations of women upon what is laudable and serious, and prevent their wasting time upon impertinent and pernicious vanity. For that lady that is studious in geometry will never affect the dissolute motions of dancing. And she that is taken with the sublime notions of Plato and Xenophon will look with disdain upon the charms and enchantments of witches and sorcerers; and if any ridiculous astrologer promises to pull the moon down from the sky, she will laugh at the ignorance and folly of the women who believe in him, being herself well grounded in astronomy, and having heard about Aganice, the daughter of Hegetor, a Thessalian lord, who understanding the reason of the eclipses of the moon, and knowing beforehand the time of her being obscured by the shadow of the earth, made the credulous women believe that it was she who at those times unhinged the moon and removed her from the sky.

True it is, that never any woman brought forth a perfect child without the assistance and society of man, but there are many whose imaginations are so strongly wrought upon by the sight or bare relation of monstrous spectacles, that they bring into the world several sorts of immature and shapeless productions. Thus, unless great care be taken by men to manure and cultivate the inclinations of their wives with wholesome and virtuous precepts, they often breed among themselves the false conceptions of extravagant and loose desires. But do thou, Eurydice, make it thy business to be familiar with the learned proverbs of wise and learned men, and always to embellish thy discourse with their profitable sentences, to the end thou mayst be the admiration of other women, that shall behold thee so richly adorned without the expense or assistance of jewels or embroideries. For pearls and diamonds are not the purchase of an ordinary purse; but the ornaments of Theano, Cleobuline, Gorgo the wife of King Leonidas, Timoclea the sister of Theagenes, the ancient Roman Claudia, or Cornelia the daughter of Scipio,—already so celebrated and renowned for their virtues,— will cost but little, yet nothing will set thee out more glorious or illustrious to the world, or render thy life more comfortable and happy. For if Sappho, only because she could compose an elegant verse, had the confidence to write to a haughty and wealthy dame in her time:

> Dead thou shalt lie forgotten in thy tomb,
> Since not for thee Pierian roses bloom,

why may it not be much more lawful for thee to boast those great perfections that give thee a greater privilege, not only to gather the flowers, but to reap the fruits themselves, which the Muses bestow upon the lovers and real owners of learning and philosophy?

Paul

During the years of Paul's intense missionary work around the middle of the first century A.D., he wrote to the Christians of the church at Corinth in Greece, a church that he himself had helped establish. Although written for the purpose of settling local disputes, Paul's letter addresses issues of universal interest to the struggling Christian Church still in its infancy. As regards the status of women in the church, Paul adheres to the traditional Jewish practice of enforcing woman's subordinate position, which entailed restricting her movements and influence lest she employ her sexuality to ensnare men. He relies heavily on the Genesis account of the creation and fall of man to support his pronouncements, which is of particular interest in light of the example of Jesus and the conflicting direction of the church in its first decades. It appears from all accounts that Jesus' approach to women was utterly unconventional by Jewish standards, since in all his dealings with them he made no derogatory comments and showed no contemptuous attitudes about them. Indeed, it is clear from the

Gospel stories that Jesus treated women as persons, frequently in a context that startled onlookers. There is evidence, consistent with Jesus' example, that women played an important part in the earliest days of the new church, even to engaging in such evangelical work as teaching the faith and converting large numbers to Christianity. Whatever his reasons, Paul explicitly objected to this new turn, and his reactionary efforts in the matter of women succeeded in setting the tone for thinking about women that would be continually reinforced in the intellectual and practical tradition in the West for the next two thousand years.

THE RELATIONSHIP OF
MEN AND WOMEN*

Now concerning the things whereof ye wrote unto me: It is good for a man not to touch a woman.

Nevertheless, to avoid fornication, let every man have his own wife, and let every woman have her own husband.

Let the husband render unto the wife due benevolence: and likewise also the wife unto the husband.

The wife hath not power of her own body, but the husband: and likewise also the husband hath not power of his own body, but the wife.

Defraud ye not one the other, except it be with consent for a time, that ye may give yourselves to fasting and prayer; and come together again, that Satan tempt you not for your incontinency.

But I speak this by permission, and not of commandment.

For I would that all men were even as I myself. But every man hath his proper gift of God, one after this manner, and another after that.

* From I Corinthians 7:1-15, 25-40; 11:2-15; 14:34-35, 40, King James Version.

I say therefore to the unmarried and widows, It is good for them if they abide even as I.

But if they cannot contain, let them marry: for it is better to marry than to burn.

And unto the married I command, yet not I, but the Lord, Let not the wife depart from her husband:

But and if she depart, let her remain unmarried, or be reconciled to her husband: and let not the husband put away his wife.

But to the rest speak I, not the Lord: If any brother hath a wife that believeth not, and she be pleased to dwell with him, let him not put her away.

And the woman which hath an husband that believeth not, and if he be pleased to dwell with her, let her not leave him.

For the unbelieving husband is sanctified by the wife, and the unbelieving wife is sanctified by the husband: else were your children unclean; but now are they holy.

But if the unbelieving depart, let him depart. A brother or a sister is not under bondage in such cases: but God hath called us to peace. . . .

Now concerning virgins I have no commandment of the Lord: yet I give my judgment, as one that hath obtained mercy of the Lord to be faithful.

I suppose therefore that this is good for the present distress, I say, that it is good for a man so to be.

Art thou bound unto a wife? seek not to be loosed. Art thou loosed from a wife? seek not a wife.

But and if thou marry, thou hast not sinned; and if a virgin marry, she hath not sinned. Nevertheless such shall have trouble in the flesh: but I spare you.

But this I say, brethren, the time is short: it remaineth, that both they that have wives be as though they had none;

And they that weep, as though they wept not, and they that rejoice, as though they rejoiced not; and they that buy, as though they possessed not;

And they that use this world, as not abusing it: for the fashion of this world passeth away.

But I would have you without carefulness. He that is unmarried careth for the things that belong to the Lord, how he may please the Lord:

But he that is married careth for the things that are of the world, how he may please his wife.

There is difference also between a wife and a virgin. The unmarried woman careth for the things of the Lord, that she may be holy both in body and in spirit: but she that is married careth for the things of the world, how she may please her husband.

And this I speak for your own profit; not that I may cast a snare upon you, but for that which is comely, and that ye may attend upon the Lord without distraction.

But if any man think that he behaveth himself uncomely toward his virgin, if she pass the flower of her age, and need so require, let him do what he will, he sinneth not: let them marry.

Nevertheless he that standeth stedfast in his heart, having no necessity, but hath power over his own will, and hath so decreed in his heart that he will keep his virgin, doeth well.

So then he that giveth her in marriage doeth well, but he that giveth her not in marriage doeth better.

The wife is bound by the law as long as her husband liveth; but if her husband be dead, she is at liberty to be married to whom she will; only in the Lord.

But she is happier if she so abide, after my judgment: and I think also that I have the spirit of God. . . .

Now I praise you, brethren, that ye remember me in all things, and keep the ordinances, as I delivered them to you.

But I would have you know, that the head of every man is Christ; and the head of the woman is the man; and the head of Christ is God.

Every man praying or prophesying, having his head covered, dishonoureth his head.

But every woman that prayeth or prophesieth with her head uncovered dishonoureth her head: for that is even all one as if she were shaven.

For if the woman be not covered, let her also be shorn: but if it be a shame for a woman to be shorn or shaven, let her be covered.

For a man indeed ought not to cover his head, forasmuch as he is the image and glory of God: but the woman is the glory of the man.

For the man is not of the woman; but the woman of the man.

Neither was the man created for the woman; but the woman for the man.

For this cause ought the woman to have power on her head because of the angels.

Nevertheless neither is the man without the woman, neither the woman without the man, in the Lord.

For as the woman is of the man, even so is the man also by the woman; but all things of God.

Judge in yourselves: is it comely that a woman pray unto God uncovered?

Doth not even nature itself teach you, that, if a man have long hair, it is a shame unto him?

But if a woman have long hair, it is a glory to her: for her hair is given her for a covering. . . .

Let your women keep silence in the churches: for it is not permitted unto them to speak; but they are commanded to be under obedience, as also saith the law.

And if they will learn any thing, let them ask their husbands at home: for it is a shame for women to speak in the church. . . .

Let all things be done decently and in order.

Augustine

Following his conversion to Christianity and subsequent consecration as bishop, Augustine began in 413 A.D. what he thought to be his masterpiece, *The City of God*, taking fourteen years to finish it. Three years prior to this, events conspired to spur Augustine to write. The devastation of Rome by the Goths ended centuries of Roman domination of the Mediterranean world, and the Christians, who were believed to have sapped Rome's strength, were held responsible. Augustine wrote *The City of God* to refute this charge. The first part is an analysis of paganism's inevitable failures and the remaining part provides Augustine's blueprint for the good human society, the "city of God" whose members are devoted to divine goodness and truth. Such a society stands as the antithesis of the earthly city in which love of self and physical things of the world predominate. Concerning woman's role in society, Augustine, like Paul, bypasses Jesus' example, further elaborating the implications of the Genesis story and, ironically, adopting the pagan Roman paterfamilias who rules his wife and may inflict physical punishment on her. In Augustine's account woman emerges in the three-fold role of temptress, wife, and mother, all of which emphasize her instrumental status in human society. As temptress, woman is the instrument of the devil's evil designs; as wife, woman is the instrument of her husband who oversees the ordered peacefulness of the family; and as mother, woman is the instrument of God's creativity. Depending on the use to which she allows herself to be put, woman is variously damned or blessed. As a member of the earthly city, where she functions in her perverted role as sex object, she is damned; in the divine city, where she functions in her natural role as helpmate serving her husband and ministering to her children, she is blessed.

WOMAN AS AUXILIARY AND
SUBJECT TO MAN *

And therefore God created only one single man, not, certainly, that he might be a solitary bereft of all society, but that by this means the unity of society and the bond of concord might be more effectually commended to him, men being bound together not only by similarity of nature, but by family affection. And indeed He did not even create the woman that was to be given him as his wife, as he created the man, but created her out of the man, that the whole human race might derive from one man. . . .

God, then, made man in His own image. For He created for him a soul endowed with reason and intelligence, so that he might excel all the creatures of earth, air, and sea, which were not so gifted. And when He had formed the man out of the dust of the earth, and had willed that his soul should be such as I have said—whether He had already made it, and now by breathing imparted it to man, or

* From Augustine, *The City of God* in *Works of Aurelius Augustine,* trans. Marcus Dods (Edinburgh: T. and T. Clark, 1871), Volume 1, Bks. XII, XIV, XIX.

rather made it by breathing, so that that breath which God made by breathing (for what else is "to breathe" than to make breath?) is the soul,—He made also a wife for him, to aid him in the work of generating his kind, and her He formed of a bone taken out of the man's side, working in a divine manner. . . .

I attribute the creating and originating work which gave being to all natures to God, to whom they themselves thankfully ascribe their existence. We do not call gardeners the creators of their fruits, for we read, "Neither is he that planteth anything, neither he that watereth, but God that giveth the increase." Nay, not even the earth itself do we call a creator, though she seems to be the prolific mother of all things which she aids in germinating and bursting forth from the seed, and which she keeps rooted in her own breast; for we likewise read, "God giveth it a body, as it hath pleased Him, and to every seed his own body." We ought not even call a woman the creatress of her own offspring; for He rather is its creator who said to His servant, "Before I formed thee in the womb, I knew thee." And although the various mental emotions of a pregnant woman do produce in the fruit of her womb similar qualities—as Jacob with his peeled wands caused piebald sheep to be produced—yet the mother as little creates her offspring, as she created herself. Whatever bodily or seminal causes, then, may be used for the production of things either by the co-operation of angels, men, or the lower animals, or by sexual generation; and whatever power the desires and mental emotions of the mother have to produce in the tender and plastic foetus, corresponding lineaments and colours; yet the natures themselves, which are thus variously affected are the production of none but the most high God. . . .

Man then lived with God for his rule in a paradise at once physical and spiritual. For neither was it a paradise only physical for the advantage of the body, and not also spiritual for the advantage of the mind; nor was it only spiritual to afford enjoyment to man by his internal sensations, and not also physical to afford him enjoyment through his external senses. But obviously it was both for

both ends. But after that proud and therefore envious angel . . .
preferring to rule with a kind of pomp of empire rather than to be
another's subject, fell from the spiritual Paradise, and essaying to
insinuate his persuasive guile into the mind of man, whose unfallen
condition provoked him to envy now that himself was fallen, he
chose the serpent as his mouthpiece in that bodily Paradise in which
it and all the other earthly animals were living with those two
human beings, the man and his wife, subject to them, and harmless;
and he chose the serpent because, being slippery, and moving in
tortuous windings, it was suitable for his purpose. And this animal
being subdued to his wicked ends by the presence and superior
force of his angelic nature, he abused as his instrument, and first
tried his deceit upon the woman, making his assault upon the
weaker part of that human alliance, that he might gradually gain
the whole, and not supposing that the man would readily give ear to
him, or be deceived, but that he might yield to the error of the
woman. For as Aaron was not induced to agree with the people
when they blindly wished him to make an idol, and yet yielded to
constraint; and as it is not credible that Solomon was so blind as to
suppose that idols should be worshipped, but was drawn over to
such sacrilege by the blandishments of women; so we cannot believe
that Adam was deceived, and supposed the devil's word to be truth,
and therefore transgressed God's law, but that he by the drawings
of kindred yielded to the woman, the husband to the wife, the one
human being to the only other human being. For not without
significance did the apostle say, "And Adam was not deceived, but
the woman being deceived was in the transgression"; but he speaks
thus, because the woman accepted as true what the serpent told her,
but the man could not bear to be severed from his only companion,
even though this involved a partnership in sin. He was not on this
account less culpable, but sinned with his eyes open. And so the
apostle does not say, "He did not sin," but "He was not deceived."
For he shows that he sinned when he says, "By one man sin
entered into the world," and immediately after more distinctly, "In
the likeness of Adam's transgression." But he meant that those are

deceived who do not judge that which they do to be sin; but he knew. Otherwise how were it true. "Adam was not deceived?" But having as yet no experience of the divine severity, he was possibly deceived in so far as he thought his sin venial. And consequently he was not deceived as the woman was deceived, but he was deceived as to the judgment which would be passed on his apology: "The woman whom thou gavest to be with me, she gave me, and I did eat." What need of saying more? Although they were not both deceived by credulity, yet both were entangled in the snares of the devil, and taken by sin. . . .

But as this divine Master inculcates two precepts—the love of God and the love of our neighbour—and as in these precepts a man finds three things he has to love—God, himself, and his neighbour—and that he who loves God loves himself thereby, it follows that he must endeavour to get his neighbour to love God, since he is ordered to love his neighbour as himself. He ought to make this endeavour in behalf of his wife, his children, his household, all within his reach, even as he would wish his neighbour to do the same for him if he needed it; and consequently he will be at peace, or in well-ordered concord, with all men, as far as in him lies. And this is the order of this concord that a man, in the first place, injure no one, and, in the second, do good to every one he can reach. Primarily, therefore, his own houshold are his care, for the law of nature and of society gives him readier access to them and greater opportunity of serving them. And hence the apostle says, "Now, if any provide not for his own, and specially for those of his own house, he hath denied the faith, and is worse than an infidel." This is the origin of domestic peace, or the well-ordered concord of those in the family who rule and those who obey. For they who care for the rest rule—the husband the wife, the parents the children, the masters the servants; and they who are cared for obey—the women their husbands, the children their parents, the servants their masters. But in the family of the just man who lives by faith and is as yet a pilgrim journeying on to the celestial city, even those who rule serve those whom they seem to command; for they rule not from a love of power, but from a sense of the duty they owe to others—not because they are proud of authority, but because they love mercy. . . .

And therefore, although our righteous fathers had slaves, and administered their domestic affairs so as to distinguish between the condition of slaves and the heirship of sons in regard to the blessings of this life, yet in regard to the worship of God, in whom we hope for eternal blessing, they took an equally loving oversight of all the members of their household. And this is so much in accordance with the natural order, that the head of the household was called *paterfamilias;* and this name has been so generally accepted, that even those whose rule is unrighteous are glad to apply it to themselves. But those who are true fathers of their households desire and endeavour that all the members of their household, equally with their own children, should worship and win God, and should come to that heavenly home in which the duty of ruling men is no longer necessary, because the duty of caring for their everlasting happiness has also ceased; but, until they reach that home, masters ought to feel their position of authority a greater burden than servants their service. And if any member of the family interrupts the domestic peace by disobedience, he is corrected either by word or blow, or some kind of just and legitimate punishment, such as society permits, that he may himself be the better for it, and be readjusted to the family harmony from which he had dislocated himself. For as it is not benevolent to give a man help at the expense of some greater benefit he might receive, so it is not innocent to spare a man at the risk of his falling into graver sin. To be innocent, we must not only do harm to no man, but also restrain him from sin or punish his sin, so that either the man himself who is punished may profit by his experience, or others be warned by his example. Since, then, the house ought to be the beginning or element of the city, and every beginning bears reference to some end of its own kind, and every element to the integrity of the whole of which it is an element, it follows plainly enough that domestic peace has a relation to civic peace—in other words, that the well-ordered concord of domestic obedience and domestic rule has a relation to the well-ordered concord of civic obedience and civic rule. And therefore it follows, further, that the father of the family ought to frame his domestic rule in accordance with the law of the city, so that the household may be in harmony with the civic order. . . .

Thomas Aquinas

By the thirteenth century the medieval Church had long since solidified its thinking about women, following the lead of Paul and Augustine. *Summa Theologica*, the multivolume work Aquinas wrote between the years 1266 and 1272, reflects official attitudes. By Aquinas' own account the *Summa* was conceived as providing a systematic treatment of the theological doctrines inherent in Scripture. He is concerned to present rational justification for these doctrines wherever possible and so relies heavily on the philosophical tradition dating from the Greeks, and in particular on Aristotle, who he felt had discovered universal truths. Aquinas' reflections on women, therefore, like much in the *Summa*, skillfully combine the Judeo-Christian and Greek traditions. For example, the Christian acceptance of the subordinate status of women finds expression in the Aristotelian idea that this is a natural state owing to man's greater rationality. Aquinas accepts Aristotle's notion that woman is a defective male lacking vital force as true of each woman, although from a Christian point of view, since God created woman, the creation of woman in general is not tainted by defect but is natural and ordered like every divine act. In addition, the Judeo-Christian attitude to man's dignity requiring the human race to descend from man, not woman, finds its parallel in Aristotle's view that the male supplies the essentially human features in reproduction while woman merely provides the nutritive material. Aquinas' *Summa Theologica,* including its treatment of women, was destined to provide the Roman Catholic Church with its official theological and philosophical dogma for centuries to come.

WOMAN AS DERIVED BEING *

We now consider the production of the woman, about which there are four points of inquiry: (1) Whether the woman should have been made in that first production of things? (2) Whether the woman should have been made from man? (3) Whether of man's rib? (4) Whether the woman was made immediately by God?

First Article.
WHETHER THE WOMAN SHOULD HAVE BEEN MADE
IN THE FIRST PRODUCTION OF THINGS?

We proceed thus to the First Article:—
Objection 1. It seems that the woman should not have been made in the first production of things. For the Philosopher says *(De Gener. Animal.* ii.), that the *female is a misbegotten male.* But nothing

* From Thomas Aquinas, *Summa Theologica,* trans. Fathers of the English Dominican Province (London: R. and T. Washbourne, Ltd., 1912), Vol. 13, Part 1, Question 92.

misbegotten or defective should have been in the first production of things. Therefore woman should not have been made at that first production.

Obj. 2. Further, subjection and limitation were a result of sin, for to the woman was it said after sin (Gen. iii. 16), *Thou shalt be under the man's power;* and Gregory says that, *Where there is no sin, we are all equal.* But woman is naturally of less strength and dignity than man: *for the agent is always more honourable than the patient,* as Augustine says *(Gen. ad lit.* xii.). Therefore woman should not have been made in the first production of things before sin.

Obj. 3. Further, occasions of sin should be *cut off.* But God foresaw that the woman would be an occasion of sin to man. Therefore He should not have made woman.

On the contrary, It is written, *It is not good for man to be alone; let us make him a helper like to himself* (Gen. ii. 18).

I answer that, It was necessary, as the Scripture says, for woman to be made as a help to man; not, indeed, as a helpmate in other works, as some say, since man can be more efficiently helped by another man in other works; but as a help in the work of generation. This can be made clear if we observe the mode of generation carried out in various living things. Some living things do not possess in themselves the power of generation, but are generated by some other specific agent, such as some plants and animals by the influence of the heavenly bodies, from some fitting matter and not from seed; others possess the active and passive generative power together; as we see in plants which are generated from seed; for the noblest vital function in plants is generation. Wherefore we observe that in these the active power of generation invariably accompanies the passive power. Among perfect animals the active power of generation belongs to the male sex, and the passive power to the female. And as among animals there is a vital operation nobler than generation, to which their life is principally directed; therefore the male sex is not found in continual union with the female in perfect animals, but only at the time of coition; so that we may consider that by this means the male and female are one, as in plants they are always united; although in some cases one of them preponderates, and in some the other. But man is yet further ordered to a still nobler vital action, and that is intellectual operation. Therefore there was greater reason for the distinction of these two forces in man; so that the female should be produced separately from the male; although they are carnally united for generation. Therefore directly after the formation of woman, it was said, *And they shall be two in one flesh* (Gen. ii. 24).

Reply Obj. 1. As regards the individual nature, woman is defective and misbegotten, for the active force in the male seed tends to the production of a perfect likeness in the masculine sex; while the production of woman comes from defect in the active force or from some material indisposition, or even from some external influence; such as that of a south wind, which is moist, as the Philosopher observes *(De Gener. Animal.* iv.). But as regards human nature in general, woman is not misbegotten, but is intended by nature, and ordered for the work of generation. Now the intention of nature depends on God, Who is the universal Author of nature. Therefore, in producing nature, God formed not only the male but also the female.

Reply Obj. 2. Subjection is twofold. One is servile, by virtue of which a superior makes use of a subject for his own benefit; and this kind of subjection began after sin. There is another kind of subjection, which is called economic or civil, whereby the superior makes use of his subjects for their own benefit and good; and this kind of subjection existed even before sin. For good order would have been wanting in the human family if some were not governed by others wiser than themselves. So by such a kind of subjection woman is naturally subject to man, because in man the discretion of reason predominates. Nor is inequality among men excluded by the state of innocence, as we shall prove (Q. XCVI., A. 3).

Reply Obj. 3. If God had deprived the world of all those things which proved an occasion of sin, the universe would have been imperfect. Nor was it fitting for the common good to be destroyed in order that individual evil might be avoided; especially as God is so powerful that He can direct any evil to a good end.

SECOND ARTICLE.
WHETHER WOMAN SHOULD HAVE BEEN MADE FROM MAN?

We proceed thus to the Second Article:—

Objection 1. It seems that woman should not have been made from man. For sex belongs both to man and animals. But in the other animals the female was not made from the male. Therefore neither should it have been so with man.

Obj. 2. Further, whatever are of the same species are of the same matter. But male and female are of the same species. Therefore, as man was made of the slime of the earth, so woman should have been made of the same, and not from man.

Obj. 3. Further, woman was made to be a helpmate to man in the work of generation. But close relationship makes a person unfit for that office; hence near relations are debarred from intermarriage, as is written (Lev. xviii. 6). Therefore woman should not have been made from man.

On the contrary, It is written (Ecclus. xvii. 5): *He created of him,* that is, out of man, *a helpmate like to himself,* that is, woman.

I answer that, When all things were first formed, it was more suitable for the woman to be made from the man than (for the female to be from the male) in other animals. Firstly, in order thus to give the first man a certain dignity consisting in this, that as God is the principle of the whole universe, so the first man, in likeness to God, was the principle of the whole human race. Wherefore Paul says that *God made the whole human race from one* (Acts. xvii. 26). Secondly, that man might love woman all the more, and cleave to her more closely, knowing her to be fashioned from himself. Hence it is written (Gen. ii. 23, 24): *She was taken out of man, wherefore a man shall leave father and mother, and shall cleave to his wife.* This was most necessary as regards the human race, in which the male and female live together for life; which is not the case with other animals. Thirdly, because, as the Philosopher says *(Ethic.* viii.), the human male and female are united, not only for generation, as with other animals, but also for the purpose of domestic life, in which each has his or her particular duty, and in which the man is the head of the woman. Wherefore it was suitable for the woman to be made out of man, as out of her principle. Fourthly, there is a sacramental reason for this. For by this is signified that the Church takes her origin from Christ. Wherefore the Apostle says (Eph. v. 32): *This is a great sacrament; but I speak in Christ and in the Church.*

Reply Obj. 1 is clear from the foregoing.

Reply Obj. 2. Matter is that from which something is made. Now created nature has a determinate principle; and since it is determined to one thing, it has also a determinate mode of proceeding. Wherefore from determinate matter it produces something in a determinate species. On the other hand, the Divine Power, being infinite, can produce things of the same species out of any matter, such as a man from the slime of the earth, and a woman from a man.

Reply Obj. 3. A certain affinity arises from natural generation, and this is an impediment to matrimony. But woman was not produced from man by natural generation, but by the Divine Power alone. Wherefore Eve is not called the daughter of Adam; and so this argument does not prove.

THIRD ARTICLE.

WHETHER THE WOMAN WAS FITTINGLY MADE FROM THE
RIB OF MAN?

We proceed thus to the Third Article:—

Objection 1. It seems that the woman should not have been formed from the rib of man. For the rib was much smaller than the woman's body. Now from a smaller thing a larger thing can be made only—either by addition (and then the woman ought to have been described as made out of that which was added, rather than out of the rib itself);—or by rarefaction, because, as Augustine says *(Gen. ad lit.* x): *A body cannot increase in bulk except by rarefaction.* But the woman's body is not more rarefied than man's—at least, not in the proportion of a rib to Eve's body. Therefore Eve was not formed from a rib of Adam.

Obj. 2. Further, in those things which were first created there was nothing superfluous. Therefore a rib of Adam belonged to the integrity of his body. So, if a rib was removed, his body remained imperfect; which is unreasonable to suppose.

Obj. 3. Further, a rib cannot be removed from man without pain. But there was no pain before sin. Therefore it was not right for a rib to be taken from the man, that Eve might be made from it.

On the contrary, It is written (Gen. ii. 22): *God built the rib, which He took from Adam, into a woman.*

I answer that, It was right for the woman to be made from a rib of man; first, to signify the social union of man and woman, for the woman should neither *use authority over man,* and so she was not made from his head; nor was it right for her to be subject to man's contempt as his slave, and so she was not made from his feet; secondly, for the sacramental signification; for from the side of Christ sleeping on the Cross the Sacraments flowed—namely, blood and water—which were to establish the Church.

Reply Obj. 1. Some say that the woman's body was formed by a material increase, without anything being added; in the same way as our Lord multiplied the five loaves. But this is quite impossible. For such an increase of matter would either be by a change of the very substance of the matter itself, or by a change of its dimensions. Not by change of the substance of the matter, both because matter, considered in itself, is quite unchangeable, since it has a potential existence, and has nothing but the nature of a subject, and because quantity and size are extraneous to the essence of the matter itself, and therefore multiplication of matter is quite unintelligible, as long as the matter itself remains the same without anything added to it; unless it receives greater dimensions. This implies rarefaction, which is for the same matter to receive greater dimensions, as the

Philosopher says *(Phys.* iv.). So to say that the same matter is enlarged, without being rarefied, is to combine contradictories—viz., the definition without the thing defined.

Wherefore, as no rarefaction is apparent in such multiplication of matter, we must admit an addition of matter: either by creation or, which is more probable, by conversion. So Augustine says *(Tract.* xxiv., *in Joan.)* that *Christ filled five thousand men with five loaves, in the same way as from a few seeds He produces the harvest of corn*—that is, by transformation of the food. Nevertheless, we say that God fed the crowds with the loaves, or made woman from the rib, because the addition was made to the already existing matter of the loaves and of the rib.

Reply Obj. 2. The rib belonged to the integral perfection of Adam, not as an individual, but as the principle of the human race; just as the semen belongs to the perfection of the begotten, and is released by a natural and pleasurable operation. Much more, therefore, was it possible that by the Divine power the body of the woman should be produced from the man's rib.

From this it is clear how to answer the third objection.

Fourth Article.
WHETHER THE WOMAN WAS FORMED IMMEDIATELY BY GOD?

We proceed thus to the Fourth Article:—

Objection 1. It seems that the woman was not formed immediately by God. For no individual is produced immediately by God from another individual alike in species. But the woman was made from a man who is of the same species. Therefore she was not made immediately by God.

Obj. 2. Further, Augustine *(De Trin.* iii.) says that corporeal things are governed by God through the angels. But the woman's body was formed from corporeal matter. Therefore it was made through the ministry of the angels, and not immediately by God.

Obj. 3. Further, those things which pre-exist in creatures as to their causal virtues are produced by the power of some creature, and not immediately by God. But the woman's body was produced in its causal virtues among the first created works, as Augustine says *(Gen. ad lit.* ix.). Therefore it was not produced immediately by God.

On the contrary, Augustine says, in the same work: *God alone, to Whom all nature owes its existence, could form or build up the woman from the man's rib.*

I answer that, as was said above (A. 2 ad 2), the natural generation of every species is from some determinate matter. Now the matter whence man is naturally begotten is the human semen of man or woman. Wherefore from any other matter an individual of the human species cannot naturally be generated. Now God alone, the Author of nature, can produce an effect into existence outside the ordinary course of nature. Therefore God alone could produce either a man from the slime of the earth, or a woman from the rib of man.

Reply Obj. 1. This argument is verified when an individual is begotten, by natural generation, from that which is like it in the same species.

Reply Obj. 2. As Augustine says *(Gen. ad lit.* ix.), we do not know whether the angels were employed by God in the formation of the woman; but it is certain that, as the body of man was not formed by the angels from the slime of the earth, so neither was the body of the woman formed by them from the man's rib.

Reply Obj. 3. As Augustine says in the same work: *The first creation of things did not demand that woman should be made thus; it made it possible for her to be thus made.* Therefore the body of the woman did indeed pre-exist in these causal virtues, in the things first created; not as regards active potentiality, but as regards a potentiality passive in relation to the active potentiality of the Creator.

Francis Bacon

During the early years of the seventeenth century when Bacon wrote his essay "Of Marriage and Single Life" (dated 1612), conditions were harsh for women in England as they were in all Europe. The example of Queen Elizabeth resulted in little if any change in women's day-to-day lot. Her successor King James I, Bacon's patron, was especially hostile to women. Persecution of women as witches, originating with the clergy who found a new way of expressing their antifemale bias, continued unabated. Brutal laws rendered a woman totally subject to her husband, without redress if he proved a tyrant, and liable to punishment if she challenged his authority. The long tradition that considered woman a necessary evil to be kept in check persisted. The ultimate check on women's influence, of course, was to avoid them altogether. This position is implicit in Bacon's preference for the single life, which follows the tradition of Paul that celibacy, the avoidance of contact with woman, particularly sexual contact, is the ideal state. Greatness of mind or soul are not compatible with the animal stirrings of sexuality. Furthermore, the private troubles and concerns brought by wives and children distract men from their public work, sapping their intellectual and material resources. While woman is not totally without merit for Bacon—she provides occasion for man to develop discipline and tenderness—nonetheless, men are best advised to avoid the married state altogether. Ironically, even the one respectable role woman is allowed to play, that of wife and mother, ultimately is a burden to man.

LOVE AND MARRIAGE AS
IMPEDIMENTS TO MAN *

He that hath wife and children hath given hostages to fortune; for they are impediments to great enterprises, either of virtue or mischief. Certainly the best works, and of greatest merit for the public, have proceeded from the unmarried or childless men, which, both in affection and means, have married and endowed the public. Yet it were great reason that those that have children should have greatest care of future times, unto which they know they must transmit their dearest pledges. Some there are, who, though they lead a single life, yet their thoughts do end with themselves, and account future times impertinencies; nay, there are some other that account wife and children but as bills of charges: nay, more, there are some foolish rich covetous men that take a pride in having no children, because they may be thought so much the richer; for, perhaps, they have heard some talk, "Such a one is a great rich man," and another except to it, "Yea, but he hath a great charge of

* From Francis Bacon, "Of Marriage and Single Life," in *Essays,* ed. Richard Whately (Boston: Lee and Shepard, 1887).

children," as if it were an abatement to his riches. But the most ordinary cause of a single life is liberty, especially in certain self-pleasing and humorous minds, which are so sensible of every restraint, as they will go near to think their girdles and garters to be bonds and shackles. Unmarried men are best friends, best masters, best servants, but not always best subjects, for they are light to run away, and almost all fugitives are of that condition. A single life doth well with churchmen, for charity will hardly water the ground where it must first fill a pool. It is indifferent for judges and magistrates; for if they be facile and corrupt, you shall have a servant five times worse than a wife. For soldiers, I find the generals commonly, in their hortatives, put men in mind of their wives and children: and I think the despising of marriage among the Turks maketh the vulgar soldier more base. Certainly the wife and children are a kind of discipline of humanity: and single men, though they be many times more charitable, because their means are less exhaust, yet, on the other side, they are more cruel and hard-hearted (good to make severe inquisitors), because their tenderness is not so oft called upon. Grave natures, led by custom, and therefore constant, are commonly loving husbands, as was said of Ulysses, "Vetulam suam praetulit immortalitati." [He preferred his old woman to immortality.] Chaste women are often proud and forward, as presuming upon the merit of their chastity. It is one of the best bonds, both of chastity and obedience, in the wife, if she thinks her husband wise, which she will never do if she finds him jealous. Wives are young men's mistresses, companions for middle age, and old men's nurses, so as a man may have a quarrel to marry when he will; but yet he was reputed one of the wise men that made answer to the question when a man should marry—"A young man not yet, an elder man not at all." It is often seen that bad husbands have very good wives; whether it be that it raiseth the price of their husband's kindness when it comes, or that the wives take a pride in their patience; but this never fails, if the bad husbands were of their own choosing, against their friends' consent: for then they will be sure to make good their own folly.

Thomas Hobbes

The social contract theory of government espoused in the seventeenth and eighteenth centuries—that is, society together with its forms of authority ultimately derives its existence from the consent of the governed—was symptomatic of an important shift in attitude toward authority. Many people had begun to suspect that society and its institutions were not entirely natural and to a certain extent arbitrary. Patriarchal authority in its civic and even in its familial form was being questioned. The sentiment that paternalism was incompatible with freedom and dignity gained a certain credence. The example of colonial governments based on popular consent raised questions concerning the divine right of kings. Hobbes was in the forefront of this rejection of paternalism. He argues in *De Cive* (1642) that being a father does not logically or naturally entail being a lord. Rather, male lordship is the result of a contract of some sort or of brute force. By nature, he says, dominion is maternal for two reasons—the identity of a child's mother alone is certain, and power over a child is initially in the hands of the mother who nourishes and trains it. As for natural right by brute force, Hobbes insists that by nature everyone is equal in the ability to overpower another, if not by superior physical strength, then by wit or cunning; hence the male cannot claim a greater right to lordship than the female on this score. Hobbes puts forth the novel idea that no case can be made for natural patriarchal right in the family, much less the state. Only by an arbitrary agreement between a man and a woman can a mother confer such a right on a man. Historically these agreements have been institutionalized in marriage, which takes various forms depending on whether the governments from which they proceed are controlled by fathers or mothers.

MATERNITY AND THE ORIGIN OF
POLITICAL POWER *

In the two foregoing chapters we have treated of an *institutive* or *framed* government, as being that which receives its original from the consent of many, who by contract and faith mutually given have obliged each other. Now follows what may be said concerning a *natural* government; which may also be called *acquired*, because it is that which is gotten by power and natural force. But we must know in the first place, by what means the right of dominion may be gotten over the persons of men. Where such a right is gotten, there is a kind of a little kingdom; for to be a *king*, is nothing else but to have dominion over many persons; and thus a great family is a kingdom, and a little kingdom a family. Let us return again to the state of nature, and consider men as if but even now sprung out of the earth, and suddenly, like mushrooms, come to full maturity, without all kind of engagement to each other. There are but three

* From Thomas Hobbes, *Philosophical Rudiments Concerning Government and Society* in *The English Works of Thomas Hobbes*, ed. Sir William Molesworth (London: John Bohn, 1841), Vol. 2, Chaps. 8, 9. Originally published as *De Cive*.

ways only, whereby one can have a dominion over the person of another; wherof the first is, if by mutual contract made between themselves, for peace and self-defence's sake, they have willingly given up themselves to the power and authority of some man, or council of men; and of this we have already spoken. The second is, if a man taken prisoner in the wars, or overcome, or else distrusting his own forces, to avoid death, promises the conqueror or the stronger party his *service,* that is, to do all whatsoever he shall command him. In which contract, the good which the vanquished or inferior in strength doth receive, is the grant of his life, which by the right of war in the natural state of men he might have been deprived of; but the good which he promises is his service and obedience. By virtue therefore of this promise, there is an absolute service and obedience due from the vanquished to the vanquisher, as possibly can be, excepting what repugns the divine laws; for he who is obliged to obey the commands of any man before he knows what he will command him, is simply and without any restriction tied to the performance of all commands whatsoever. Now he that is thus tied, is called a *servant;* he to whom he is tied, a *lord.* Thirdly, there is a right acquired over the person of a man by generation. . . .

SOCRATES *is a man, and therefore a living creature,* is right reasoning; and that most evident, because there is nothing needful to the acknowledging of the truth of the consequence, but that the word *man* be understood; because *a living creature* is in the definition itself of a *man,* and every one makes up the proposition which was desired, namely this, *man is a living creature.* And this, *Sophroniscus is Socrates' father, and therefore his lord,* is perhaps a true inference, but not evident; because the word *lord* is not in the definition of a *father:* wherefore it is necessary, to make it more evident, that the connexion of *father* and *lord* be somewhat unfolded. Those that have hitherto endeavoured to prove the dominion of a parent over his children, have brought no other argument than that of *generation;* as if it were of itself evident, that what is begotten by me is mine; just as if a man should think, that because there is a triangle, it appears presently, without any further discourse, that its angles are equal to two right. Besides, since dominion, that is, supreme power is indivisible, insomuch as no man can serve two masters; but two persons, male and female, must concur in the act of generation; it is impossible that dominion should at all be acquired by generation only. Wherefore we will, with the more diligence, in this place inquire into the original of *paternal government.*

We must therefore return to the state of nature, in which, by reason of equality of nature, all men of riper years are to be accounted equal. There *by right of nature* the conqueror is lord of the conquered. By the right therefore of *nature*, the dominion over the infant first belongs to him who first hath him in his power. But it is manifest that he who is newly born, is in the *mother's* power before any others; insomuch as she may rightly, and at her own will, either breed him up or adventure him to fortune.

If therefore she breed him, because the state of nature is the state of war, she is supposed to bring him up on this condition; that being grown to full age he become not her enemy; which is, that he obey her. For since by natural necessity we all desire that which appears good unto us, it cannot be understood that any man hath on such terms afforded life to another, that he might both get strength by his years, and at once become an enemy. But each man is an enemy to that other, whom he neither obeys nor commands. And thus in the state of nature, every woman that bears children, becomes both a *mother* and a *lord.* But what some say, that in this case the *father,* by reason of the pre-eminence of sex, and not the *mother* becomes *lord,* signifies nothing. For both reason shows the contrary; because the inequality of their natural forces is not so great, that the man could get the dominion over the woman without war. And custom also contradicts not; for women, namely Amazons, have in former times waged war against their adversaries, and disposed of their children at their own wills. And at this day, in divers places women are invested with the principal authority; neither do their husbands dispose of their children, but themselves;

which in truth they do *by the right of nature;* forasmuch as they who have the supreme power, are not tied at all (as hath been shewed) to the civil laws. Add also, that in the state of nature it cannot be known who is the *father,* but by the testimony of the *mother;* the child therefore is his whose the mother will have it, and therefore hers. Wherefore original dominion over *children* belongs to the *mother*: and among men no less than other creatures, the birth follows the belly.

The dominion passes from the mother to others, divers ways. First, if she quit and forsake her right by *exposing* the child. He therefore that shall bring up the child thus exposed, shall have the same dominion over it which the mother had. For that life which the mother had given it, (not by *getting* but *nourishing* it), she now by *exposing* takes from it. Wherefore the obligation also which arose from the benefit of life, is by this exposition made void. Now the preserved oweth all to the preserver, whether in regard of his education as to a *mother,* or of his service as to a *lord.* For although the mother in the state of nature, where all men have a right to all things, may recover her son again, namely, by the same right that anybody else might do it; yet may not the son rightly transfer himself again unto his mother.

Secondly, if the mother be taken prisoner, her son is his that took her; because that he who hath dominion over the person, hath also dominion over all belonging to the person; wherefore over the son also, as hath been shewed in the foregoing chapter, in the fifth article. Thirdly, if the mother be a subject under what government soever, he that hath the supreme authority in that government, will also have the dominion over him that is born of her; for he is lord also of the mother, who is bound to obey him in all things. Fourthly, if a woman for society's sake give herself to a man on this condition, that he shall bear the sway; he that receives his being from the contribution of both parties, is the *father's,* in regard of the command he hath over the *mother.* But if a woman bearing rule shall have children, by a subject, the children are the *mother's;* for otherwise the woman can have no children without prejudice to her authority. And universally, if the society of the male and female be such an union, as the one have subjected himself to the other, the children belong to him or her that commands.

But in the state of nature, if a man and woman contract so, as neither is subject to the command of the other, the children are the mother's, for the reasons above given in the third article, unless by pacts it be otherwise provided. For the *mother* may by pact dispose of her right as she lists; as heretofore hath been done by the Amazons, who of those children which have been begotten by their neighbours, have by pact allowed them the *males,* and retained the *females* to themselves. But in a civil government, if there be a contract of marriage between a man and woman, the children are the *father's;* because in all cities, to wit, constituted of *fathers,* not *mothers* governing their families, the domestical command belongs to the man; and such a contract, if it be made according to the civil laws, is called matrimony. But if they agree only to lie together, the children are the *father's* or the *mother's* variously, according to the differing civil laws of divers cities.

John Locke

As a social contract theorist, Locke too rejected the patriarchal concept of civil authority that had historically been used to support the rights of kings. In particular he rejected the idea advanced by some that Adam was granted a divine right to rule and argued that even if God had conferred such authority, it was not necessarily passed down to his male heirs. Like Hobbes, he turned to the family to provide an account of the origin of authority, and like Hobbes, he rejected the idea that a father rules his family by virtue of natural right. However, he disagreed with Hobbes' assertion that power over children, derived from the reproductive act, is by nature invested in the mother. Locke wrote in his *Second Treatise of Civil Government* (1690) that familial power is vested equally in mother and father, not in one or the other. He supported this position on rational and scriptural grounds: Scripture reveals that children owe obedience to both father and mother, while reason reveals that the child's physical and intellectual weakness and inability to give consent render it temporarily under the jurisdiction of both parents, each of whom has a share in its existence. Natural law, that is, the divine order inherent in the nature of things, cannot be contradicted by parental or civil authority but can only be enforced by them in order to preserve and enhance the freedom of the individual. While Locke is often referred to as the most representative thinker in the English-American political system, his ideas on the equal rights and authority of women and men have been virtually ignored by people who adopted his other ideas wholesale. When Thomas Jefferson, who is often accused of plagiarizing the *Second Treatise* in his Declaration of Independence, copied the phrase "all men are created equal" from Locke, he did not mean what Locke had meant—*all* men, male and female.

MATERNITY, PATERNITY, AND THE ORIGIN OF POLITICAL POWER *

To understand political power right, and derive it from its original, we must consider what state all men are naturally in, and that is, a state of perfect freedom to order their actions and dispose of their possessions and persons, as they think fit, within the bounds of the law of nature; without asking leave, or depending upon the will of any other man.

A state also of equality, wherein all the power and jurisdiction is reciprocal, no one having more than another; there being nothing more evident, than that creatures of the same species and rank, promiscuously born to all the same advantages of nature, and the use of the same faculties, should also be equal one amongst another without subordination or subjection; unless the lord and master of them all should, by any manifest declaration of his will, set one above another, and confer on him, by an evident and clear appointment, an undoubted right to dominion and sovereignty. . . .

*From John Locke, *Second Treatise of Civil Government* in *The Works of John Locke* (London: C. and G. Rivington, etc., 1824), Vol. 4, Chaps. II, VI.

It may perhaps be censured as an impertinent criticism, in a discourse of this nature, to find fault with words and names, that have obtained in the world: and yet possibly it may not be amiss to offer new ones, when the old are apt to lead men into mistakes, as this of paternal power probably has done; which seems so to place the power of parents over their children wholly in the father, as if the mother had no share in it: whereas, if we consult reason or revelation, we shall find she hath an equal title. This may give one reason to ask, whether this might not be more properly called parental power? For whatever obligation nature and the right of generation lays on children, it must certainly bind them equally to both concurrent causes of it. And accordingly we see the positive law of God every where joins them together without distinction, when it commands the obedience of children: "Honour thy father and thy mother," Exod. xx. 12. "Whosoever curseth his father or his mother," Lev. xx. 9. "Ye shall fear every man his mother and his father," Lev. xix. 5. "Children, obey your parents," etc., Eph. vi. 1, is the style of the Old and New Testament.

Had but this one thing been well considered, without looking any deeper into the matter, it might perhaps have kept men from running into those gross mistakes they have made, about this power of parents; which, however it might, without any great harshness, bear the name of absolute dominion, and regal authority, when under the title of paternal power it seemed appropriated to the father, would yet have sounded but oddly, and in the very name shown the absurdity, if this supposed absolute power over children had been called parental; and thereby have discovered, that it belonged to the mother too: for it will but very ill serve the turn of those men, who contend so much for the absolute power and authority of the fatherhood, as they call it, that the mother should have any share in it; and it would have but ill supported the monarchy they contend for, when by the very name it appeared that that fundamental authority, from whence they would derive their government of a single person only, was not placed in one, but two persons jointly. But to let this of names pass.

Though I have said above, chap. ii. "That all men by nature are equal," I cannot be supposed to understand all sorts of equality: age or virtue may give men a just precedency: excellency of parts and merit may place others above the common level: birth may subject some, and alliance or benefits others, to pay an observance to those whom nature, gratitude, or other respects, may have made it due: and yet all this consists with the equality, which all men are in, in respect of jurisdiction or dominion one over another; which was the equality I there spoke of, as proper to the business in hand, being that equal right, that every man hath, to his natural freedom, without being subjected to the will or authority of any other man.

Children, I confess, are not born in this state of equality, though they are born to it. Their parents have a sort of rule and jurisdiction over them, when they come into the world, and for some time after; but it is but a temporary one. The bonds of this subjection are like the swaddling clothes they are wrapt up in, and supported by, in the weakness of their infancy: age and reason as they grow up loosen them, till at length they drop quite off, and leave a man at his own free disposal.

Adam was created a perfect man, his body and mind in full possession of their strength and reason, and so was capable from the first instant of his being to provide for his own support and preservation; and govern his actions according to the dictates of the law of reason which God had implanted in him. From him the world is peopled with his descendants, who are all born infants, weak and helpless, without knowledge or understanding: but to supply the defects of this imperfect state, till the improvement of growth and age hath removed them, Adam and Eve, and after them all parents were, by the law of nature, "under an obligation to preserve, nourish, and educate the children," they had begotten; not as their own workmanship, but the workmanship of their own maker, the Almighty, to whom they were to be accountable for them.

The law, that was to govern Adam, was the same that was to govern all his posterity, the law of reason. But his offspring having another way of entrance into the world, different from him, by a natural birth, that produced them ignorant and without the use of reason, they were not presently under that law; for nobody can be under a law, which is not promulgated to him; and this law being promulgated or made known by reason only, he that is not come to the use of his reason, cannot be said to be under this law; and Adam's children, being not presently as soon as born, under this law of reason, were not presently free: for law, in its true notion, is not so much the limitation, as the direction of a free and intelligent agent to his proper interest, and prescribes no farther than is for the general good of those under that law: could they be happier without it, the law, as a useless thing, would of itself vanish; and that ill deserves the name of confinement which hedges us in only from bogs and precipices. So that, however it may be mistaken, the end of law is not to abolish or restrain, but to preserve and enlarge freedom: for in all the states of created beings capable of laws, "where there is no law, there is no freedom;" for liberty is to be free from restraint and violence from others; which cannot be where there is not law: but freedom is not, as we are told, "a liberty for every man to do what he lists": (for who could be free, when every other man's humour might domineer over him?) but a liberty to dispose, and order as he lists, his person, actions, possessions, and his whole property, within the allowance of those laws under which he is, and therein not to be subject to the arbitrary will of another, but freely follow his own.

The power, then, that parents have over their children, arises from that duty which is incumbent on them, to take care of their offspring during the imperfect state of childhood. To inform the mind, and govern the actions of their yet ignorant nonage, till reason shall take its place, and ease them of that trouble, is what the children want, and the parents are bound to: for God having given man an understanding to direct his actions, has allowed him a freedom of will, and liberty of acting, as properly belonging thereunto, within the bounds of that law he is under. But whilst he is in an estate, wherein he has not understanding of his own to direct his will, he is not to have any will of his own to follow: he that understands for him, must will for him too; he must prescribe to his will, and regulate his actions: but when he comes to the estate that made his father a freeman, the son is a freeman too. . . .

But what reason can hence advance this care of the parents due to their offspring into an absolute arbitrary dominion of the father, whose power reaches no farther than, by such a discipline as he finds most effectual, to give such strength and health to their bodies, such vigour and rectitude to their minds, as may best fit his children to be most useful to themselves and others: and, if it be necessary to his condition, to make them work, when they are able, for their own subsistence. But in this power the mother too has her share with the father.

Nay, this power so little belongs to the father by any peculiar right of nature, but only as he is guardian of his children, that when he quits his care of them, he loses his power over them, which goes along with their nourishment and education, to which it is inseparable annexed; and it belongs as much to the foster-father of an exposed child, as to the natural father of another. So little power does the bare act of begetting give a man over his issue; if all his care ends there, and this be all the title he hath to the name and authority of a father. And what will become of this paternal power in that part of the world, where one woman hath more than one husband at a time? or in those parts of America, where, when the husband and wife part, which happens frequently, the children are all left to the mother, follow her, and are wholly under her care and provision? If the father die whilst the children are young, do they not naturally every where owe the same obedience to their mother, during the minority, as to their father were he alive; and will any one say, that the mother hath a legislative power over her children? that she can make standing rules, which shall be of perpetual obligation, by which they ought to regulate all the concerns of their property, and bound their liberty all the course of their lives? or can she enforce the observation of them with capital punishments? for this is the proper power of the magistrate, of which the father hath not so much as the shadow. His command over his children is but temporary, and reaches not their life or property: it is but a help to the weakness and imperfection of their nonage, a discipline necessary to their education: and though a father may dispose of his own possessions as he pleases, when his children are out of danger of perishing for want, yet his power extends not to the lives or goods, which either their own industry, or another's bounty has made theirs; nor to their liberty neither, when they are once arrived to the infranchisement of the years of discretion. The father's empire then ceases, and can from thenceforwards no more dispose of the liberty of his son, than that of any other man: and it must be far from an absolute or perpetual jurisdiction, from which a man may withdraw himself, having licence from divine authority to "leave father and mother, and cleave to his wife." . . .

A man may owe honour and respect to an ancient, or wise man; defence to his child or friend; relief and support to the distressed; and gratitude to a benefactor, to such a degree, that all he has, all he can do, cannot sufficiently pay it: but all these give no authority, no right to any one, of making laws over him from whom they are owing. And it is plain, all this is due not only to the bare title of father; not only because, as has been said, it is owing to the mother too, but because these obligations to parents, and the degrees of what is required of children, may be varied by the different care and kindness, trouble and expense, which are often employed upon one child more than another.

This shows the reason how it comes to pass, that parents in societies, where they themselves are subjects, retain a power over their children, and have as much right to their subjection as those who are in the state of nature. Which could not possibly be, if all political power were only paternal, and that in truth they were one and the same thing: for then, all paternal power being in the prince, the subject could naturally have none of it. But these two powers, political and paternal, are so perfectly distinct and separate, are built upon so different foundations, and given to so different ends, that every subject that is a father, has as much a paternal power over his children, as the prince has over his: and every prince, that has parents, owes them as much filial duty and obedience, as the meanest of his subjects do to theirs; and cannot therefore contain any part or degree of that kind of dominion which a prince or magistrate has over his subjects. . . .

To conclude then, though the father's power of commanding extends no farther than the minority of his children, and to a degree only fit for the discipline and government of that age; and though that honour and respect, and all that which the Latins called piety, which they indispensably owe to their parents all their lifetime, and in all estates, with all that support and defence which is due to them, gives the father no power of governing, i.e., making laws and enacting penalties on his children; though by all this he has no dominion over the property or actions of his son; yet it is obvious to conceive how easy it was, in the first ages of the world, and in places still, where the thinness of people gives families leave to separate into unpossessed quarters, and they have room to remove or plant themselves in yet vacant habitations, for the father of the family to become the prince [1] of it; he had been a ruler from the beginning of the infancy of his children: and since without some government it would be hard for them to live together, it was likeliest it should, by the express or tacit consent of the children when they were grown up, be in the father, where it seemed without any change barely to continue; when indeed nothing more

[1] It is no improbable opinion, therefore, which the arch-philosopher was of, "That the chief person in every household was always, as it were, a king: so when numbers of households joined themselves in civil societies together, kings were the first kind of governors amongst them, which is also, as it seemeth, the reason why the name of fathers continued still in them, who, of fathers, were made rulers; as also the ancient custom of governors to do as Melchizedeck, and being kings, to exercise the office of priests, which fathers did at the first, grew perhaps by the same occasion. Howbeit, this is not the only kind of regiment that has been received in the world. The inconveniencies of one kind have caused sundry others to be devised; so that, in a word, all public regiment, of what kind soever, seemeth evidently to have risen from the deliberate advice, consultation, and composition between men, judging it convenient and behoveful; there being no impossibility in nature considered by itself, but that man might have lived without any public regiment." Hooker's Eccl. P. 1.i. sect. 10.

was required to it, than the permitting the father to exercise alone, in his family, that executive power of the law of nature, which every free man naturally hath, and by that permission resigning up to him a monarchical power, whilst they remained in it. But that this was not by any paternal right, but only by the consent of his children, is evident from hence, that nobody doubts, but if a stranger, whom chance or business had brought to his family, had there killed any of his children, or committed any other fact, he might condemn and put him to death, or otherwise punish him, as well as any of his children: which it was impossible he should do by virtue of any paternal authority over one who was not his child, but by virtue of that executive power of the law of nature, which, as a man, he had a right to: and he alone could punish him in his family, where the respect of his children had laid by the exercise of such a power, to give way to the dignity and authority they were willing should remain in him, above the rest of his family.

Thus it was easy, and almost natural for children, by a tacit, and scarce avoidable consent, to make way for the father's authority and government. They had been accustomed in their childhood to follow his direction, and to refer their little differences to him; and when they were men, who fitter to rule them? Their little properties, and less covetousness, seldom afforded greater controversies; and when any should arise, where could they have a fitter umpire than he, by whose care they had every one been sustained and brought up, and who had a tenderness for them all? It is no wonder that they made no distinction betwixt minority and full age; nor looked after one and twenty, or any other age that might make them the free disposers of themselves and fortunes, when they could have no desire to be out of their pupilage: the government they had been under during it, continued still to be more their protection than restraint: and they could no-where find a greater security to their peace, liberties, and fortunes, than in the rule of a father.

Thus the natural fathers of families by an insensible change became the politic monarchs of them too: and as they chanced to live long, and leave able and worthy heirs, for several successions, or otherwise; so they laid the foundations of hereditary, or elective kingdoms, under several constitutions and manners, according as chance, contrivance, or occasions happened to mould them. But if princes have their titles in their fathers right, and it be a sufficient proof of the natural right of fathers to political authority, because they commonly were those in whose hands we find, de facto, the exercise of government: I say, if this argument be good, it will as strongly prove, that all princes, nay princes only, ought to be priests, since it is as certain, that in the beginning, "the father of the family was priest, as that he was ruler in his own household."

Jean Jacques Rousseau

Under Rousseau, the social contract theory took an invidious turn. The social contract was conceived by Hobbes and Locke as requiring the consent of all the governed and predicated on the belief that all are by nature equal in their individual human rights. Rousseau reduced the "all" to "men." In his famous *Social Contract* he does not mention women, nor indeed could he without exposing a contradiction between his ideas about women and his radical egalitarian ideals. One of the consistent themes of his life and works was that women are inferior and subordinate beings who should be nurtured for the sole purpose of serving men and providing them pleasure. He preached that women should be restricted to domestic chores and excluded from liberal education, urging that they be "trained to bear the yoke from the first, so that they may not feel it." In *A Discourse on Political Economy* (1755), he states that the primary function of the family is to "preserve and increase the patrimony of the father" so that he may pass it on to his heirs. He insists that the patriarchal structure of the family is natural, while denying any analogy with the state. Men may govern women but not men. Rousseau's rigid apportionment of sex roles was at once reactionary and pacesetting. It was a reaction against women's attempts to expand their prerogatives, especially via the so-called blue-stocking salons springing up throughout Europe; it was also a model for subsequent relations between men and women, particularly after the French Revolution, which, ironically, women vigorously supported. The architects of the Revolution adopted not only his radical egalitarianism, if only in principle, but also his elitist pronouncements on women.

PATERNITY AND THE ORIGIN OF
POLITICAL POWER *

The word Economy, or Oeconomy, is derived from ὀικός, a house, and νόμας, law, and meant originally only the wise and legitimate government of the house for the common good of the whole family. The meaning of the term was then extended to the government of that great family, the State. To distinguish these two senses of the word, the latter is called *general* or *political* economy, and the former domestic or particular economy. The first only is discussed in the present discourse.

Even if there were as close an analogy as many authors maintain between the State and the family, it would not follow that the rules of conduct proper for one of these societies would be also proper for the other. They differ too much in extent to be regulated in the same manner; and there will always be a great difference between domestic government, in which a father can see everything for

* From Jean Jacques Rousseau, *A Discourse on Political Economy* in *The Social Contract and Discourses,* trans. G.D.H. Cole (London: J.M. Dent and Sons, Ltd., 1913).

himself, and civil government, where the chief sees hardly anything save through the eyes of others. To put both on an equality in this respect, the talents, strength, and all the faculties of the father would have to increase in proportion to the size of his family, and the soul of a powerful monarch would have to be, to that of an ordinary man, as the extent of his empire is to that of a private person's estate.

But how could the government of the State be like that of the family, when the basis on which they rest is so different? The father being physically stronger than his children, his paternal authority, as long as they need his protection, may be reasonably said to be established by nature. But in the great family, all the members of which are naturally equal, the political authority, being purely arbitrary as far as its institution is concerned, can be founded only on conventions, and the Magistrate can have no authority over the rest, except by virtue of the laws. The duties of a father are dictated to him by natural feelings, and in a manner that seldom allows him to neglect them. For rulers there is no such principle, and they are really obliged to the people only by what they themselves have promised to do, and the people have therefore a right to require of them. Another more important difference is that since the children have nothing but what they receive from their father, it is plain that all the rights of property belong to him, or emanate from him; but quite the opposite is the case in the great family, where the general administration is established only to secure individual property, which is antecedent to it. The principal object of the work of the whole house is to preserve and increase the patrimony of the father in order that he may be able some day to distribute among his children without impoverishing them; whereas the wealth of the exchequer is only a means, often ill understood, of keeping the individuals in peace and plenty. In a word, the little family is destined to be extinguished, and to resolve itself some day into several families of a similar nature; but the great family, being constituted to endure for ever in the same condition, need not, like the small one, increase for the purpose of multiplying, but need only maintain itself; and it can easily be proved that any increase does it more harm than good.

In the family, it is clear, for several reasons which lie in its very nature, that the father ought to command. In the first place, the authority ought not to be equally divided between father and mother; the government must be single, and in every division of opinion there must be one preponderant voice to decide. Secondly, however lightly we may regard the disadvantages peculiar to women, yet, as they necessarily occasion intervals of inaction, this is a sufficient reason for excluding them from this supreme authority: for when the balance is perfectly even, a straw is enough to turn the scale. Besides, the husband ought to be able to superintend his wife's conduct, because it is of importance for him to be assured that the children, whom he is obligated to acknowledge and maintain, belong to no one but himself. Thirdly, children should be obedient to their father, at first of necessity, and afterwards from gratitude: after having had their wants satisfied by him during one half of their lives, they ought to consecrate the other half to providing for his. Fourthly, servants owe him their services in exchange for the provision he makes for them, though they may break off the bargain as soon as it ceases to suit them. I say nothing here of slavery, because it is contrary to nature, and cannot be authorized by any right or law.

There is nothing of all this in political society, in which the chief is so far from having any natural interest in the happiness of the individuals, that it is not uncommon for him to seek his own in their misery. If the magistracy is hereditary, a community of men is often governed by a child. If it be elective, innumerable inconveniences arise from such election; while in both cases all the advantages of paternity are lost. If you have but a single ruler, you lie at the discretion of a master who has no reason to love you: and if you have several, you must bear at once their tyranny and their divisions. In a word, abuses are inevitable and their consequences fatal in every society where the public interest and the laws have no natural force, and are perpetually attacked by personal interest and the passions of the ruler and the members.

Although the functions of the father of a family and those of the chief magistrate ought to make for the same object, they must do so in such different ways, and their duty and rights are so essentially distinct, that we cannot confound them without forming very false ideas about the fundamental laws of society, and falling into errors which are fatal to mankind. In fact, if the voice of nature is the best counsellor to which a father can listen in the discharge of his duty, for the Magistrate it is a false guide, which continually prevents him for performing this, and leads sooner or later to the ruin of himself and of the State, if he is not restrained by the most sublime virtue. The only precaution necessary for the father of a family is to guard himself against depravity, and prevent his natural inclinations from being corrupted; whereas it is these themselves which corrupt the Magistrate. In order to act aright, the first has only to consult his heart; the other becomes a traitor the moment he listens to his. Even his own reason should be suspect to him, nor should he follow any rule other than the public reason, which is the law. Thus nature has made a multitude of good fathers of families; but it is doubtful whether, from the very beginning of the world, human wisdom has made ten men capable of governing their peers.

David Hume

As part of his criticism of social-contract theories, Hume denied that agreement alone explains why some people obey others. For example, how can we explain the fact, cited by Hobbes, that women have agreed in the marriage contract to confer patriarchal rights on men? According to Hume this agreement, like all conventional agreements, must ultimately be explained on grounds of utility. In his famous *Treatise of Human Nature* (1740), he agrees with Hobbes that men labor under a considerable disadvantage, since the paternity of a child is virtually impossible to ascertain. Given that society's interest is served by the propagation and nurture of the species, it is clear that something must be done to assure men that their wives' children are their own. Without such assurance, men are unlikely to make the sacrifices necessary to assist women in the care and education of children. Hume recognizes that a marriage contract in itself could not provide this assurance, that the problem is ultimately a psychological one: how to instill in women an obligation to bear children, but at the same time render everything to do with sex repulsive. Society, namely male society, accomplishes its end through an elaborate process of habituation beginning in infancy when the female mind is plastic and impressionable, and admits of no exception (even for old and sterile women), lest the reason for different standards for the sexes should become evident. With characteristic honesty, Hume affirms that these demands on women have no basis in justice, merely in utility. Hume's views bear a striking resemblance to later male-conspiracy theories.

THE CONVENTIONAL ORIGIN OF

FEMALE VIRTUES *

If any difficulty attend this system concerning the laws of nature and nations, 'twill be with regard to the universal approbation or blame, which follows their observance or transgression, and which some may not think sufficiently explained from the general interests of society. To remove, as far as possible, all scruples of this kind, I shall here consider another set of duties, *viz.* the *modesty* and *chastity* which belong to the fair sex: And I doubt not but these virtues will be found to be still more conspicuous instances of the operation of those principles, which I have insisted on.

There are some philosophers, who attack the female virtues with great vehemence, and fancy they have gone very far in detecting popular errors, when they can show, that there is no foundation in nature for all that exterior modesty, which we require in the expressions, and dress, and behaviour of the fair sex. I believe I may spare myself the trouble of insisting on so obvious a subject,

* From David Hume, *A Treatise of Human Nature*, ed. L.A. Selby-Bigge (London: Oxford University Press, 1888), Bk. III, Part 2, Sect. 12.

and may proceed, without farther preparation to examine after what manner such notions arise from education, from the voluntary conventions of men, and from the interest of society.

Whoever considers the length and feebleness of human infancy, with the concern which both sexes naturally have for their offspring, will easily perceive, that there must be an union of male and female for the education of the young, and that this union must be of considerable duration. But in order to induce the men to impose on themselves this restraint, and undergo cheerfully all the fatigues and expences, to which it subjects them, they must believe, that the children are their own, and that their natural instinct is not directed to a wrong object, when they give a loose to love and tenderness. Now if we examine the structure of the human body, we shall find, that this security is very difficult to be attained on our part; and that since, in the copulation of the sexes, the principle of generation goes from the man to the woman, an error may easily take place on the side of the former, tho' it be utterly impossible with regard to the latter. From this trivial and anatomical observation is derived that vast difference betwixt the education and duties of the two sexes.

Were a philosopher to examine the matter *a priori,* he wou'd reason after the following manner. Men are induc'd to labour for the maintenance and education of their children, by the persuasion that they are really their own; and therefore 'tis reasonable, and even necessary, to give them some security in this particular. This security cannot consist entirely in the imposing of severe punishments on any transgressions of conjugal fidelity on the part of the wife; since these public punishments cannot be inflicted without legal proof, which 'tis difficult to meet with in this subject. What restraint, therefore, shall we impose on women, in order to counterbalance so strong a temptation as they have to infidelity? There seems to be no restraint possible, but in the punishment of bad fame or reputation; a punishment, which has a mighty influence on the human mind, and at the same time is inflicted by the world upon surmises, and conjectures, and proofs, that wou'd never be receiv'd in any court of judicature. In order, therefore, to impose a due restraint on the female sex, we must attach a peculiar degree of shame to their infidelity, above what arises merely from its injustice, and must bestow proportionable praises on their chastity.

But tho' this be a very strong motive to fidelity, our philosopher wou'd quickly discover, that it wou'd not alone be sufficient to that purpose. All human creatures, especially of the female sex, are apt to over-look remote motives in favour of any present temptation: The temptation is here the strongest imaginable: Its approaches are insensible and seducing: And a woman easily finds, or flatters herself she shall find, certain means of securing her reputation, and preventing all the pernicious consequences of her pleasures. 'Tis necessary, therefore, that, beside the infamy attending such licences, there shou'd be some preceding backwardness or dread, which may prevent their first approaches, and may give the female sex a repugnance to all expressions, and postures, and liberties, that have an immediate relation to that enjoyment.

Such wou'd be the reasoning of our speculative philosopher: But I am persuaded, that if he had not a perfect knowledge of human nature, he wou'd be apt to regard them as mere chimerical speculations, and wou'd consider the infamy attending infidelity, and backwardness to all its approaches, as principles that were rather to be wish'd than hop'd for in the world. For what means, wou'd he say, of persuading mankind, that the transgressions of conjugal duty are more infamous than any other kind of injustice, when 'tis evident they are more excusable, upon account of the greatness of the temptation? And what possibility of giving a backwardness to the approaches of a pleasure, to which nature has inspir'd so strong a propensity; and a propensity that 'tis absolutely necessary in the end to comply with, for the support of the species?

But speculative reasonings, which cost so much pains to philosophers, are often form'd by the world naturally, and without reflection: As difficulties, which seem unsurmountable in theory, are easily got over in practice. Those, who have an interest in the fidelity of women, naturally disapprove of their infidelity, and all the approaches to it. Those, who have no interest, are carried along with the stream. Education takes possession of the ductile minds of the fair sex in their infancy. And when a general rule of this kind is once establish'd, men are apt to extend it beyond those principles, from which it first arose. Thus batchelors, however debauch'd, cannot chuse but be shock'd with any instance of lewdness or impudence in women. And tho' all these maxims have a plain reference to generation, yet women past child-bearing have no more privilege in this respect, than those who are in the flower of their youth and beauty. Men have undoubtedly an implicit notion, that all those ideas of modesty and decency have a regard to generation; since they impose not the same laws, *with the same force,* on the male sex, where that reason takes not place. The exception is there obvious and extensive, and founded on a remarkable difference, which produces a clear separation and disjunction of ideas. But as the case is not the same with regard to the different ages of women, for this reason, tho' men know, that these notions are founded on the public interest, yet the general rule carries us beyond the original principle, and makes us extend the notions of modesty over the whole sex, from their earliest infancy to their extremest old-age and infirmity.

Courage, which is the point of honour among men, derives its merit, in a great measure, from artifice, as well as the chastity of women; tho' it has also some foundation in nature, as we shall see afterwards.

As to the obligations which the male sex lie under, with regard to chastity, we may observe, that according to the general notions of the world, they bear nearly the same proportion to the obligations of women, as the obligations of the law of nations do to those of the law of nature. 'Tis contrary to the interest of civil society, that men shou'd have an *entire* liberty of indulging their appetites in venereal enjoyment. But as this interest is weaker than in the case of the female sex, the moral obligation, arising from it, must be proportionably weaker. And to prove this we need only appeal to the practice and sentiments of all nations and ages.

Immanuel Kant

By the eighteenth century a picture of the ideal woman had formed: the "lady." The idea of the lady was born in the Middle Ages when aristocratic women became the object of romantic love in chivalric literature. The medieval concept of the ideal woman who evoked courtesy and adoration in well-bred men marked a significant break with the Christian tradition and its literature, in which neither woman nor passionate love had any significant place. In one form or another the concept of the lady was destined for a long life stretching across centuries. This is the image Kant extolls in his *Observations on the Feeling of the Beautiful and the Sublime* (1764), an essay that deals with kinds of pleasure and their relation to beauty and sublimity. Complementarity is the foundation of Kant's belief that each sex contributes a different principle to marriage, forming together a "single moral person." The noble male contributes rationality and learning; the beautiful female contributes taste and pleasantry. The outstanding criterion of femininity is charm, which Kant regards as a kind of magic exercised on men. So important is charm that Kant admonishes women against the pursuit of learning, an endeavor sure to weaken their power to attract men. Even woman's vanity cannot be condemned, since it enhances her charm. Women have no sense of duty because they live by feeling, while men live by reason. Morality in women amounts to a feeling of propriety, Kant says, avoiding evil because it is ugly, not because it is wrong. Finally, although nobility and sublimity are characteristic of men, women rise to nobility in modesty and to sublimity in their ability to treasure men.

THE INTERRELATIONS OF THE
TWO SEXES *

He who first conceived of woman under the name of the *fair sex*
probably wanted to say something flattering, but he has hit upon it
better than even he himself might have believed. For without
taking into consideration that her figure in general is finer, her
features more delicate and gentler, and her mien more engaging
and more expressive of friendliness, pleasantry, and kindness than in
the male sex, and not forgetting what one must reckon as a secret
magic with which she makes our passion inclined to judgments
favorable to her—even so, certain specific traits lie especially in the
personality of this sex which distinguish it clearly from ours and
chiefly result in making her known by the mark of the beautiful.
On the other side, we could make a claim on the title of the *noble
sex*, if it were not required of a noble disposition to decline honorific
titles and rather to bestow than to receive them. It is not to be
understood by this that woman lacks noble qualities, or that the

* From Immanuel Kant, *Observations on the Feeling of the Beautiful and Sublime*,
trans. John T. Goldthwait (Berkeley: University of California Press, 1960), Sect. 3.

male sex must do without beauty completely. On the contrary, one expects that a person of either sex brings both together, in such a way that all the other merits of a woman should unite solely to enhance the character of the beautiful, which is the proper reference point; and on the other hand, among the masculine qualities the sublime clearly stands out as the criterion of his kind. All judgments of the two sexes must refer to these criteria, those that praise as well as those that blame; all education and instruction must have these before its eyes, and all efforts to advance the moral perfection of the one or the other—unless one wants to disguise the charming distinction that nature has chosen to make between the two sorts of human being. For here it is not enough to keep in mind that we are dealing with human beings; we must also remember that they are not all alike.

Women have a strong inborn feeling for all that is beautiful, elegant, and decorated. Even in childhood they like to be dressed up, and take pleasure when they are adorned. They are cleanly and very delicate in respect to all that provokes disgust. They love pleasantry and can be entertained by trivialities if only these are merry and laughing. Very early they have a modest manner about themselves, know how to give themselves a fine demeanor and be self-possessed—and this at an age when our well-bred male youth is still unruly, clumsy, and confused. They have many sympathetic sensations, goodheartedness, and compassion, prefer the beautiful to the useful, and gladly turn abundance of circumstance into parsimony, in order to support expenditure on adornment and glitter. They have very delicate feelings in regard to the least offense, and are exceedingly precise to notice the most trifling lack of attention and respect toward them. In short, they contain the chief cause in human nature for the contrast of the beautiful qualities with the noble, and they refine even the masculine sex.

I hope the reader will spare me the reckoning of the manly qualities, so far as they are parallel to the feminine, and be content only to consider both in comparison with each other. The fair sex has just as much understanding as the male, but it is a *beautiful understanding,* whereas ours should be a *deep understanding,* an expression that signifies identity with the sublime.

To the beauty of all actions belongs above all the mark that they display facility, and appear to be accomplished without painful toil. On the other hand, strivings and surmounted difficulties arouse admiration and belong to the sublime. Deep meditation and a long-sustained reflection are noble but difficult, and do not well befit a person in whom unconstrained charms should show nothing else than a beautiful nature. Laborious learning or painful pondering, even if a woman should greatly succeed in it, destroy the merits that are proper to her sex, and because of their rarity they can make of her an object of cold admiration; but at the same time they will weaken the charms with which she exercises her great power over the other sex. A woman who has a head full of Greek, like Mme Dacier, or carries on fundamental controversies about mechanics, like the Marquise de Châtelet, might as well even have a beard; for perhaps that would express more obviously the mien of profundity for which she strives. The beautiful understanding selects for its objects everything closely related to the finer feeling, and relinquishes to the diligent, fundamental, and deep understanding abstract speculations or branches of knowledge useful but dry. A woman therefore will learn no geometry; of the principle of sufficient reason or the monads she will know only so much as is needed to perceive the salt in a satire which the insipid grubs of our sex have censured. The fair can leave Descartes his vortices to whirl forever without troubling themselves about them, even though the suave Fontenelle wished to afford them company among the planets; and the attraction of their charms loses none of its strength even if they know nothing of what Algarotti has taken the trouble to sketch out for their benefit about the gravitational attraction of matter according to Newton. In history they will not fill their heads with battles, nor in geography with fortresses, for it becomes them just as little to reek of gunpowder as it does the males to reek of musk.

It appears to be a malicious stratagem of men that they have wanted to influence the fair sex to this perverted taste. For, well aware of their weakness before her natural charms and of the fact that a single sly glance sets them more in confusion than the most difficult problem of science, so soon as woman enters upon this taste they see themselves in a decided superiority and are at an advantage that otherwise they hardly would have, being able to succor their vanity in its weakness by a generous indulgence toward her. The content of woman's great science, rather, is humankind, and among humanity, men. Her philosophy is not to reason, but to sense. In the opportunity that one wants to give to women to cultivate their beautiful nature, one must always keep this relation before his eyes. One will seek to broaden their total moral feeling and not their memory, and that of course not by universal rules but by some judgment upon the conduct that they see about them. The examples one borrows from other times in order to examine the influence the fair sex has had in culture, the various relations to the masculine in which it has stood in other ages or in foreign lands, the character of both so far as it can be illustrated by these, and the changing taste in amusements—these comprise her whole history and geography. For the ladies, it is well to make it a pleasant diversion to see a map setting forth the entire globe or the principal parts of the world. This is brought about by showing it only with the intention of portraying the different characters of peoples that dwell there, and the differences of their taste and moral feeling, especially in respect to the effect these have upon the relations of the sexes—together with a few easy illustrations taken from the differences of their climates, or their freedom or slavery. It is of little consequence whether or not the women know the particular subdivisions of these lands, their industry, power, and sovereigns. Similarly, they will need to know nothing more of the cosmos than is necessary to make the appearance of the heavens on a beautiful evening a stimulating sight to them, if they can conceive to some extent that yet more worlds, and in them yet more beautiful creatures, are to be found. Feeling for expressive painting and for music, not so far as it manifests artistry but sensitivity—all this refines or elevates the taste of this sex, and always has some connection with moral impulses. Never a cold and speculative instruction but always feelings, and those indeed which remain as close as possible to the situation of her sex. Such instruction is very rare because it demands talents, experience, and a heart full of feeling; and a woman can do very well without any other, as in fact without this she usually develops very well by her own efforts.

The virtue of a woman is a *beautiful virtue.*[1] That of the male sex should be a *noble virtue.* Women will avoid the wicked not because it is unright, but because it is ugly; and virtuous actions mean to them such as are morally beautiful. Nothing of duty, nothing of compulsion, nothing of obligation! Woman is intolerant of all commands and all morose constraint. They do something only because it pleases them, and the art consists in making only that please them which is good. I hardly believe that the fair sex is capable of principles, and I hope by that not to offend, for these are also extremely rare in the male. But in place of it Providence has put in their breast kind and benevolent sensations, a fine feeling for propriety, and a complaisant soul. One should not at all demand sacrifices and generous self-restraint. A man must never tell his wife if he risks a part of his fortune on behalf of a friend. Why should he fetter her merry talkativeness by burdening her mind with a weighty secret whose keeping lies solely upon him? Even many of her weaknesses are, so to speak, *beautiful faults.* Offense or misfortune moves her tender soul to sadness. A man must never weep other than magnanimous tears. Those he sheds in pain or over circumstances of fortune make him contemptible. *Vanity,* for which one reproaches the fair sex so frequently, so far as it is a fault in that sex, yet is only a beautiful fault. For—not to mention that the men who so gladly flatter a woman would be left in a strait if she were not inclined to take it well—by that they actually enliven their charms. This inclination is an impulsion to exhibit pleasantness and

[1] Above, in a strict judgment this was called adoptive virtue; here, where on account of the character of the sex it deserves a favorable justification, it is generally called a beautiful virtue.

good demeanor, to let her merry wit play, to radiate through the changing devices of dress, and to heighten her beauty. Now in this there is not at all any offensiveness toward others, but rather so much courtesy, if it is done with good taste, that to scold against it with peevish rebukes is very ill-bred. A woman who is too inconstant and deceitful is called a coquette; which expression yet has not so harsh a meaning as what, with a changed syllable, is applied to man, so that if we understand each other, it can sometimes indicate a familiar flattery. If vanity is a fault that in a woman much merits excuse, a *haughty bearing* is not only as reproachable in her as in people in general, but completely disfigures the character of her sex. For this quality is exceedingly stupid and ugly, and is set completely in opposition to her captivating, modest charms. Then such a person is in a slippery position. She will suffer herself to be judged sharply and without any pity; for whoever presumes an esteem invites all around him to rebuke. Each disclosure of even the least fault gives everyone a true joy, and the word *coquette* here loses its mitigated meaning. One must always distinguish between vanity and conceit. The first seeks approbation and to some extent honors those on whose account it gives itself the trouble. The second believes itself already in full possession of approbation, and because it never strives to gain any, it wins none.

If a few ingredients of vanity do not deform a woman in the eyes of the male sex, still, the more apparent they are, the more they serve to divide the fair sex among themselves. Then they judge one another very severely, because the one seems to obscure the charms of the other, and in fact, those who make strong presumptions of conquest actually are seldom friends of one another in a true sense.

Nothing is so much set against the beautiful as disgust, just as nothing sinks deeper beneath the sublime than the ridiculous. On this account no insult can be more painful to a man than being called a *fool*, and to a woman, than being called *disgusting*. The English *Spectator* maintains that no more insulting reproach could be made to a man than if he is considered a liar, and to a woman none more bitter than if she is held unchaste. I will leave this for what it is worth so far as it is judged according to strictness in morals. But here the question is not what of itself deserves the greatest rebuke, but what is actually felt as the harshest of all. And to that point I ask every reader whether, when he sets himself to thinking upon this matter, he must not assent to my opinion. The maid Ninon Lenclos made not the least claims upon the honor of chastity, and yet she would have been implacably offended if one of her lovers should have gone so far in his pronouncements; and one knows the gruesome fate of Monaldeschi, on account of an insulting expression of that sort, at the hands of a princess who had wanted to be thought no Lucretia. It is intolerable that one should never once be capable of doing something wicked if one actually wanted to, because then even the omission of it remains only a very ambiguous virtue.

In order to remove ourselves as far as possible from these disgusting things, *neatness,* which of course well becomes any person, in the fair sex belongs among the virtues of first rank and can hardly be pushed too high among them, although in a man it sometimes rises to excess and then becomes trifling.

Sensitivity to *shame* is a secrecy of nature addressed to setting bounds to a very intractable inclination, and since it has the voice of nature on its side, seems always to agree with good moral qualities even if it yields to excess. Hence it is most needed, as a supplement to principles, for there is no instance in which inclination is so ready to turn Sophist, subtly to devise complaisant principles, as in this. But at the same time it serves to draw a curtain of mystery before even the most appropriate and necessary purposes of nature, so that a too familiar acquaintance with them might not occasion disgust, or indifference at least, in respect to the final purpose of an impulse onto which the finest and liveliest inclinations of human nature are grafted. This quality is especially peculiar to the fair sex and very becoming to it. There is also a coarse and contemptible rudeness in putting delicate modesty to embarrassment or annoyance by the sort of vulgar jests called obscenities. However, although one may go as far around the secret as one ever will, the sexual inclination still ultimately underlies all her remaining charms, and a woman, ever as a woman, is the pleasant object of a well-mannered conversation; and this might perhaps explain why otherwise polite men occasionally take the liberty to let certain fine allusions show through, by a little mischief in their jests, which make us call them *loose* or *waggish*. Because they neither affront by searching glances nor intend to injure anyone's esteem, they believe it justified to call the person who receives it with an indignant or brittle mien a *prude*. I mention this practice only because it is generally considered as a somewhat bold trait in polite conversation, and also because in point of fact much wit has been squandered upon it; however, judgment according to moral strictness does not belong here, because what I have to observe and explain in the sensing of the beautiful is only the appearances.

The noble qualities of this sex, which still, as we have already noted, must never disguise the feeling of the beautiful, proclaim themselves by nothing more clearly and surely than by *modesty*, a sort of noble simplicity and innocence in great excellences. Out of it shines a quiet benevolence and respect toward others, linked at the same time with a certain *noble trust* in oneself, and a reasonable self-esteem that is always to be found in a sublime disposition. Since this fine mixture at once captivates by charms and moves by respect, it puts all the remaining shining qualities in security against the mischief of censure and mockery. Persons of this temperament also have a heart for friendship, which in a woman can never be valued highly enough, because it is so rare and moreover must be so exceedingly charming.

As it is our purpose to judge concerning feelings, it cannot be unpleasant to bring under concepts, if possible, the difference of the impression that the form and features of the fair sex make on the masculine. This complete fascination is really overlaid upon the sex instinct. Nature pursues its great purpose, and all refinements that join together, though they may appear to stand as far from that as they will, are only trimmings and borrow their charm ultimately from that very source. A healthy and *coarse taste*, which always stays very close to this impulse, is little tempted by the charms of demeanor, of facial features, of eyes, and so on, in a woman, and because it really pertains only to sex, it oftentimes sees the delicacy of others as empty flirting.

If this taste is not fine, nevertheless it is not on that account to be disdained. For the largest part of mankind complies by means of it with the great order of nature, in a very simple and sure way.[2] Through it the greatest number of marriages are brought about, and indeed by the most diligent part of the human race; and because the man does not have his head full of fascinating expressions, languishing eyes, noble demeanor, and so forth, and understands nothing of all this, he becomes that much the more attentive to householders' virtues, thrift and such, and to the dowry. As for what relates to the somewhat finer taste, on whose account it might be necessary to make a distinction among the exterior charms of women, this fixed either upon what in the form and the expression of the face is moral, or upon what is non-moral. In respect to the last-named sort of pleasantness, a lady is called *pretty*. A well-proportioned figure, regular features, colors of eyes and face which contrast prettily, beauties pure and simple which are also pleasing in a bouquet and gain a cool approbation. The face itself says nothing, although it is pretty, and speaks not to the heart. What is moral in the expression of the features, the eyes, and mien pertains to the feeling either of the sublime or of the beautiful. A woman in whom the agreeableness beseeming her sex particularly makes manifest the moral expression of the sublime is called *beautiful* in the proper sense; so far as the moral composition makes itself discernible in the mien or facial features, she whose features show qualities of beauty is *agreeable,* and if she is that to a high degree, *charming*. The first, under a mien of composure and a noble

[2] As all things in the world have their bad side, regarding this taste it is only to be regretted that easier than another it degenerates into dissoluteness. For as any other can extinguish the fire one person has lighted, there are not enough obstacles that can confine an intractable inclination.

demeanor, lets the glimmer of a beautiful understanding play forth through discreet glances, and as in her face she portrays a tender feeling and a benevolent heart, she seizes possession of the affection as well as the esteem of a masculine heart. The second exhibits merriment and wit in laughing eyes, something of fine mischief, the playfulness of jest and sly coyness. She charms, while the first moves; and the feeling of love of which she is capable and which she stimulates in others is fickle but beautiful, whereas the feeling of the first is tender, combined with respect, and constant. I do not want to engage in too detailed an analysis of this sort, for in doing so the author always appears to depict his own inclination. I shall still mention, however, that the liking many women have for a healthy but pale color can be explained here. For this generally accompanies a disposition of more inward feeling and delicate sensation, which belongs to the quality of the sublime; whereas the rosy and blooming complexion proclaims less of the first, but more of the joyful and merry disposition—but it is more suitable to vanity to move and to arrest, than to charm and to attract. On the other hand there can be very pretty persons completely without moral feeling and without any expression that indicates feeling; but they will neither move nor charm, unless it might be the coarse taste of which we have made mention, which sometimes grows somewhat more refined and then also selects after its fashion. It is too bad that this sort of beautiful creatures easily fall into the fault of *conceit*, through the consciousness of the beautiful figure their mirror shows them, and from a lack of finer sensations, for then they make all indifferent to them except the flatterer, who has ulterior motives and contrives intrigues.

Perhaps by following these concepts one can understand something of the different effect the figure of the same woman has upon the tastes of men. I do not concern myself with what in this impression relates too closely to the sex impulse and may be of a piece with the particular sensual illusion with which the feeling of everyone clothes itself, because it lies outside the compass of finer taste. Perhaps what M. Buffon supposes may be true: that the figure that makes the first impression, at the time when this impulse is still new and is beginning to develop, remains the pattern all feminine figures in the future must more or less follow so as to be able to stir the fanciful ardor, whereby a rather coarse inclination is compelled to choose among the different objects of a sex. Regarding the somewhat finer taste, I affirm that the sort of beauty we have called the *pretty figure* is judged by all men very much alike, and that opinions about it are not so different as one generally maintains. The Circassian and Georgian maidens have always been considered extremely pretty by all Europeans who travel through their lands. The Turks, the Arabs, the Persians are apparently of one mind in this taste, because they are very eager to beautify their races through such fine blood, and one also notes that the Persian race has actually succeeded in this. The merchants of Hindustan likewise do not fail to draw great profit from a wicked commerce in such beautiful creatures, for they supply them to the self-indulgent rich men of their land. And it appears that, as greatly as the caprice of taste in these different quarters of the world may diverge, still, whatever is once known in any of these as especially pretty will also be considered the same in all the others. But whenever what is moral in the features mingles in the judgment upon the fine figure, the taste of different men is always very different, both because their moral feeling itself is dissimilar, and also on account of the different meaning that the expression of the face may have in every fancy. One finds that those formations that at first glance do not have any particular effect, because they are not pretty in any decided way, generally appear far more to captivate and to grow constantly more beautiful as soon as they begin to please upon nearer acquaintance. On the other hand, the pretty appearance that proclaims itself at once is later received with greater indifference. This probably is because moral charms, when they are evident, are all the more arresting because they are set in operation only on the occasion of moral sensations, and let themselves be discovered in this way, each disclosure of a new charm causing one to suspect still more of these; whereas all the agreeable features that do not at all conceal themselves, after exercising their entire effect at the beginning, can subsequently do nothing more than to cool off the enamored curiosity and bring it gradually to indifference.

Along with these observations, the following comment naturally presents itself. The quite simple and coarse feeling in the sexual inclination leads directly to the great purpose of nature, and as it fulfills her claims it is fitted to make the person himself happy without digression; but because of its great universality it degenerates easily into excess and dissoluteness. On the other hand, a very refined taste serves to take away the wildness of an impetuous inclination, and although it limits this to few objects, to make it modest and decorous, such an inclination usually misses the great goal of nature. As it demands or expects more than nature usually offers, it seldom takes care to make the person of such delicate feeling happy. The first disposition becomes uncouth, because it is attracted to all the members of a sex; the second becomes oversubtle, because actually it is attracted to none. It is occupied only with an object that the enamored inclination creates in thought, and ornaments with all the noble and beautiful qualities that nature seldom unites in one human being and still more seldom brings to him who can value them and perhaps would be worthy of such a possession. Thence arises the postponement and finally the full abandonment of the marital bond; or what is perhaps just as bad, a peevish regret after making a choice that does not fulfill the great expectations one had made oneself—for not seldom the Aesopian cock finds a pearl when a common barleycorn would have been better suited to him.

From this we can perceive in general that as charming as the impressions of the delicate feeling may be, one still might have cause to be on guard in its refinement, lest by excessive sensibility we subtly fabricate only much discontent and a source of evil. To noble souls I might well propose to refine as much as they can the feeling with respect to qualities that become them, or with respect to actions that they themselves perform, but to maintain this taste in its simplicity respecting what they enjoy or expect from others—

if only I saw how this were possible to achieve. But if it were approached, they would make others happy and also be happy themselves. It is never to be lost sight of that in whatever way it might be, one must make no very high claims upon the raptures of life and the perfection of men; for he who always expects only something ordinary has the advantage that the result seldom refutes his hope, but sometimes he is surprised by quite unexpected perfections.

Finally age, the great destroyer of beauty, threatens all these charms; and if it proceeds according to the natural order of things, gradually the sublime and noble qualities must take the place of the beautiful, in order to make a person always worthy of a greater respect as she ceases to be attractive. In my opinion, the whole perfection of the fair sex in the bloom of years should consist in the beautiful simplicity that has been brought to its height by a refined feeling toward all that is charming and noble. Gradually, as the claims upon charms diminish, the reading of books and the broadening of insight could refill unnoticed the vacant place of the Graces with the Muses, and the husband should be the first instructor. Nevertheless, when the epoch of growing old, so terrible to every woman, actually approaches, she still belongs to the fair sex, and that sex disfigures itself if in a kind of despair of holding this character longer, it gives way to a surly and irritable mood.

An aged person who attends a gathering with a modest and friendly manner, is sociable in a merry and sensible way, favors with a pleasant demeanor the pleasures of youth in which she herself no longer participates, and, as she looks after everything, manifests contentment and benevolence toward the joys that are going on around her, is yet a finer person than a man of like age and perhaps even more attractive than a girl, although in another sense. Indeed the platonic love might well be somewhat too mystical, which an ancient philosopher asserted when he said of the object of his inclination, "The Graces reside in her wrinkles, and my soul seems to hover upon my lips when I kiss her withered mouth"; but such claims must then be relinquished. An old man who acts infatuated is a fool, and the like presumptions of the other sex at that age are disgusting. It never is due to nature when we do not appear with a good demeanor, but rather to the fact that we turn her upside down.

In order to keep close to my text, I want to undertake a few reflections on the influence one sex can have upon the other, to beautify or ennoble its feeling. Woman has a superior feeling for the beautiful, so far as it pertains to herself; but for the noble, so far as it is encountered in the male sex. Man on the other hand has a decided feeling for the noble, which belongs to his qualities, but for the beautiful, so far as it is to be found in woman. From this it must follow that the purposes of nature are directed still more to ennoble man, by the sexual inclination, and likewise still more to beautify woman. A woman is embarrassed little that she does not possess certain high insights, that she is timid, and not fit for serious employments, and so forth; she is beautiful and captivates, and that is enough. On the other hand, she demands all these qualities in a man, and the sublimity of her soul shows itself only in that she knows to treasure these noble qualities so far as they are found in him. How else indeed would it be possible that so many grotesque male faces, whatever merits they may possess, could gain such well-bred and fine wives! Man on the other hand is much more delicate in respect to the beautiful charms of woman. By their fine figure, merry naïveté, and charming friendliness he is sufficiently repaid for the lack of book learning and for other deficiencies that he must supply by his own talents. Vanity and fashion can give these natural drives a false direction and make out of many a male a *sweet gentleman,* but out of a woman either a prude or an Amazon; but still nature always seeks to reassert her own order. One can thereby judge what powerful influences the sexual inclination could have especially upon the male sex, to ennoble it, if instead of many dry instructions the moral feeling of woman were seasonably developed to sense properly what belongs to the dignity and the sublime qualities of the other sex, and were thus prepared to look upon the trifling fops with disdain and to yield to no other qualities than the merits. It is also certain that the power of her charms on the whole would gain through that; for it is apparent that their fascination for the most part works only upon nobler souls; the others are not fine enough to sense them. Just as the poet Simonides said, when someone advised him to let the Thessalians hear his beautiful songs: "These fellows are too stupid to be beguiled by such a man as I am." It has been regarded moreover as an effect of association with the fair sex that men's customs have become gentler, their conduct more polite and refined, and their bearing more elegant; but the advantage of this is only incidental.[3] The principal object is that the man should become more perfect as a man, and the woman as a wife; that is, that the motives of the sexual inclination work according to the hint of nature, still more to ennoble the one and to beautify the qualities of the other. If all comes to the extreme, the man, confident in his merits, will be able to say: "Even if you do not love me, I will constrain you to esteem me," and the woman, secure in the might of her charms, will answer: "Even if you do not inwardly admire me, I will still constrain you to love me." In default of such principles one sees men take on femininity in order to please, and women occasionally (although much more seldom) affect a masculine demeanor in order to stimulate esteem; but whatever one does contrary to nature's will, one always does very poorly.

In matrimonial life the united pair should, as it were, constitute a single moral person, which is animated and governed by the understanding of the man and the taste of the wife. For not only can one credit more insight founded on experience to the former, and more freedom and accuracy in sensation to the latter; but also, the more sublime a disposition is, the more inclined it is to place

---

[3] This advantage itself is really much reduced by the observation that one will have made, that men who are too early and too frequently introduced into company where woman sets the tone generally become somewhat trifling, and in male society they are boring or even contemptible because they have lost the taste for conversation, which must be merry, to be sure, but still of actual content—witty, to be sure, but also useful through its earnest discourse.

the greatest purpose of its exertions in the contentment of a beloved object, and likewise the more beautiful it is, the more it seeks to requite these exertions by complaisance. In such a relation, then, a dispute over precedence is trifling and, where it occurs, is the surest sign of a coarse or dissimilarly matched taste. If it comes to such a state that the question is of the right of the superior to command, then the case is already utterly corrupted; for where the whole union is in reality erected solely upon inclination, it is already half destroyed as soon as the "duty" begins to make itself heard. The presumption of the woman in this harsh tone is extremely ugly, and of the man is base and contemptible in the highest degree. However, the wise order of things so brings it about that all these niceties and delicacies of feeling have their whole strength only in the beginning, but subsequently gradually become duller through association and domestic concerns, and then degenerate into familiar love. Finally, the great skill consists in still preserving sufficient remainders of those feelings so that indifference and satiety do not put an end to the whole value of the enjoyment on whose account it has solely and alone been worth the trouble to enter such a union.

Mary Wollstonecraft

Toward the end of the eighteenth century, in the midst of the revolutionary fever in Europe, a book appeared that was destined to become the manifesto of the feminist movement in England and America during the next century. Wollstonecraft's *A Vindication of the Rights of Woman,* published in 1792, was a response to Rousseau's program for training women. Although an early disciple of his egalitarian views, she objected to his assumption that man's nature and virtues differ from woman's nature and virtues, the essence of the distinction lying in the old belief that women are deficient in reason. Since reason is the fundamental human characteristic, Wollstonecraft argued, to deny women a full measure of rationality amounts to denying their humanity. Further, since reason is necessary for the development of the moral virtues, Rousseau's female virtues—passivity, gentleness, and sensitivity—can be only pseudo virtues, since they do not proceed from rational activity. The early feminists supported Wollstonecraft's contention that women are not debased by anything inherent in their nature, but by the lifelong habituation to which females are subjected by social forces. Wollstonecraft argued, contrary to popular belief, that the traditional training for girls made them empty-headed, frivolous, selfish, and mean creatures—ladies—instead of good and noble women, and did not even render them competent to raise children and be companions to their husbands. Ultimately, she argued, such beliefs and practices damaged not only women themselves, but the family and society as a whole. Wollstonecraft was, of course, urging equal rights for women, though she addressed herself mainly to the problems of middle- and upper-class women of her day; it remained for the likes of Mill, Marx, and Engels to address the plight of lower-class women.

THE EFFECTS OF DISCRIMINATION
AGAINST WOMEN *

From the respect paid to property flow, as from a poisoned fountain, most of the evils and vices which render this world such a dreary scene to the contemplative mind. For it is in the most polished society that noisome reptiles and venomous serpents lurk under the rank herbage; and there is voluptuousness pampered by the still sultry air, which relaxes every good disposition before it ripens into virtue.

One class presses on another; for all are aiming to procure respect on account of their property: and property, once gained, will procure the respect due only to talents and virtue. Men neglect the duties incumbent on man, yet are treated like demi-gods; religion is also separated from morality by a ceremonial veil, yet men wonder that the world is almost, literally speaking, a den of sharpers or oppressors.

There is a homely proverb, which speaks a shrewd truth, that

* From Mary Wollstonecraft, *A Vindication of the Rights of Woman,* 2nd ed. (London: J. Johnson, 1792), Chap. 9.

whoever the devil finds idle he will employ. And what but habitual idleness can hereditary wealth and titles produce? For man is so constituted that he can only attain a proper use of his faculties by exercising them, and will not exercise them unless necessity, of some kind, first set the wheels in motion. Virtue likewise can only be acquired by the discharge of relative duties; but the importance of these sacred duties will scarcely be felt by the being who is cajoled out of his humanity by the flattery of sycophants. There must be more equality established in society, or morality will never gain ground, and this virtuous equality will not rest firmly even when founded on a rock, if one half of mankind be chained to its bottom by fate, for they will be continually undermining it through ignorance or pride.

It is vain to expect virtue from women till they are, in some degree, independent of men; nay, it is vain to expect that strength of natural affection, which would make them good wives and mothers. Whilst they are absolutely dependent on their husbands they will be cunning, mean, and selfish, and the men who can be gratified by the fawning fondness of spaniellike affection, have not much delicacy, for love is not to be bought, in any sense of the words, its silken wings are instantly shrivelled up when any thing beside a return in kind is sought. Yet whilst wealth enervates men; and women live, as it were, by their personal charms, how can we expect them to discharge those ennobling duties which equally require exertion and self-denial. Hereditary property sophisticates the mind, and the unfortunate victims to it, if I may so express myself, swathed from their birth, seldom exert the locomotive faculty of body or mind; and, thus viewing every thing through one medium, and that a false one, they are unable to discern in what true merit and happiness consist. False, indeed, must be the light when the drapery of situation hides the man, and makes him stalk in masquerade, dragging from one scene of dissipation to another the nerveless limbs that hang with stupid listlessness, and rolling round the vacant eye which plainly tells us that there is no mind at home.

I mean, therefore, to infer that the society is not properly organized which does not compel men and women to discharge their respective duties, by making it the only way to acquire that countenance from their fellow-creatures, which every human being wishes some way to attain. The respect, consequently, which is paid to wealth and mere personal charms, is a true north-east blast, that blights the tender blossoms of affection and virtue. Nature has wisely attached affections to duties, to sweeten toil, and to give that vigour to the exertions of reason which only the heart can give. But, the affection which is put on merely because it is the appropriated insignia of a certain character, when its duties are not fulfilled, is one of the empty compliments which vice and folly are obliged to pay to virtue and the real nature of things.

To illustrate my opinion, I need only observe, that when a woman is admired for her beauty, and suffers herself to be so far intoxicated by the admiration she receives, as to neglect to discharge the indispensable duty of a mother, she sins against herself by neglecting to cultivate an affection that would equally tend to make her useful and happy. True happiness, I mean all the contentment, and virtuous satisfaction, that can be snatched in this imperfect state, must arise from well regulated affections; and an affection includes a duty. Men are not aware of the misery they cause, and the vicious weakness they cherish, by only inciting women to render themselves pleasing; they do not consider that they thus make natural and artificial duties clash, by sacrificing the comfort and respectability of a woman's life to voluptuous notions of beauty, when in nature they all harmonize.

Cold would be the heart of a husband, were he not rendered unnatural by early debauchery, who did not feel more delight at seeing his child suckled by its mother, than the most artful wanton tricks could ever raise; yet this natural way of cementing the matrimonial tie, and twisting esteem with fonder recollections, wealth leads women to spurn. To preserve their beauty, and wear the flowery crown of the day, which gives them a kind of right to reign for a short time over the sex, they neglect to stamp impressions on their husbands' hearts, that would be remembered with more tenderness when the snow on the head began to chill the bosom, than even their virgin charms. The maternal solicitude of a reasonable affectionate woman is very interesting, and the chastened dignity with which a mother returns the caresses that she and her child receive from a father who has been fulfilling the serious duties of his station, is not only a respectable, but a beautiful sight. So singular, indeed, are my feelings, and I have endeavoured not to catch factitious ones, that after having been fatigued with the sight of insipid grandeur and the slavish ceremonies that with cumberous pomp supplied the place of domestic affections, I have turned to some other scene to relieve my eye by resting it on the refreshing green every where scattered by nature. I have then viewed with pleasure a woman nursing her children, and discharging the duties of her station with, perhaps, merely a servant maid to take off her hands the servile part of the household business. I have seen her prepare herself and children, with only the luxury of cleanliness, to receive her husband, who returning weary home in the evening found smiling babes and a clean hearth. My heart has loitered in the midst of the group, and has even throbbed with sympathetic emotion, when the scraping of the well known foot has raised a pleasing tumult.

Whilst my benevolence has been gratified by contemplating this artless picture, I have thought that a couple of this description, equally necessary and independent of each other, because each fulfilled the respective duties of their station, possessed all that life could give.—Raised sufficiently above abject poverty not to be obliged to weigh the consequence of every farthing they spend, and having sufficient to prevent their attending to a frigid system of economy, which narrows both heart and mind. I declare, so vulgar are my conceptions, that I know not what is wanted to render this the happiest as well as the most respectable situation in the world, but a taste for literature, to throw a little variety and interest into social converse, and some superfluous money to give to the needy and to buy books. For it is not pleasant when the heart is opened by compassion and the head active in arranging plans of usefulness, to have a prim urchin continually twitching back the elbow to prevent the hand from drawing out an almost empty purse, whispering at the same time some prudential maxim about the priority of justice.

Destructive, however, as riches and inherited honours are to the human character, women are more debased and cramped, if possible, by them, than men, because men may still, in some degree, unfold their faculties by becoming soldiers and statesmen.

As soldiers, I grant, they can now only gather, for the most part, vain glorious laurels, whilst they adjust to a hair the European balance, taking especial care that no bleak northern nook or sound incline the beam. But the days of true heroism are over, when a citizen fought for his country like a Fabricius or a Washington, and then returned to his farm to let his virtuous fervour run in a more placid, but not a less salutary, stream. No, our British heroes are oftener sent from the gaming table than from the plow; and their passions have been rather inflamed by hanging with dumb suspense on the turn of a die, than sublimated by panting after the adventurous march of virtue in the historic page.

The statesman, it is true, might with more propriety quit the Faro Bank, or card-table, to guide the helm, for he has still but to shuffle and trick. The whole system of British politics, if system it may courteously be called, consisting in multiplying dependents and contriving taxes which grind the poor to pamper the rich; thus a war, or any wild goose chase, is, as the vulgar use the phrase, a lucky turnup of patronage for the minister, whose chief merit is the art of keeping himself in place. It is not necessary then that he should have bowels for the poor, so he can secure for his family the odd trick. Or should some shew of respect, for what is termed with ignorant ostentation an Englishman's birth-right, be expedient to bubble the gruff mastiff that he has to lead by the nose, he can make an empty shew, very safely, by giving his single voice, and suffering his light squadron to file off to the other side. And when a question of humanity is agitated he may dip a sop in the milk of human kindness, to silence Cerberus, and talk of the interest which his heart takes in an attempt to make the earth no longer cry for vengeance as it sucks in its children's blood, though his cold hand may at the very moment rivet their chains, by sanctioning the abominable traffick. A minister is no longer a minister, than while he can carry a point, which he is determined to carry.—Yet it is not necessary that a minister should feel like a man, when a bold push might shake his feat.

But, to have done with these episodical observations, let me return to the more specious slavery which chains the very soul of woman, keeping her for ever under the bondage of ignorance.

The preposterous distinctions of rank, which render civilization a curse, by dividing the world between voluptuous tyrants, and cunning envious dependents, corrupt, almost equally, every class of people, because respectability is not attached to the discharge of the relative duties of life, but to the station, and when the duties are not fulfilled the affections cannot gain sufficient strength to fortify the virtue of which they are the natural reward. Still there are some loop-holes out of which a man may creep, and dare to think and act for himself; but for a woman it is an herculean task, because she has difficulties peculiar to her sex to overcome, which require almost superhuman powers.

A truly benevolent legislator always endeavours to make it the interest of each individual to be virtuous; and thus private virtue becoming the cement of public happiness, an orderly whole is consolidated by the tendency of all the parts towards a common centre. But, the private or public virtue of woman is very problematical; for Rousseau, and a numerous list of male writers, insist that she should all her life be subjected to a severe restraint, that of propriety. Why subject her to propriety—blind propriety, if she be capable of acting from a nobler spring, if she be an heir of immortality? Is sugar always to be produced by vital blood? Is one half of the human species, like the poor African slaves, to be subject to prejudices that brutalize them, when principles would be a surer guard, only to sweeten the cup of man? Is not this indirectly to deny woman reason? for a gift is a mockery, if it be unfit for use.

Women are, in common with men, rendered weak and luxurious by the relaxing pleasures which wealth procures; but added to this they are made slaves to their persons, and must render them alluring that man may lend them his reason to guide their tottering steps aright. Or should they be ambitious, they must govern their tyrants by sinister tricks, for without rights there cannot be any incumbent duties. The laws respecting woman, which I mean to discuss in a future part, make an absurd unit of a man and his wife; and then, by the easy transition of only considering him as responsible, she is reduced to a mere cypher.

The being who discharges the duties of its station is independent; and, speaking of women at large, their first duty is to themselves as rational creatures, and the next, in point of importance, as citizens, is that, which includes so many, of a mother. The rank in life which dispenses with their fulfilling this duty, necessarily degrades them by making them mere dolls. Or, should they turn to something more important than merely fitting drapery upon a smooth block, their minds are only occupied by some soft platonic attachment; or, the actual management of an intrigue may keep their thoughts in motion; for when they neglect domestic duties, they have it not in their power to take the field and march and countermarch like soldiers, or wrangle in the senate to keep their faculties from rusting.

I know that, as a proof of the inferiority of the sex, Rousseau has exultingly exclaimed, How can they leave the nursery for the camp!—And the camp has by some moralists been termed the school of the most heroic virtues; though, I think, it would puzzle a keen casuist to prove the reasonableness of the greater number of wars that have dubbed heroes. I do not mean to consider this question critically; because, having frequently viewed these freaks of ambition as the first natural mode of civilization, when the ground must be torn up, and the woods cleared by fire and sword, I do not choose to call them pests; but surely the present system of war has little connection with virtue of any denomination, being rather the school of *finesse* and effeminacy, than of fortitude.

Yet, if defensive war, the only justifiable war, in the present advanced state of society, where virtue can shew its face and ripen amidst the rigours which purify the air on the mountain's top, were alone to be adopted as just and glorious, the true heroism of antiquity might again animate female bosoms.—But fair and softly, gentle reader, male or female, do not alarm thyself, for though I have compared the character of a modern soldier with that of a civilized woman, I am not going to advise them to turn their distaff into a musket, though I sincerely wish to see the bayonet converted into a pruning-hook. I only recreated an imagination, fatigued by contemplating the vices and follies which all proceed from a feculent stream of wealth that has muddied the pure rills of natural affection, by supposing that society will some time or other be so constituted, that man must necessarily fulfil the duties of a citizen, or be despised, and that while he was employed in any of the departments of civil life, his wife, also an active citizen, should be equally intent to manage her family, educate her children, and assist her neighbours.

But, to render her really virtuous and useful, she must not, if she discharge her civil duties, want, individually, the protection of civil laws; she must not be dependent on her husband's bounty for her subsistence during his life, or support after his death—for how can a being be generous who has nothing of its own? or, virtuous, who is not free? The wife, in the present state of things, who is faithful to her husband, and neither suckles nor educates her children, scarcely deserves the name of a wife, and has no right to that of a citizen. But take away natural rights, and duties become null.

Women then must be considered as only the wanton solace of men, when they become so weak in mind and body, that they cannot exert themselves, unless to pursue some frothy pleasure, or to invent some frivolous fashion. What can be a more melancholy sight to a thinking mind, than to look into the numerous carriages that drive helter-skelter about this metropolis in a morning full of pale-faced creatures who are flying from themselves. I have often wished, with Dr. Johnson, to place some of them in a little shop with half a dozen children looking up to their languid countenances for support. I am much mistaken, if some latent vigour would not soon give health and spirit to their eyes, and some lines drawn by the exercise of reason on the blank cheeks, which before were only undulated by dimples, might restore lost dignity to the character, or rather enable it to attain the true dignity of its nature. Virtue is not to be acquired even by speculation, much less by the negative supineness that wealth naturally generates.

Besides, when poverty is more disgraceful than even vice, is not morality cut to the quick? Still to avoid misconstruction, though I consider that women in the common walks of life are called to fulfil the duties of wives and mothers, by religion and reason, I cannot help lamenting that women of a superiour cast have not a road open by which they can pursue more extensive plans of usefulness and independence. I may excite laughter, by dropping an hint, which I mean to pursue, some future time, for I really think that women ought to have representatives, instead of being arbitrarily governed without having any direct share allowed them in the deliberations of government.

But, as the whole system of representation is now, in this country, only a convenient handle for despotism, they need not complain, for they are as well represented as a numerous class of hard working mechanics, who pay for the support of royalty when they can scarcely stop their children's mouths with bread. How are they represented whose very sweat supports the splendid stud of an heir apparent, or varnished the chariot of some female favourite who looks down on shame? Taxes on the very necessaries of life, enable an endless tribe of idle princes and princesses to pass with stupid pomp before a gaping crowd, who almost worship the very parade which costs them so dear. This is mere gothic grandeur, something like the barbarous useless parade of having sentinels on horseback at Whitehall, which I could never view without a mixture of contempt and indignation.

How strangely must the mind be sophisticated when this sort of state impresses it! But, till these monuments of folly are levelled by virtue, similar follies will leaven the whole mass. For the same character, in some degree, will prevail in the aggregate of society: and the refinements of luxury, or the vicious repinings of envious poverty, will equally banish virtue from society, considered as the characteristic of that society, or only allow it to appear as one of the stripes of the harlequin coat, worn by the civilized man.

In the superiour ranks of life, every duty is done by deputies, as if duties could ever be waved, and the vain pleasures which consequent idleness forces the rich to pursue, appear so enticing to the next rank, that the numerous scramblers for wealth sacrifice every thing to tread on their heels. The most sacred trusts are then considered as sinecures, because they were procured by interest, and only sought to enable a man to keep *good company*. Women, in particular, all want to be ladies. Which is simply to have nothing to do, but listlessly to go they scarcely care where, for they cannot tell what.

But what have women to do in society? I may be asked, but to loiter with easy grace; surely you would not condemn them all to suckle fools and chronicle small beer! No. Women might certainly study the art of healing, and be physicians as well as nurses. And midwifery, decency seems to allot to them, though I am afraid the word midwife, in our dictionaries, will soon give place to *accoucheur,* and one proof of the former delicacy of the sex be effaced from the language.

They might, also, study politics, and settle their benevolence on the broadest basis; for the reading of history will scarcely be more useful than the perusal of romances, if read as mere biography; if the character of the times, the political improvements, arts, &c., be not observed. In short, if it be not considered as the history of man; and not of particular men, who filled a niche in the temple of fame, and dropped into the black rolling stream of time, that silently sweeps all before it, into the shapeless void called—eternity.—For shape, can it be called, "that shape hath none?"

Business of various kinds, they might likewise pursue, if they were educated in a more orderly manner, which might save many from common and legal prostitution. Women would not then marry for a support, as men accept of places under government, and neglect the implied duties; nor would an attempt to earn their own subsistence, a most laudable one! sink them almost to the level of those poor abandoned creatures who live by prostitution. For are not milliners and mantua-makers reckoned the next class? The few employments open to women, so far from being liberal, are menial; and when a superiour education enables them to take charge of the education of children as governesses, they are not treated like the tutors of sons, though even clerical tutors are not always treated in a manner calculated to render them respectable in the eyes of their pupils, to say nothing of the private comfort of the individual. But as women educated like gentlewomen, are never designed for the humiliating situation which necessity sometimes forces them to fill; these situations are considered in the light of a degradation; and they know little of the human heart, who need to be told, that nothing so painfully sharpens sensibility as such a fall in life.

Some of these women might be restrained from marrying by a proper spirit or delicacy, and others may not have had it in their power to escape in this pitiful way from servitude; is not that government then very defective, and very unmindful of the happiness of one half of its members, that does not provide for honest, independent women, by encouraging them to fill respectable stations? But in order to render their private virtue a public benefit, they must have a civil existence in the state, married or single; else we shall continually see some worthy woman, whose sensibility has been rendered painfully acute by undeserved contempt, droop like "the lily broken down by a plow-share."

It is melancholy truth; yet such is the blessed effect of civilization! the most respectable women are the most oppressed; and, unless they have understandings far superiour to the common run of understandings, taking in both sexes, they must, from being treated like contemptible beings, become contemptible. How many women thus waste life away the prey of discontent, who might have practised as physicians, regulated a farm, managed a shop, and stood erect, supported by their own industry, instead of hanging their heads surcharged with the dew of sensibility, that consumes the beauty to which it at first gave lustre; nay, I doubt whether pity and love are so near akin as poets feign, for I have seldom seen much compassion excited by the helplessness of females, unless they were fair; then, perhaps, pity was the soft handmaid of love, or the harbinger of lust.

How much more respectable is the woman who earns her own bread by fulfilling any duty, than the most accomplished beauty!—

beauty did I say?—so sensible am I of the beauty of moral loveliness, or the harmonious propriety that attunes the passions of a well-regulated mind, that I blush at making the comparison; yet I sigh to think how few women aim at attaining this respectability by withdrawing from the giddy whirl of pleasure, or the indolent calm that stupefies the good sort of women it sucks in.

Proud of their weakness, however, they must always be protected, guarded from care, and all the rough toils that dignify the mind.—If this be the fiat of fate, if they will make themselves insignificant and contemptible, sweetly to waste "life away," let them not expect to be valued when their beauty fades, for it is the fate of the fairest flowers to be admired and pulled to pieces by the careless hand that plucked them. In how many ways do I wish, from the purest benevolence, to impress this truth on my sex; yet I fear that they will not listen to a truth that dear bought experience has brought home to many an agitated bosom, nor willingly resign the privileges of rank and sex for the privileges of humanity, to which those have no claim who do not discharge its duties.

Those writers are particularly useful, in my opinion, who make man feel for man, independent of the station he fills, or the drapery of factitious sentiments. I then would fain convince reasonable men of the importance of some of my remarks; and prevail on them to weigh dispassionately the whole tenor of my observations.—I appeal to their understandings; and, as a fellow-creature, claim in the name of my sex, some interest in their hearts. I entreat them to assist to emancipate their companion, to make her a *help meet* for them!

Would men but generously snap our chains, and be content with rational fellowship instead of slavish obedience, they would find us more observant daughters, more affectionate sisters, more faithful wives, more reasonable mothers—in a word, better citizens. We should then love them with true affection, because we should learn to respect ourselves; and the peace of mind of a worthy man would not be interrupted by the idle vanity of his wife, nor the babes sent to nestle in a strange bosom, having never found a home in their mother's.

Georg Hegel

Consistent with his concern for the universal as opposed to the merely individual, Hegel treats of marriage as a unity that transcends and subsumes the individual personalities of the couple involved. In *The Philosophy of Right,* dated 1821, Hegel writes that marriage is an ethical principle that overcomes the accidental features of private feelings that otherwise constitute its individual members. What this means, in effect, is that within marriage the husband and wife renounce their individual personalities. However, this does not amount to the same thing for the man and the woman. Woman's whole sphere, Hegel maintains, is within the family, and hence for her the renunciation of individuality is final and complete. Man's sphere, on the other hand, is only accidentally the family. His life lies essentially in the state and in his profession, and therefore his personality is not completely renounced in marriage. The reason for this distinction is the different nature possessed by women and men. Pursuing an ancient theme, Hegel holds that women lack the ability to reason on the universal level, acting instead out of feeling and opinion. Their minds function on the aesthetic level but cannot cope with abstract ideas. Man, of course, is able to attain rationality and to him falls the serious responsibility of tending the state and the sciences. Hegel's analogy is explicit enough—men and women differ in proportion as animal and plant differ respectively. Hegel has captured a frequent theme in the history of ideas—the necessity for women to approach life in a spirit of total self-sacrifice and self-negation, to suppress their individuality in the interests of marriage and the family.

MARRIAGE AND THE FAMILY *

Marriage, as the elementary social relation, contains firstly the factor of natural life. As marriage is also a substantive fact, natural life must be viewed in its totality as the realization of the species, and the process which the realization involves. But, secondly, the merely inner, potential and, when actualized, external unity of the sexes is transformed in self-consciousness into the spiritual unity of self-conscious love.

Marriage is essentially an ethical relation. Formerly, in the majority of what are called rights of nature, marriage was interpreted on its physical or natural side. It has thus been looked upon simply as a sexual relation, and as excluding all the other features of marriage. But such a view is no more crude than to conceive of marriage merely as civil contract, a view found in Kant. In accordance with this view, individuals form a compact through mere caprice, and marriage is degraded to a bargain for mutual use. A

* From Georg Hegel, *The Philosophy of Right,* trans. S.W. Dyde (London: George Bell and Sons, 1896), Part 3, Sect. 161-173.

third doctrine, equally reprehensible, bases marriage on love only. Love, which is feeling, admits the accidental on every side, as the ethical cannot do. Hence, marriage is to be defined more exactly as legal ethical love. Out of marriage has disappeared the love which is merely subjective.

As a subjective starting-point for marriage either the special inclination of two persons for each other may be the more observable, or else the provision and general arrangements of the parents. The objective point of departure, however, is the free consent of the two to become one person. They give up their natural and private personality to enter a unity, which may be regarded as a limitation, but, since in it they attain to a substantive self-consciousness, is really their liberation.

That an individual may be objective, and so fulfil his ethical duty, he should marry. The circumstances attending the external starting-point are naturally a matter of chance, depending largely upon the state of reflective culture. In this there may be either of two extremes. Either well-meaning parents arrange beforehand for the marriage of two persons, who, when they have made each other's acquaintance as prospective husband and wife, are then expected to love each other. Or, on the other hand, inclination is supposed first to appear in the two persons, left absolutely to their private selves. The extreme, in which marriage is resolved on prior to inclination, and both resolution and inclination are then present in the actual marriage, is the more ethical. In the other extreme, it is the individual's private and unformed nature, which makes good its pretensions. This extreme is in close alliance with the subjective principle of the modern world.

Modern dramas and other works of art produce an atmosphere of the chilliest indifference, by the way in which they represent the motive of sexual love. This feeling of indifference is due to the association in the drama of ardent passion with the most utter contingency, the whole interest being made to depend simply upon merely private persons. The event is, doubtless, of the very last importance to these persons, but not in itself.

Amongst nations where women are held in slight esteem, parents arrange the marriage of their children, without ever consulting them. The children submit, because the particularity of feeling as yet makes no claim at all. The maiden is simply to have a husband, the man a wife. In other circumstances regard may be had to means, connections, political hopes. To make marriage the means for other ends may cause great hardship. But in modern times the subjective point of departure, i.e., being in love, is thought to be the only thing of consequence. In this it is taken for granted that each one must wait till his hour has struck, and that he can bestow his love upon one and only one individual.

The ethical side of marriage consists in the consciousness that the union is a substantive end. Marriage thus rests upon love, confidence, and the socializing of the whole individual existence. In this social disposition and reality natural impulse is reduced to the mode of a merely natural element, which is extinguished in the moment of its satisfaction. On the other hand, the spiritual bond of union, when its right as a substantive fact is recognized, is raised above the chances of passion and of temporary particular inclination and is of itself indissoluble.

It has already been remarked that there is no contract in connection with the essential character of marriage. Marriage leaves behind and transcends the standpoint of contract, occupied by the person who is sufficient for himself. Substance is such as to be in essential relation to its accidents. The union of personalities, whereby the family becomes one person, and its members its accidents, is the ethical spirit. The ethical spirit, stripped of the many external phases which it has in particular individuals and transitory interests, has been by picture-thought given independent form, and reverenced as the Penates, etc. In this attitude of mind is found that religious side of marriage and the family, which is called piety. It is a further abstraction, when the divine and substantive reality is separated from its physical embodiment. The result of this procedure is that feeling and the consciousness of spiritual unity become what is falsely called Platonic love. This separation is in keeping with the monastic doctrine, in which natural vitality is regarded simply as negative, and is given by this very separation an infinite importance.

Marriage is distinguished from concubinage, since in concubinage the chief factor is the satisfaction of natural impulse, while in marriage this satisfaction is subordinate. Hence, in marriage one speaks without blushing of occurrences, which apart from the marriage relation cause a sense of shame. Therefore, also, is marriage to be esteemed as in itself indissoluble. The end of marriage is ethical, and therefore occupies so high a place that every thing opposing it seems secondary and powerless. Marriage shall not be liable to dissolution through passion, since passion is subject to it. But, after all, it is only in itself indissoluble, for, as Christ says, divorce is permitted, but only because of hardness of heart. Marriage, since it contains feeling, is not absolute, but open to fluctuations, and has in it the possibility of dissolution. Yet the laws must make the possibility as difficult as can be, and must retain intact the right of the ethical against inclination.

Just as in the case of contract it is the explicit stipulation, which constitutes the true transference of property, so in the case of the ethical bond of marriage the public celebration of consent, and the corresponding recognition and acceptance of it by the family and the community, constitute its consummation and reality. The function of the church is a separate feature, which is not to be considered here. Thus the union is established and completed ethically, only when preceded by social ceremony, the symbol of language being the most spiritual embodiment of the spiritual. The sensual element pertaining to the natural life has place in the ethical relation only as an after result and accident belonging to the external reality of the ethical union. The union can be expressed fully only in mutual love and assistance.

When the question as to the chief end of marriage is asked with a view to enact or recast laws, it means: Which particular side of the reality of marriage must be accepted as the most essential? But no one separate phase of marriage comprises the whole range of its absolute ethical content; and one or other phase of its existence may be wanting without injury to its essence.—In the celebration of marriage the essence of the union is clearly understood to be an ethical principle, freed from the accidents of feeling and private inclination. If the solemnization be taken for an external formality, or a so-called mere civil requisition, the act loses all purpose except that of edification, or of an attestation to the civic regulation. Indeed, there may perhaps remain only the positive arbitrariness of a civil or ecclesiastical command. Now, not only is a command of this kind indifferent to the nature of marriage, but in so far as the two persons have because of it ascribed value to the formality, and counted it as a condition precedent to complete abandonment to each other, it is an alien thing, bringing discord into the disposition of love, and thwarting the inner nature of the union. The opinion that the marriage ceremony is a mere civic mandate professes to contain the loftiest conception of the freedom, intensity, and completeness of love; but in point of fact it denies the ethical side of it, which implies a limitation and repression of the mere natural tendency. Reserve is already found naturally in a sense of shame, and is by the more articulate spiritual consciousness raised to the higher form of modesty and chastity. In a word, the view of marriage just criticised rejects the ethical side, by virtue of which consciousness gathers itself out of its native and subjective condition, and attains to the thought of the substantive. Instead of always holding before itself the accidental character of sensual inclination, it casts off the fetters of this state and engages itself to what is substantive and binding, namely, the Penates. The sensual element is reduced and conditioned by the recognition of marriage as an ethical bond. Insolent is the view of the mere understanding, which is unable to apprehend marriage in its speculative nature. This substantive relation, however, is in harmony with the unsophisticated ethical sense, and with the laws of Christian nations.

It is laid down by Friedrich von Schlegel, in "Lucinde," and by a follower of his in the "Letters of an Unknown" (Lübeck and Leipzig, 1800), that the marriage-ceremony is a superfluous formality. They argue that by the form of marriage love, which is the substantive factor, loses its value; they represent that the abandonment to the sensual is necessary as proof of the freedom and inner reality of love. This style of argument is usual with seducers. Besides, as regards the relation of man to woman, it is woman who, in yielding to sense, gives up her dignity, whereas man has another field than the family for his ethical activity. The sphere of woman is essentially marriage. Her rightful claim is that love should assume the form of marriage, and that the different elements existing in love should be brought into a truly rational connection.

The natural office of the sexes receives, when rationalized, intellectual and social significance. This significance is determined by the distinction which the ethical substance, as conception, introduces by its own motion into itself, in order to win out of the distinction its own life or concrete unity.

In one sex the spiritual divides itself into two phases, independent, personal self-sufficiency, and knowing and willing of free universality. These two together are the self-consciousness of the conceiving thought, and the willing of the objective final cause. In the other sex the spiritual maintains itself in unity and concord. This sex knows and wills the substantive in the form of concrete individuality and feeling. In relation to what is without one sex exhibits power and mastery, while the other is subjective and passive. Hence the husband has his real essential life in the state, the sciences, and the like, in battle and in struggle with the outer world and with himself. Only by effort does he, out of this disruption of himself, reach self-sufficing concord. A peaceful sense of this concord, and an ethical existence, which is intuitive and subjective, he finds in the family. In the family the wife has her full substantive place, and in the feeling of family piety realizes her ethical disposition.

Hence piety is in the "Antigone" of Sophocles most superbly presented as the law of the woman, the law of the nature, which realizes itself subjectively and intuitively, the law of an inner life, which has not yet attained complete realization, the law of the ancient gods, and of the underworld, the eternal law, of whose origin no one knows, in opposition to the public law of the state. This opposition is in the highest sense ethical, and hence also tragic; it is individualized in the opposing natures of man and woman.

Women can, of course, be educated, but their minds are not adapted to the higher sciences, philosophy, or certain of the arts. These demand a universal faculty. Women may have happy inspirations, taste, elegance, but they have not the ideal. The difference between man and woman is the same as that between animal and plant. The animal corresponds more closely to the character of the man, the plant to that of the woman. In woman there is a more peaceful unfolding of nature, a process, whose principle is the less clearly determined unity of feeling. If women were to control the government, the state would be in danger, for they do not act according to the dictates of universality, but are influenced by accidental inclinations and opinions. The education of woman goes on one hardly knows how, in the atmosphere of picture-thinking, as it were, more through life than through the acquisition of knowledge. Man attains his position only through stress of thought and much specialized effort.

Marriage in its essence is monogamy, because in this relation it is the personality, the directly exclusive individuality which subsides and resigns itself. The true inner side of marriage, the subjective form of the real substantive institution, issues only out of such a mutual renunciation of personaltiy as is shared in by no one else. Personality acquires the right of being conscious of itself in another, only in so far as the other appears in this identity as a person or atomic individuality.

Marriage, or monogamy, rather, is one of the principles on which the ethical life of a community depends most absolutely. Hence the institution of marriage is represented as one of the features of the divine or heroic founding of the state.

Since marriage proceeds out of the free resignation by both sexes of that personality which is infinitely peculiar to themselves, it must not occur within the bounds of natural identity, which involves great intimacy and unlimited familiarity. Within such a circle individuals have no exclusive personality. Marriage must rather take place in families that are unconnected, and between persons who are distinct in their origin. Between persons related by blood, therefore, marriage is contrary to the conception of it. It is an ethical act done in freedom, and not controlled by direct natural conditions and their impulses. Marriage within these limits is likewise contrary to true natural feeling.

To regard marriage as grounded not on a right of nature, but on natural sexual impulse, to view it as a capricious contract, to give such an external reason for monogamy as the number of men in relation to the number of women, and to give only vague feelings as cause sufficient to prohibit marriage between blood connections, all such theories are due to the current idea of a state of nature, and to the opinion that such a state possesses rights. They are, however, devoid of the conception of rationality and freedom.

Consanguineous marriages find opposition, in the first instance, in the sense of shame. This feeling of hesitation is justified by the conception. What is already united cannot be first of all united by marriage. As to the relation of mere nature, it is known that amongst animals copulation within one stock produces weaker offspring. What is to be joined ought to be at first distinct and separate. The power of production, both of spirit and body, is greater, the deeper are the oppositions out of which it restores itself. Familiarity, intimacy, habituation due to the same course of action, ought not to occur previous to marriage, but should be found for the first time in the married state. Their appearance after marriage has richer results and a higher value, the more numerous have been the points of difference.

The family, as person, has its external reality in property. If it is to furnish a basis for the substantive personality of the family, it must take the form of means.

It is not enough that the family has property, but, as a universal and lasting person, it needs a permanent and sure possession, or means. When property is treated abstractly, there occur at random the particular needs of the mere individual, and also the self-seeking of the appetites. These now take on an ethical aspect, and are changed into provision for a common interest.

In the wise sayings concerning the founding of states, the institution of a sure property makes its appearance in connection with the institution of marriage, or at least with the introduction of an orderly social life.—When we come to the civic community, we shall see in what family competence consists, and how it is to be secured.

The husband is the head of the family, and when it, as a legal person, collides with other families, he is its representative. It is expected of him, further, to go out and earn its living, care for its needs, and administer the family means. This means is a common possession, to which each member has a common but not a special right. This general right and the husband's right to dispose of the property may conflict, because the ethical sentiment, which in the family is still in its simplest form, is subject to chance and violence.

Marriage establishes a new family, which has its own independent footing as against the stems or houses from which it has proceeded. The connection of the new family with these stems is con-sanguinity, but the principle of the new family is ethical love. Thus, the individual's property is essentially allied to his marriage, and less intimately to his original stock or house.

A marriage-settlement, which imposes a limit to the common possession of goods by the wedded couple, or any other arrange-ment by which the right of the wife is retained, is intended to be security against the dissolution of the marriage-tie by death or divorce. In such an event the different members of the family are by this arrangement apportioned their shares of the common possession.

In many law codes the more extended range of the family circle is retained. It is looked upon as the real bond of union, while the tie of the single family is regarded as comparatively unimportant. Thus in the older Roman law the wife of the lax marriage is more closely allied to her relatives than to her husband and children. In feudal times, also, the necessity of preserving the *splendor familiae* led to reckoning under the family only its male members. Thus the whole family connection was the chief object of concern, and the newly-formed family was placed in the background. Notwithstanding this, every new family is more essential than the wider circle bounded by the tie of consanguinity. A married couple with their children form a nucleus of their own in opposition to the more extended household. Hence the financial status of individuals must be more vitally connected with marriage than with the wider family union.

The unity of marriage which, as substantive, exists only as an inner harmony and sentiment, but, so far as it exists actually, is separated in the two married persons, becomes in the children a unity, which has actual independent existence, and is an independent object. This new object the parents love as an embodiment of their love.—The presupposition of the direct presence of the two people as parents becomes, when taken on its merely natural side, a result. This process expands into an infinite series of generations, which beget and are presupposed. At this finite and natural standpoint the existence of the simple spirit of the Penates is represented as species or kind.

Between husband and wife the relation of love is not yet objective. Though feeling is a substantive unity, it has as yet no footing in reality. This foothold parents attain only in their children, in whom the totality of their alliance is visibly embodied. In the child the mother loves her husband, and the father his wife. In the child both parents have their love before their eyes. Whereas in means the marriage tie exists only in an external object, in children it is present in a spiritual being, in whom the parents are loved, and whom they love.

Søren Kierkegaard

The setting of the following scene from *Stages on Life's Way* (1845) is a banquet given by Constantine Constantius at which he and his friends speak about "Woman." Consistent with Kierkegaard's practice of ascribing his works to pseudonymous authors, each speaker represents a different point of view. Yet they all have in common an inability to grasp the nature of human existence, in this case, woman's human existence. As an existentialist, Kierkegaard is committed to the view that there is no single view of "human being." There are only individuals, in the radical sense that the conscious ego, which defines each person, must constantly make decisions in a context of infinite possibilities. In other words, an individual is constantly making him- or herself; there is no static self, only a continually dynamic, striving person. "Man" as such is a fiction, a Hegelian fantasy; individual, subjective reality is the only reality. Hence, all attempts to know other human beings are doomed to failure, not only because each conscious ego is isolated and subjective but also because all such attempts require the application of fixed, abstract categories, which pervert human reality. This is precisely what the speakers at the banquet fail to understand. They claim to know "woman" as such; they subsume "her" life under universal, abstract stereotypes, totally unmindful of real individuals. Constantine categorizes woman as a type of jest; Victor Eremita denies her life any significance; the Ladies Tailor identifies her with external situations and appearances; Johannes the Seducer reduces her to the instrumentality of gods and men. Yet with characteristic irony, Kierkegaard makes his speakers unwittingly say such perceptive things as "woman cannot be exhaustively expressed by any formula but is an infinity of finitudes."

THE ESSENCE OF WOMAN*

Constantine spoke as follows: . . .

"And now for woman, the subject on which I would speak. I too have pondered, and I have fathomed her category; I too have sought, but I have also found, making a peerless discovery which I impart to you herewith. She can only be rightly construed under the category of jest. It is man's part to be absolute, to act absolutely, to give expression to the absolute; woman has her being in relationships. Between two such different beings no genuine reciprocal action can take place. This incongruity is precisely what constitutes jest, and it is with woman jest first came into the world. It follows, however, as a matter of course that man must know how to keep himself under the category of the absolute, for otherwise nothing comes of it, that is to say, there comes of it something only too universal, that man and woman tally with one another, he as a half-man and she as a half-man.

* From Søren Kierkegaard, "The Banquet," in *Stages on Life's Way*, trans. Walter Lowrie (Princeton: Princeton University Press, 1940).

"Jest is not an aesthetic but an imperfect ethical category. Its effect upon thought is like the effect upon one's frame of mind at hearing a man who begins a speech, and after reciting a phrase or two with the same eloquence, says, 'Hm'—and then dead silence. So it is with woman. One aims at her with the ethical category, one shuts one's eyes, one thinks of the absolute in the way of requirements, one thinks the thought of man, one opens one's eyes, one fixes one's glance upon the demure little miss upon whom one is experimenting to see if she meets the specifications; one becomes uneasy and says to oneself, 'Ah, this surely is jest.' For the jest consists in applying the category, in subsuming her under it, because with her the serious never can become serious; but precisely this is jest, for if one might require seriousness of her, it would not be jest. To put her under a vacuum pump and pump all the air out of her would be cruel and would not be in the least amusing, but to pump air into her, to pump her up to supernatural size, to let her suppose she has attained all the ideality a little miss of sixteen years can imagine she wants to have—this is the beginning of the performance, and the beginning of a highly entertaining performance. No young man has half so much imaginary ideality as a young girl. But 'there is a rebate on that,' as said the tailor, for all her ideality is illusion.

"If one does not regard woman in this way, she may do irreparable harm; with my interpretation she becomes harmless and amusing. There is nothing more dreadful for a man than to catch himself in the act of twaddling. With this all genuine ideality is brought to naught; for to have been a knave is a thing one can repent of, not having meant one word of all one said one can regret, but to have meant all one said, and lo, it turned out to be twaddle—even repentance turns away from that in disgust. It is different with woman. She has a prescriptive right to be transformed in less than twenty-four hours into the most innocent and pardonable galimatias; far be it from her candid soul to want to deceive anyone, she meant all she said, now she says the contrary, but with the same lovable frankness, for she is ready to die for the contrary. In case a man in all seriousness surrenders himself to love, he can say that he has lots of assurance, if only he can get any assurance company to take the risk, for a material so inflammable as woman must always make the insurer suspicious. What has he done? He has identified himself with her: if on New Year's Eve she goes off like a rocket, he goes with her, or if that does not occur, he has nevertheless come into pretty close affinity with danger. And what does he stand to lose? He can lose everything; for there is only one absolute opposite to the absolute, and that is twaddle. He is not to seek asylum in a society for persons morally depraved, for he is not morally depraved, far from it, he is merely reduced *in absurdum* and rendered beatific by nonsense, he has made a fool of himself. Between man and man this situation can never occur. If in this fashion a man fizzles out in nonsense, I despise him; if he dupes me by his shrewdness, I have merely to apply to him the ethical category and the danger is very insignificant; if the thing is carried too far—well, then I put a bullet through his head. But to challenge a woman to a duel—what is that? Who does not know? It is jest—as when Xerxes gave orders to have the sea scourged. . . .

"To shoot a woman, to challenge her to a duel, to show contempt for her, only makes the poor man more ridiculous, for woman is the weaker sex. This consideration is brought forward everywhere and brings everything to confusion. If she does something great she is more admired than a man would be, because people did not suppose they might venture to require it of her; if she is deceived, she has all the pathos in her favor whereas when a man is deceived, people have a little sympathy and a little patience so long as he is present, only to laugh at him when he is gone.

"One had better be prompt, therefore, to regard woman as a jest. The entertainment is peerless. Let one regard her as a fixed quantity and make a relative quantity of oneself. One is not to contradict her, far from it, that would only be to play into her hands. Just because she is unable to set limits to herself, she shows off to the best advantage, seriously speaking, when one contradicts her a bit. One is never to doubt what she says, far from it, every word must be believed. With a rapturous look of blissful intoxication one must dance attendance upon her with the mincing step of an idolatrous worshipper—one falls upon one's knees, one pines, one raises one's eyes to her, one pines, one breathes again. One is to do everything she says, like an obedient slave. Now comes the spice of it. It requires no proof that a woman can talk, i.e. *verba facere.* Unfortunately, she does not possess sufficient power of reflection to insure her against self-contradiction for any considerable time, say a week at the maximum, if the male does not help her regulatively by contradicting her. So the consequence is that in a short while the confusion is in full swing. If one had not done what she told one to do, the confusion would have passed unnoticed, for she forgets again as promptly as she is prompt to talk. But since her adorer has done everything she wanted and been entirely at her service, the confusion is palpable. The more gifted a woman is, the more amusing. The more gifted, so much the more imagination has she. The more imaginative, so much the more potent is she at the instant, and so much the more does confusion reveal itself the next instant. This amusement is rarely witnessed in life because such blind obedience to a woman's whim is very rare. If it is to be found in the languishing shepherd, he hasn't wit enough to perceive the amusement. . . .

"Forgive me now, dear boon companions, if I have spoken too long, and now drain a glass to love and woman. Fair is she and lovely when regarded aesthetically—that no one can deny. But since it so often is said, I too will say: one should not remain standing, but 'go further.' So regard her ethically, and the thing becomes a jest. Even Plato and Aristotle [1] take it that woman is an incomplete form, that is, an irrational quantity, which perhaps some time in a better existence might be brought back to the male form. In this life one must take her as she is. What this is will soon appear, for she too is not satisfied with the aesthetic sphere, she 'goes further,'

[1] Aristotle, Politics, I, 13, ascribes to woman "incomplete reflection"; Plato, Timaias, Chap. 14, lets men who in their former life were imperfect become women in the next.

she would be emancipated—that she is man enough to say, Let that come to pass, and the jest will be beyond all bounds."

When Constantine ceased speaking he instantly commanded Victor Eremita to begin. He spoke as follows:

"Plato, as you know, gave thanks to the gods for four things, and the fourth was that he was contemporary with Socrates. An earlier Greek philosopher [2] had already expressed his gratitude for the first three of them, [3] so I conclude that they were worth it. But I, alas supposing I were desirous of expressing my gratitude like those Greeks, cannot very well give thanks for privileges which are denied me, and so I will muster all the powers of my soul to express gratitude for the one boon which was accorded me: that I became a man and not a woman.

"To be a woman is something so strange, so mixed, so complex, that no predicate expresses it, and the many predicates one might use contradict one another so sharply that only a woman can endure it, and, still worse, can enjoy it. The fact that she actually has less significance than man is not what constitutes her misfortune, even if she were to come to know it, for after all this is something that can be endured. No, the misfortune is that, owing to the romantic way in which she is regarded, her life has become meaningless, so that one moment she has the utmost significance and the next moment none whatever, without ever coming to know what her significance really is—yet this is not the whole of her misfortune, for the worst of it is that she can never come to know it because she is a woman. For my part, if I were a woman, I had rather be a woman in the orient where I would be a slave, for to be a slave, neither more or less, is at any rate something definite, in comparison with being hurrah boys and nothing whatever.

"Even if the life of a woman did not present such contrasts, the distinction which she enjoys and which is rightly assumed to belong to her *qua* woman, a distinction which she does not share with man,

[2] Thales of Miletos, according to Diogenes Laertius, I, 33.

[3] That he had been created a human, not an animal; a man, not a woman; a Greek, not a barbarian.

already indicates the meaningless of her life. This distinction is that of gallantry. Now gallantry consists quite simply in construing by means of fantastic categories the person towards whom one is gallant. Hence gallantry showed toward a man is an insult, for a man deprecates the application of fantastic categories to him. On the other hand it is a tribute to the fair sex, a distinction essentially due to her. Alas, alack! If it were only a single cavalier that was gallant, it would not be so serious a matter, after all. But such is by no means the case. At bottom every man is gallant, he is instinctively gallant. Accordingly, this signifies that nature itself has bestowed this perquisite upon the fair sex. On the other hand, woman instinctively accepts this homage. Once more a misfortune; for if only one woman here and there were to accept it, a different explanation might be given. So here again we have the irony of life. If there is to be truth in gallantry, it must be reciprocal, and gallantry would then be the current rate quoted on the bourse for the difference between beauty and strength, cunning and might. But this is not the way of it, gallantry is essentially woman's due, and the fact that she accepts it instinctively may be explained as an instance of nature's tender care for the weak, for those who have had a hard deal, to whom an illusion gives more than adequate compensation. But this illusion is precisely the calamity. Not infrequently nature comes to the aid of an ill-favored man by consoling him with the belief that he is the most beautiful. Thus nature has made good the deficiency, the man possesses in fact even more than he could reasonably desire.[4] But to possess this in a vain conceit, not to be enslaved to wretchedness, but to be fooled into a conceit, is in fact a still worse mockery. In the sense of being ill-favored it cannot be said that woman suffers from nature's neglect, yet she does suffer in another sense, inasmuch as she never can free herself from the illusion with which life has consoled her. . . .

"Woman's significance is wholly negative, as compared with that her positive significance is nil, indeed it is even pernicious. This is

[4] This is the "over-compensation" with which analytical psychology has made us familiar.

the truth which existence has hidden from her, while it consoles her with a vain conceit which surpasses everything that can enter into any man's brain and with fatherly care has so arranged it all that language unites with everything else to confirm her in the conceit. Even when she is conceived of as the very opposite of inspiring, as the one from whom all depravity issues—whether it be that sin came into the world through her, or that it is her infidelity which is the ruin of everything—the conception is always gallant. For on hearing such talk one might think that woman was capable of becoming infinitely more guilty than man—which after all is a prodigious appreciation of her. Alas, the situation is in reality quite different. There is a secret way of reading this verdict which woman does not understand; for the very next instant existence as a whole accepts the very same conclusion as the state, which makes man responsible for his wife. People condemn her in a way they never have condemned any man, for he gets only a real sentence, and with a woman the thing ends, not with getting a milder sentence (for then her life would not be all illusion), but by quashing the case, leaving the public, i.e. existence, to pay the costs. At one instant she is supposed to be in possession of all possible cunning, the next instant they laugh at the man she deceived, which surely is a contradiction, and even over Potiphar's wife there hovers the possibility of being able to give the impression that she was seduced. Thus woman has a possibility such as no man has, a prodigious possibility, but her reality is in inverse proportion to that, and the most dreadful thing of all is the sorcery of illusion in which she feels happy.

"So let Plato thank the gods that he was contemporary with Socrates, I envy him; let him give thanks for being a Greek, I envy him; but when he gives thanks that he became a man, not a woman, I join in that with my whole heart. If I had become a woman and could understand what I now understand—how dreadful! If I had become a woman and consequently could not even understand that—how much more dreadful!

"But if such be the case, it follows that one had better keep out of any positive relationship with her. Wherever woman is involved one has that inevitable hiatus which renders her blissful because she does not notice it, but kills a man if he discovers it.

"A negative relationship to a woman may exalt a man to infinity. Let that always be said in honor of woman, and it may be said without any qualification; for essentially it does not depend upon any particular quality of the woman, upon her loveliness, or upon the lasting quality of her loveliness; it depends upon the fact that she appears at the right instant, when ideality is acquiring the power of vision. It is a brief instant, and then she would do well to vanish again. For a positive relationship to woman reduces a man to finiteness in the greatest conceivable degree. The highest thing, therefore, a woman can do for a man is to come within his range of vision at the right instant, but that, after all, she cannot do, it is the kindness of fate—but then comes the greatest thing she can do for a man, and that is, to be unfaithful to him, the sooner the better. The first ideality will assist him to reach an ideality of a higher power, and then he is succored absolutely. It is true, this second ideality is bought with the sharpest pain, but it is also the greatest bliss; it is true, he cannot by any means wish it before it has come to pass, but afterwards he thanks her for it; and since after all, humanly speaking, he has no great reason for being so very grateful, all is for the best. But woe unto him if she remains faithful.

"So I thank the gods for the fact that I became a man, not a woman; then in the next place I thank the gods that no woman with a lifelong tenure constrains me constantly to think too late.

"What a strange invention marriage is! And what makes it still stranger is the fact that it is regarded as an 'immediate' step. And yet there is no step so decisive, for there is nothing so self-willed and domineering in relation to a human life as is marriage. A thing so decisive as that, one is to do, not reflectively, but 'immediately'! And yet marriage is not a simple thing but something extremely complex and ambiguous. Just as the meat of the turtle savors of all kinds of meat, so has marriage a savor of everything; and as the turtle is a slow-moving beast, so also is marriage. A love affair is a simple thing after all—but marriage! Is it something pagan or something Christian or something pious or something worldly or a little of everything, is it the expression of that inexplicable erotic sentiment, that concordant elective affinity of souls, or is it a duty or a partnership or expediency or use and wont in certain lands, or is it a little of all that; is one to engage the town band to play the music, or the organist, or a little of both; is it the parson or the police magistrate who is to make the address and inscribe their names in the book of life—I mean the parish register. . . .

"If any positive relationship to woman is to be thought of, it must be so thoroughly reflected that by reason of so much reflection it would not become any relationship to her. To be an excellent husband, and yet in secret to seduce every girl; to seem to be a seducer, and yet to cherish secretly within one's heart all the glow of romanticism—that would be something, and in such a case the concession made in the first potency would be obliterated by the second. Man, however, possesses his true ideality only in a reduplication. Every immediate existence must be annihilated, and the annihilation must constantly be insured by a false expression. Such a reduplication woman is unable to grasp, to her it makes man's nature unpronounceable. If a woman could live and move and have her being in such a reduplication, no erotic relationship with her would be thinkable, and her nature being what it notoriously is, the erotic relationship is disturbed by man's nature, which constantly lives and moves in the annihilation of the very thing in which she lives.

"So I perhaps am preaching the monastic life and am called with good reason Eremita? Not a bit of it. Away with the cloister. After all, that too is only an 'immediate' expression for spirit, and spirit cannot be expressed 'immediately.' It is a matter of indifference whether somebody uses gold or silver or paper money, but the man who never pays out a farthing unless it is false will understand what I mean. The man for whom every direct expression is only a *falsum* is better insured than if he entered a monastery, he continues to be a hermit even though he rides day and night in an omnibus."

Hardly had Victor finished than the Ladies' Tailor sprang to his feet, upset a bottle of wine standing in front of him and began as follows:

"Well-spoken, dear boon companions, well-spoken, the more I hear you talk, the more I am convinced that you are co-conspirators; I hail you as such, I understand you as such, for conspirators understand one another from afar. And yet what do you know? What is your bit of theory worth to which you give the semblance of experience, your bit of experience which you revamp into a theory? And after all, you now and then believe in her for an instant and are captivated for an instant. No, I know woman on her weak side, that is to say, I know her. I shun no terror in the pursuit of my studies and shun no measures calculated to confirm what I have understood. For I am a madman, and one must be mad in order to understand her, and if one was not mad before, he must be so when he has understood her. As the robber has his haunt near the noisy highway, and the ant-lion his funnel in the loose sand, and the pirate his hiding-place near the roaring sea, so have I my *maison* of fashion in the midst of the human swarm, seductive, irresistible to a woman, as the Venusberg is to man. Here in a *maison* of fashion one learns to know her practically and from the bottom up, without any theoretical fuss. Oh, if fashion meant nothing more than that a woman in the heat of desire were to throw off all her clothes, well, that would be something. But that is not all of it, fashion is not undisguised sensuality, not tolerated debauchery, but a contraband trade in indecency licensed as decorum. As in heathen Prussia a marriageable girl wore a bell which served as a signal to the men, so likewise is the existence of a woman of fashion a perpetual bell-ringing, not for debauchees but for lickerish voluptuaries. It is believed that fortune is a woman—oh, yes, it is changeable, to be sure, but it is changeable in something, for it is able to give much, and to that extent it is not a woman. No it is fashion that is a woman, for fashion is changeable in nonsense, is logically consistent only in becoming more and more crazy. One hour in my *maison* is worth more than a year and a day outside of it, if one wants to learn to know woman. I say in my *maison,* for it is the only one in the capital of Denmark, no one thinks of competing. . . .

"You wonder whether it is true? Well, just put it to the test: at the moment his sweetheart sinks blissfully upon his breast and whispers incoherently, 'Thine forever,' as she hides her face against his bosom, let the lover say to her, 'Dear Kitty, your curls are not in the fashion.' Perhaps men don't think about this, but the man who knows it and has the reputation of knowing it is the most dangerous man in the kingdom. What blissful hours the lover passes with his sweetheart before the wedding, I do not know, but the blissful hours she passes in my *maison* he has no inkling of. Without my royal license and sanction a wedding is an invalid act, or at least it is a very plebeian affair. Suppose the moment has already arrived when they are about to meet in front of the altar, suppose she is marching up with the best conscience in the world, knowing that everything was bought in my place and was tried on in my presence, and I rush up and say, 'But, my God! gracious lady, the myrtle wreath is all awry!'—perhaps then the ceremony would be postponed. But men know nothing about this sort of thing, one must be a *modiste* to know it. It requires such prodigious reflection to keep track of a woman's reflection that only a man who sacrifices himself to that task is sufficient for it, and then only in case he has a native gift. A man is fortunate therefore if he never takes up with any woman, in any case she doesn't belong to him, even if she doesn't belong to any other man, she belongs to that phantom which is formed by the unnatural intercourse of feminine reflection with feminine reflection, i.e. fashion. For this reason a woman ought always to swear by fashion, then her oath would have some force, for fashion after all is the one thing she is always thinking about, the one thing she is able to think together with and in everything else. From my *maison de mode* has gone out to the world of elegance the glad tidings for every lady of distinction that fashion commands the use of a special sort of headdress when one goes to church, and again that the headdress must be somewhat different for high mass and for evensong. When the bells are ringing the equipages begin to drew up at my door—for it has also been proclaimed that nobody can properly adjust the headdress but me, the arbiter of fashion. I rush out to meet her with a low bow and lead her into my salon. While she vegetates languidly I adjust everything as it should be. The work is finished, she has looked at herself in the glass. Swift as a messenger of the gods I hasten on before her, I have opened the door of the salon and bowed, I hasten to the door of the *maison,* I fold my arms upon my breast like an oriental slave, but encouraged by a gracious curtsy I venture even to throw her an adoring and admiring kiss—she takes her seat in the carriage, ah! she has forgotten her prayer-book, I make haste and hand it to her through the window, permitting myself to remind her once more to hold her head a little to the right and to rearrange things herself a little if in alighting her headdress should become a trifle disordered. She drives away and is edified.

"You think perhaps that only ladies in high society do homage to fashion. Far from it. Just look at my seamstresses, upon whose toilet I spare no pains in order that the dogmas of fashion may be emphatically proclaimed from my *maison.* They compose a chorus of nitwits, and I the high priest go before them as a shining example, prepared to squander everything if only by the help of fashion I may make every woman ridiculous. For when a seducer boasts that the virtue of every woman is vendible to the right bidder, I don't believe him, but I do believe that before long every woman will be satanized by the crazy and defiling self-reflection of fashion, which depraves her more thoroughly than if she were to be seduced. I have put it to the proof more than once. If I am not able to accomplish it by myself, I egg her on by the help of the female slaves of fashion who belong to her own class. For as one can train rats to bite rats, so is the bite of a satanized woman like that of a tarantula, and it is dangerous above all when a man takes part in it. Whether I am serving the devil or serving God, I do not know, but I am in the right, I will be in the right, I will it, I will it as long as I have a single farthing left, I will it until the blood spurts from my fingers. The physiologist draws the form of a woman to show the dreadful effect of corsets, and alongside of this he draws the normal form. That's all very well, but only the one drawing has the validity of truth—for they all wear corsets. Describe in this way the miserable stunted extravagance of the fashion-mad woman, describe the insidious self-reflection which consumes her, and describe the womanly modesty which knows about itself last of all; do this well, and with that thou hast passed judgment upon woman, and in reality hast passed a damning judgment. If ever I discover such a girl, contented and humble, who is not yet depraved by indecent intercourse with women, she shall fall nevertheless. I entangle her in my toils, now she stands at the place of sacrifice, i.e. in my *maison*. With the most disdainful look a haughty nonchalance can arm itself with I take her measures, she is ready to perish with fright, a peal of laughter from the adjoining room where my trained assistants sit annihilates her. Dressed up in the fashion she looks as crazy as a lunatic, as crazy even as one who could not be admitted into a lunatic asylum. Then she departs from me full of bliss, no man, nor even a god, could terrify her, for she is indeed in the fashion.

"You understand me now, you understand why I call you co-conspirators, though at a great distance from me. You understand now my interpretation of woman. Everything in life is a matter of fashion, the fear of God is a matter of fashion and love, and hoopskirts, and a ring in the nose. So with all my might I will abet the lofty genius who desires to laugh at the most ludicrous of all animals. Since woman has reduced everything to fashion, I by the aid of fashion will prostitute her as she deserves. I give myself no rest, I, the Ladies' Tailor; my soul chafes when I think of my task, she must yet come to the point of wearing a ring in her nose. Therefore seek no sweetheart, forego love as you would shun the most dangerous neighborhood, for also your sweetheart would have to come to the point of wearing a ring in her nose."

Thereupon Johannes the Seducer spoke as follows:

"Esteemed boon companions, is Satan plaguing you? You talk

like undertakers, your eyes are red with tears and not with wine. You move me almost to tears, for an unfortunate lover is very sadly situated in life. *Hinc illae lacrymae.* Now I am a fortunate lover, and my only desire is to remain such constantly. Perhaps this is a concession to woman, which Victor is so much afraid of? Why not? It is a concession. The fact that I undo the wire of this champagne bottle is also a concession, that I let its foam spurt into the goblet is also a concession, that I raise the goblet to my lips is also a concession—now I have drained it—*concedo.* Now, however, the goblet is empty, so I make no more concessions. Thus it is with the girls. If some unlucky lover has bought a kiss too dearly, that only proves to me that he knows neither how to help himself to a dish nor to abstain from it. I never buy it too dearly, I leave that to the girls. What is the meaning of this? To me it means the most beautiful, the most delicious, and pretty nearly the most persuasive *argumentum ad hominum*; but since every woman at least once in her life possesses this primitive power of argumentation, why should I not let myself be persuaded? Our young friend would like to *think* the thing. In fact he can buy what the confectioner calls a 'kiss,' just to look at it. I want to enjoy. No nonsense! Hence an old song says about a kiss, *Es ist kaum zu sehen, es ist nur für Lippen, die genau sich verstehen* [5]—which understand one another so perfectly that reflection is impertinence and folly. The man who is twenty years old and does not comprehend that there is a categorical imperative: Enjoy thyself—that man is a fool. And he who does not seize the opportunity is a Wesleyan Methodist.[6] But you are unfortunate lovers, hence you want to remodel woman. God forbid it. I like her as she is, exactly as she is. Even Constantine's notion that she is a jest implies a secret wish. I, on the other hand, am gallant—and why not? Gallantry costs nothing and brings in everything and is the condition of all erotic enjoyment. Gallantry is the

[5] It is hardly to be seen, it is only for lips which understand one another perfectly.

[6] Literally, a Christianfelder, Christianfeld being the name of a town in South Jutland where the Moravian Brethren were numerous.

Freemasonry of sensuousness and sensuality as between man and woman. It is a primitive language of nature, like love's language in general. It is not made up of sounds but of masked desires which are constantly changing their roles. I can understand very well that an unfortunate lover is ungallant enough to want to convert his deficit into a bill of exchange on eternity. Yet at the same time I do not understand it, for to me woman possesses abundant intrinsic value. . . .

"Originally there was one sex, that of the man—so the Greeks report. Gloriously endowed was he, so that he reflected honor upon the gods who created him, so gloriously endowed that the gods were in the position in which a poet sometimes finds himself when he has expended all his forces upon a poetic creation: they became envious of man. Yea, what was worse, they feared him, lest he might bow unwillingly to their yoke. They feared though it was without reason, that he might cause heaven itself to totter. So then they had conjured up a power they hardly thought themselves capable of curbing. Then there was concern and commotion in the council of the gods. Much had they lavished upon the creation of man, that was magnanimous; now everything must be risked, for everything was at stake, this was self-defense. So thought the gods. And it was impossible to revoke him, as a poet may revoke his thought. By force he could not be compelled, or else the gods themselves might have compelled him, but it was precisely about this they had misgivings. He must then be taken captive and compelled by a power which was weaker than his own and yet stronger, strong enough to compel. What a marvellous power that must be! Necessity, however, teaches the gods to surpass themselves in inventiveness. They sought and pondered and found. This power was woman, the miracle of creation, even in the eyes of the gods a greater miracle than man, a discovery for which the gods in their naïveté could not help patting themselves on the back. What more can be said in honor of her than that she should be able to do what even the gods did not think themselves capable of doing, what more can be said than that she was able? How marvellous she must be to be capable of it! This was a ruse of the gods. Cunningly the enchantress was fashioned; the very instant she had enchanted man she transformed herself and held him captive in all the prolixities of finiteness. This is what the gods wanted. But what can be more delicious, more pleasurable, more enchanting, than this which the gods as they were fighting for their own power devised as the only thing that could decoy man? And verily it is so, for woman is the unique and the most seductive power in heaven and on earth. In this comparison man is something exceedingly imperfect.

"And the ruse of the gods succeeded. However, it did not always succeed. In every generation there were some men, individuals, who became aware of the deception. They perceived her loveliness, it is true, more than did any of the others, but they had an inkling what it was all about. These are what I call erotics, and I reckon myself among them; men call them seducers, woman has no name for them, such a type is for her unmentionable. These erotics are the fortunate ones. They live more luxuriously than the gods, for they eat constantly only that which is more precious than ambrosia and drink what is more delicious than nectar; they dine upon the most seductive fancy which issued from the most artful thought of the gods, they dine constantly upon bait. Oh, luxury beyond compare! Oh, blissful mode of living! They dine constantly upon bait—and are never caught. The other men set to and eat bait as the vulgar eat caviar, and are caught. Only the erotic knows how to appreciate bait, to appreciate it infinitely. Woman divines this, and hence there is a secret understanding between him and her. But he knows also that it is bait, and this is a secret he keeps to himself.

"That nothing more marvellous, nothing more delicious, nothing more seductive can be devised than a woman, the gods vouch for, and the necessity which sharpened their invention; and in turn it vouches for them that they risked their all and in the forming of her nature set heaven and earth in commotion.

"I leave for a moment the myth. The concept of man corresponds exactly to the idea of man. One therefore can think of a single man existing and nothing more than that. On the other hand, the idea of woman is a generality which is not exhaustively exemplified in any single woman. She is not *ebenbürtig* with man but is later, is a part of man, and yet more complete than he. Whether it be that the gods took a part of him while he slept (fearful of awakening him if they took too much), or that they divided him in equal parts so that woman is a half—in any case it is man that was divided. So it is only as a subdivision she is related to man as his mate. She is a deception, but that she is only in her second phase and for him who is deceived. She is finiteness, but in her first phase she is finiteness raised to the highest power in the delusive infinity of all divine and human illusions. Not yet is the deception—but one more instant and a man is deceived. She is finiteness, and so she is a collective term, to say one woman means many women. This the erotic alone understands, and hence he is so prompt to love many, never being deceived, but sucking up all the voluptuous delights the cunning gods were capable of preparing. Therefore woman cannot be exhaustively expressed by any formula but is an infinity of finitudes. He who is bent upon thinking her idea is like one who gazes into a sea of nebulous shapes which are constantly forming, or like one who is bewildered by looking at the billows with their foaming crests which constantly elude him; for her idea is only a workshop of possibilities, and for the erotic these possibilities are the never-failing source of enthusiasm."

Arthur Schopenhauer

Schopenhauer's essay "On Women" (1851) has come to be known among twentieth-century feminists as a classic of misogynist writing. He combines virtually all the negative aspects of traditional ideas on womankind and adds one or two of his own. Schopenhauer's basic contention is twofold—first, that women's qualities (their behavior, virtues, vices, etc.) are natural, and second, that by nature women are in all respects inferior to men. This inferiority is both qualitative (men have certain qualities that women lack) and quantitative (women are deficient in the qualities they share with men). Specifically, women are deficient in reason, in physical strength, and in love, and—a new twist—in the aesthetic faculty. All these flaws have serious consequences. Woman's deficient intelligence accounts for her lifelong childishness, her willfulness, and her lack of a sense of justice, since justice depends on deliberation, and explains why woman must obey and man rule by nature. She is not physically strong, and so nature made her cunning, a master of pretence and lying. This natural cunning, in turn, explains why women are by nature false, unfaithful, hypocritical ingrates, among other things. Woman's deficiency in love makes her hate her own sex and unable to love her own childen on any level other than the purely instinctive. She is capable only of genuinely loving man, since this is her whole goal in life. Finally, she has no aesthetic faculty (which goes with her naturally ugly appearance) and so cannot appreciate any fine art. In short, to reverence woman in a chivalric spirit is to flout nature at every turn.

THE WEAKNESS OF WOMAN*

Schiller's poem in honor of women, *Würde der Frauen*, is the result of much careful thought, and it appeals to the reader by its antithetic style and its use of contrast; but as an expression of the true praise which should be accorded to them, it is, I think, inferior to these few words of Jouy's: *Without women, the beginning of our life would be helpless; the middle, devoid of pleasure; and the end, of consolation.* The same thing is more feelingly expressed by Byron in *Sardanapalus:*

> The very first
> *Of human life must spring from woman's breast,*
> *Your first small words are taught you from her lips,*
> *Your first tears quench'd by her, and your last sighs*
> *Too often breathed out in a woman's hearing,*
> *When men have shrunk from the ignoble care*
> *Of watching the last hour of him who led them.*
>
> (Act I. Scene 2)

* From Arthur Schopenhauer, "Of Women," in *Studies in Pessimism*, trans. T. Bailey Saunders (London: Swan Sonnenschein and Company, 1893).

These two passages indicate the right standpoint for the appreciation of women.

You need only look at the way in which she is formed, to see that woman is not meant to undergo great labor, whether of the mind or of the body. She pays the debt of life not by what she does, but by what she suffers; by the pains of childbearing and care for the child, and by submission to her husband, to whom she should be a patient and cheering companion. The keenest sorrows and joys are not for her, nor is she called upon to display a great deal of strength. The current of her life should be more gentle, peaceful and trivial than man's, without being essentially happier or unhappier.

Women are directly fitted for acting as the nurses and teachers of our early childhood by the fact that they are themselves childish, frivolous and short-sighted; in a word, they are big children all their life long—a kind of intermediate stage between the child and the full-grown man, who is man in the strict sense of the word. See how a girl will fondle a child for days together, dance with it and sing to it; and then think what a man, with the best will in the world, could do if he were put in her place.

With young girls Nature seems to have had in view what, in the language of the drama, is called *a striking effect;* as for a few years she dowers them with a wealth of beauty and is lavish in her gift of charm, at the expense of all the rest of their life; so that during those years they may capture the fantasy of some man to such a degree that he is hurried away into undertaking the honorable care of them, in some form or other, as long as they live—a step for which there would not appear to be any sufficient warranty if reason only directed his thoughts. Accordingly, Nature has equipped woman, as she does all her creatures, with the weapons and implements requisite for the safeguarding of her existence, and for just as long as it is necessary for her to have them. Here, as elsewhere, Nature proceeds with her usual economy; for just as the female ant, after fecundation, loses her wings, which are then superfluous, nay, actually a danger to the business of breeding; so, after giving birth to one or two children, a woman generally loses her beauty; probably, indeed, for similar reasons.

And so we find that young girls, in their hearts, look upon domestic affairs or work of any kind as of secondary importance, if not actually as a mere jest. The only business that really claims their earnest attention is love, making conquests, and everything connected with this—dress, dancing, and so on.

The nobler and more perfect a thing is, the later and slower it is in arriving at maturity. A man reaches the maturity of his reasoning powers and mental faculties hardly before the age of twenty-eight; a woman at eighteen. And then, too, in the case of woman, it is only reason of a sort—very niggard in its dimensions. That is why women remain children their whole life long; never seeing anything but what is quite close to them, cleaving to the present moment, taking appearance for reality, and preferring trifles to matters of the first importance. For it is by virtue of his reasoning faculty that man does not live in the present only, like the brute, but looks about him and considers the past and the future; and this is the origin of prudence, as well as of that care and anxiety which so many people exhibit. Both the advantages and the disadvantages which this involves, are shared in by the woman to a smaller extent because of her weaker power of reasoning. She may, in fact, be described as intellectually short-sighted, because, while she has an intuitive understanding of what lies quite close to her, her field of vision is narrow and does not reach to what is remote; so that things which are absent, or past, or to come, have much less effect upon women than upon men. This is the reason why women are more often inclined to be extravagant, and sometimes carry their inclination to a length that borders upon madness. In their hearts, women think that it is men's business to earn money and theirs to spend it—if possible during their husband's life, but, at any rate, after his death. The very fact that their husband hands them over his earnings for purposes of housekeeping, strengthens them in this belief.

However many disadvantages all this may involve, there is at least this to be said in its favor; that the woman lives more in the present than the man, and that, if the present is at all tolerable, she enjoys it more eagerly. This is the source of that cheerfulness which is peculiar to women, fitting her to amuse man in his hours of recreation, and, in case of need, to console him when he is borne down by the weight of his cares.

It is by no means a bad plan to consult women in matters of difficulty, as the Germans used to do in ancient times; for their way of looking at things is quite different from ours, chiefly in the fact that they like to take the shortest way to their goal, and, in general, manage to fix their eyes upon what lies before them; while we, as a rule, see far beyond it, just because it is in front of our noses. In cases like this, we need to be brought back to the right standpoint, so as to recover the near and simple view.

Then, again, women are decidedly more sober in their judgment than we are, so that they do not see more in things than is really there; whilst, if our passions are aroused, we are apt to see things in an exaggerated way, or imagine what does not exist.

The weakness of their reasoning faculty also explains why it is that women show more sympathy for the unfortunate than men do, and so treat them with more kindness and interest; and why it is that, on the contrary, they are inferior to men in point of justice, and less honorable and conscientious. For it is just because their reasoning power is weak that present circumstances have such a hold over them, and those concrete things, which lie directly before their eyes, exercise a power which is seldom counteracted to any extent by abstract principles of thought, by fixed rules of conduct, firm resolutions, or, in general, by consideration for the past and the future, or regard for what is absent and remote. Accordingly, they possess the first and main elements that go to make a virtuous character, but they are deficient in those secondary qualities which are often a necessary instrument in the formation of it.[1]

---

[1] In this respect they may be compared to an animal organism which contains a liver but no gall-bladder. Here let me refer to what I have said in my treatise on *The Foundation of Morals, §.17.*

Hence, it will be found that the fundamental fault of the female character is that it has *no sense of justice.* This is mainly due to the fact, already mentioned, that women are defective in the powers of reasoning and deliberation; but it is also traceable to the position which Nature has assigned to them as the weaker sex. They are dependent, not upon strength, but upon craft; and hence their instinctive capacity for cunning, and their ineradicable tendency to say what is not true. For as lions are provided with claws and teeth, and elephants and boars with tusks, bulls with horns, and cuttle fish with its clouds of inky fluid, so Nature has equipped woman, for her defence and protection, with the arts of dissimulation; and all the power which Nature has conferred upon man in the shape of physical strength and reason, has been bestowed upon women in this form. Hence, dissimulation is innate in woman, and almost as much a quality of the stupid as of the clever. It is natural for them to make use of it on every occasion as it is for those animals to employ their means of defence when they are attacked; they have a feeling that in doing so they are only within their rights. Therefore a woman who is perfectly truthful and not given to dissimulation is perhaps an impossibility, and for this very reason they are so quick at seeing through dissimulation in others that it is not a wise thing to attempt it with them. But this fundamental defect which I have stated, with all that it entails, gives rise to falsity, faithlessness, treachery, ingratitude, and so on. Perjury in a court of justice is more often committed by women than by men. It may, indeed, be generally questioned whether women ought to be sworn in at all. From time to time one finds repeated cases everywhere of ladies, who want for nothing, taking things from shop-counters when no one is looking, and making off with them.

Nature has appointed that the propagation of the species shall be the business of men who are young, strong and handsome; so that the race may not degenerate. This is the firm will and purpose of Nature in regard to the species, and it finds its expression in the passions of women. There is no law that is older or more powerful than this. Woe, then, to the man who sets up claims and interests that will conflict with it; whatever he may say and do, they will be unmercifully crushed at the first serious encounter. For the innate rule that governs women's conduct, though it is secret and unformulated, nay, unconscious in its working, is this: *We are justified in deceiving those who think they have acquired rights over the species by paying little attention to the individual, that is, to us. The constitution and, therefore, the welfare of the species have been placed in our hands and committed to our care, through the control we obtain over the next generation, which proceeds from us; let us discharge our duties conscientiously.* But women have no abstract knowledge of this leading principle; they are conscious of it only as a concrete fact; and they have no other method of giving expression to it than the way in which they act when the opportunity arrives. And then their conscience does not trouble them so much as we fancy; for in the darkest recesses of their heart, they are aware that in committing a breach of their duty towards the individual, they have all the better fulfilled their duty towards the species, which is infinitely greater.[2]

And since women exist in the main solely for the propagation of the species, and are not destined for anything else, they live, as a rule, more for the species than for the individual, and in their hearts take the affairs of the species more seriously than those of the individual. This gives their whole life and being a certain levity; the general bent of their character is in a direction fundamentally different from that of man; and it is this to which produces that discord in married life which is so frequent, and almost the normal state.

The natural feeling between men is mere indifference, but between women it is actual enmity. The reason of this is that trade-jealousy—*odium figulinum*—which, in the case of men does not go beyond the confines of their own particular pursuit; but, with women, embraces the whole sex; since they have only one kind of business. Even when they meet in the street, women look at one another like Guelphs and Ghibellines. And it is a patent fact that

[2] A more detailed discussion of the matter in question may be found in my chief work, *Die Welt als Wille und Vorstellung,* vol. ii, ch. 44.

when two women make first acquaintance with each other, they behave with more constraint and dissimulation than two men would show in a like case; and hence it is that an exchange of compliments between two women is a much more ridiculous proceeding than between two men. Further, whilst a man will, as a general rule, always preserve a certain amount of consideration and humanity in speaking to others, even to those who are in a very inferior position, it is intolerable to see how proudly and disdainfully a fine lady will generally behave towards one who is in a lower social rank (I do not mean a woman who is in her service), whenever she speaks to her. The reason of this may be that, with women, differences of rank are much more precarious than with us; because, while a hundred considerations carry weight in our case, in theirs there is only one, namely, with which man they have found favor; as also that they stand in much nearer relations with one another than men do, in consequence of the one-sided nature of their calling. This makes them endeavor to lay stress upon differences of rank.

It is only the man whose intellect is clouded by his sexual impulses that could give the name of *the fair sex* to that under-sized, narrow-shouldered, broad-hipped, and short-legged race; for the whole beauty of the sex is bound up with this impulse. Instead of calling them beautiful, there would be more warrant for describing women as the unaesthetic sex. Neither for music, nor for poetry, nor for fine art, have they really and truly any sense or susceptibility; it is a mere mockery if they make a pretence of it in order to assist their endeavor to please. Hence, as a result of this, they are incapable of taking a *purely objective interest* in anything; and the reason of it seems to me to be as follows. A man tries to acquire *direct* mastery over things, either by understanding them, or by forcing them to do his will. But a woman is always and everywhere reduced to obtaining this mastery *indirectly,* namely, through a man; and whatever direct mastery she may have is entirely confined to him. And so it lies in woman's nature to look upon everything only as a means for conquering man; and if she takes an interest in anything else, it is simulated—a mere roundabout way of gaining her ends by coquetry, and feigning what she does not feel. Hence, even Rousseau declared: *Women have, in general, no love for any art; they have no proper knowledge of any; and they have no genius.*[3]

No one who sees at all below the surface can have failed to remark the same thing. You need only observe the kind of attention women bestow upon a concert, an opera, or a play—the childish simplicity, for example, with which they keep on chattering during the finest passages in the greatest masterpieces. If it is true that the Greeks excluded women from their theatres they were quite right in what they did; at any rate you would have been able to hear what was said upon the stage. In our day, besides, or in lieu of saying, *Let a woman keep silence in the church,* it would be much to the point to say *Let a woman keep silence in the theatre.* This might, perhaps, be put up in big letters on the curtain.

And you cannot expect anything else of women if you consider that the most distinguished intellects among the whole sex have never managed to produce a single achievement in the fine arts that is really great, genuine, and original; or given to the world any work of permanent value in any sphere. This is most strikingly shown in regard to painting, where mastery of technique is at least as much within their power as within ours—and hence they are diligent in cultivating it; but still, they have not a single great painting to boast of, just because they are deficient in that objectivity of mind which is so directly indispensable in painting. They never get beyond a subjective point of view. It is quite in keeping with this that ordinary women have no real susceptibility for art at all; for Nature proceeds in strict sequence—*non facit saltum.* And Huarte in his *Examen de ingenios para las scienzias*—a book which has been famous for three hundred years—denies women the possession of all the higher faculties. The case is not altered by particular and partial exceptions; taken as a whole, women are, and remain, thoroughgoing Philistines, and quite incurable. Hence, with that absurd arrangement which allows them to share the rank and title of their husbands they are a constant

[3] Lettre à d'Alembert. Note xx.

stimulus to his ignoble ambitions. And, further, it is just because they are Philistines that modern society, where they take the lead and set the tone, is in such a bad way. Napoleon's saying—that *women have no rank*—should be adopted as the right standpoint in determining their position in society; and as regards their other qualities Chamfort makes the very true remark: *They are made to trade with our own weaknesses and our follies, but not with our reason. The sympathies that exist between them and men are skin-deep only, and do not touch the mind or the feelings or the character.* They form the *sexus sequior*—the second sex, inferior in every respect to the first; their infirmities should be treated with consideration; but to show them great reverence is extremely ridiculous, and lowers us in their eyes. When Nature made two divisions of the human race, she did not draw the line exactly through the middle. These divisions are polar and opposed to each other, it is true; but the difference between them is not qualitative merely, it is also quantitative.

This is just the view which the ancients took of woman, and the view which people in the East take now; and their judgment as to her proper position is much more correct than ours, with our old French notions of gallantry and our preposterous system of reverence—that highest product of Teutonico-Christian stupidity. These notions have served only to make women more arrogant and overbearing; so that one is occasionally reminded of the holy apes in Benares, who in the consciousness of their sanctity and inviolable position, think they can do exactly as they please.

But in the West, the woman, and especially the *lady*, finds herself in a false position; for woman, rightly called by the ancients, *sexus sequior*, is by no means fit to be the object of our honor and veneration, or to hold her head higher than man and be on equal terms with him. The consequences of this false position are sufficiently obvious. Accordingly, it would be a very desirable thing if this Number-Two of the human race were in Europe also relegated to her natural place, and an end put to that lady nuisance, which not only moves all Asia to laughter, but would have been ridiculed by Greece and Rome as well. It is impossible to calculate the good effects which such a change would bring about in our social, civil and political arrangements. There would be no necessity for the Salic law: it would be a superfluous truism. In Europe the *lady*, strictly so-called, is a being who should not exist at all; she should be either a housewife or a girl who hopes to become one; and she should be brought up, not to be arrogant, but to be thrifty and submissive. It is just because there are such people as *ladies* in Europe that the women of the lower classes, that is to say, the great majority of the sex, are much more unhappy than they are in the East. And even Lord Byron says: *Thought of the state of women under the ancient Greeks—convenient enough. Present state, a remnant of the barbarism of the chivalric and the feudal ages—artificial and unnatural. They ought to mind home—and be well fed and clothed—but not mixed in society. Well educated, too, in religion—but to read neither poetry nor politics—nothing but books of piety and cookery. Music—drawing—dancing—also a little gardening and ploughing now and then. I have seen them mending the roads in Epirus with good success. Why not, as well as hay-making and milking?*

The laws of marriage prevailing in Europe consider the woman as the equivalent of the man—start, that is to say, from a wrong position. In our part of the world where monogamy is the rule, to marry means to halve one's rights and double one's duties. Now, when the laws gave women equal rights with man, they ought to have also endowed her with a masculine intellect. But the fact is, that just in proportion as the honors and privileges which the laws accord to women, exceed the amount which nature gives, is there a diminution in the number of women who really participate in these privileges; and all the remainder are deprived of their natural rights by just so much as is given to the others over and above their share. For the institution of monogamy, and the laws of marriage which it entails, bestow upon the woman an unnatural position of privilege, by considering her throughout as the full equivalent of the man, which is by no means the case; and seeing this, men who are shrewd and prudent very often scruple to make so great a sacrifice and to acquiesce in so unfair an arrangement.

Consequently, whilst among polygamous nations every woman is provided for, where monogamy prevails the number of married women is limited; and there remains over a large number of women without stay or support, who, in the upper classes, vegetate as useless old maids, and in the lower succumb to hard work for which they are not suited; or else become *filles de joie,* whose life is as destitute of joy as it is of honor. But under the circumstances they become a necessity; and their position is openly recognized as serving the special end of warding off temptation from those women favored by fate, who have found, or may hope to find, husbands. In London alone there are 80,000 prostitutes. What are they but the women, who, under the institution of monogamy have come off worse? Theirs is a dreadful fate: they are human sacrifices offered up on the altar of monogamy. The women whose wretched position is here described are the inevitable set-off to the European lady with her arrogance and pretension. Polygamy is therefore a real benefit to the female sex if it is taken as a whole. And, from another point of view, there is no true reason why a man whose wife suffers from chronic illness, or remains barren, or has gradually become too old for him, should not take a second. The motives which induce so many people to become converts to Mormonism appear to be just those which militate against the unnatural institution of monogamy.

Moreover, the bestowal of unnatural rights upon women has imposed upon them unnatural duties, and, nevertheless, a breach of these duties makes them unhappy. Let me explain. A man may often think that his social or financial position will suffer if he marries, unless he makes some brilliant alliance. His desire will then be to win a woman of his own choice under conditions other than those of marriage, such as will secure her position and that of the children. However fair, reasonable, fit and proper these conditions may be, and the woman consents by foregoing that undue amount of privilege which marriage alone can bestow, she to some extent loses her honor, because marriage is the basis of civic society; and she will lead an unhappy life, since human nature is so constituted that we pay an attention to the opinion of other people which is out of all proportion to its value. On the other hand, if she does not consent, she runs the risk either of having to be given in marriage to a man whom she does not like, or of being landed high and dry as an old maid; for the period during which she has a chance of being settled for life is very short. And in view of this aspect of the institution of monogamy, Thomasius' profoundly learned treatise, *de Concubinatu*, is well worth reading; for it shows that, amongst all nations and in all ages, down to the Lutheran Reformation, concubinage was permitted; nay, that it was an institution which was to a certain extent actually recognized by law, and attended with no dishonor. It was only the Lutheran Reformation that degraded it from this position. It was seen to be a further justification for the marriage of the clergy; and then, after that, the Catholic Church did not dare to remain behind-hand in the matter.

There is no use arguing about polygamy; it must be taken as *de facto* existing everywhere, and the only question is as to how it shall be regulated. Where are there, then, any real monogamists? We all live, at any rate, for a time, and most of us, always, in polygamy. And so, since every man needs many women, there is nothing fairer than to allow him, nay, to make it incumbent upon him, to provide for many women. This will reduce woman to her true and natural position as a subordinate being; and the *lady*—that monster of European civilization and Teutonico-Christian stupidity—will disappear from the world, leaving only *women,* but no more *unhappy women,* of whom Europe is now full.

In India, no woman is ever independent, but in accordance with the law of Manu,[4] she stands under the control of her father, her husband, her brother or her son. It is, to be sure, a revolting thing that a widow should immolate herself upon her husband's funeral pyre; but it is also revolting that she should spend her husband's money with her paramours—the money for which he toiled his whole life long, in the consoling belief that he was providing for his children. Happy are those who have kept the middle course—*medium tenuere beati.*

The first love of a mother for her child is, with the lower animals

4 Ch. V., v. 148.

as with men, of a purely *instinctive* character, and so it ceases when the child is no longer in a physically helpless condition. After that, the first love should give way to one that is based on habit and reason; but this often fails to make its appearance, especially where the mother did not love the father. The love of a father for his child is of a different order, and more likely to last; because it has its foundation in the fact that in the child he recognizes his own inner self; that is to say, his love for it is metaphysical in its origin.

In almost all nations, whether of the ancient or the modern world, even amongst the Hottentots,[5] property is inherited by the male descendants alone; it is only in Europe that a departure has taken place; but not amongst the nobility, however. That the property which has cost men long years of toil and effort, and been won with so much difficulty, should afterwards come into the hands of women, who then, in their lack of reason, squander it in a short time, or otherwise fool it away, is a grievance and a wrong as serious as it is common, which should be prevented by limiting the right of women to inherit. In my opinion, the best arrangement would be that by which women, whether widows or daughters, should never receive anything beyond the interest for life on property secured by mortgage, and in no case the property itself, or the capital, except where all male descendants fail. The people who make money are men, not women; and it follows from this that women are neither justified in having unconditional possession of it, nor fit persons to be entrusted with its administration. When wealth, in any true sense of the word, that is to say, funds, houses or land, is to go to them as an inheritance they should never be allowed the free disposition of it. In their case a guardian should always be appointed; and hence they should never be given the free control of their own children, wherever it can be avoided. The vanity of women, even though it should not prove to be greater than that of men, has this much danger in it, that it takes an entirely material direction. They are vain, I mean, of their personal beauty, and then of finery, show and magnificence. That is just why

5 Leroy, *Lettres philosophiques sur l'intelligence et la perfectibilité des animaux, avec quelques lettres sur l'homme,* p. 298, Paris, 1802.

they are so much in their element in society. It is this, too, which makes them so inclined to be extravagant, all the more as their reasoning power is low. Accordingly we find an ancient writer describing woman as in general of an extravagant nature—Γὴ τὸ σύνολον ἔστι δαπανηρὸν Φύσει.[6] But with men vanity often takes the direction of non-material advantages, such as intellect, learning, courage.

In the *Politics* [7] Aristotle explains the great disadvantage which accrued to the Spartans from the fact that they conceded too much to their women, by giving them the right of inheritance and dower, and a great amount of independence; and he shows how much this contributed to Sparta's fall. May it not be the case in France that the influence of women, which went on increasing steadily from the time of Louis XIII., was to blame for that gradual corruption of the Court and the Government, which brought about the Revolution of 1789, of which all subsequent disturbances have been the fruit? However that may be, the false position which women occupy, demonstrated as it is, in the most glaring way, by the institution of the *lady,* is a fundamental defect in our social scheme, and this defect, proceeding from the very heart of it, must spread its baneful influence in all directions.

.   .   .   .

That woman is by nature meant to obey may be seen by the fact that every woman who is placed in the unnatural position of complete independence, immediately attaches herself to some man, by whom she allows herself to be guided and ruled. It is because she needs a lord and master. If she is young, it will be a lover; if she is old, a priest.

[6] Brunck's *Gnomici poetae graeci,* v. 115.
[7] Bk. I., ch. 9.

Ralph Waldo Emerson

The long struggle to achieve women's suffrage in America officially began in 1848 at the Woman's Rights Convention held in Seneca Falls, New York. It was a time of intellectual and social ferment for Americans—utopian experiments were springing up, the abolition of slavery was being preached, a religious revival was spreading, and Transcendentalism was being established. The infant women's rights cause, often identifying itself with these other movements, proclaimed its commitment to the political, economic, and social equality of women. During these early years, the women's movement attracted many prominent men to its cause, among them, Emerson, who spoke in their behalf at the 1855 National Women's Rights Convention in Boston. The text of that speech is presented here. It is of particular interest, since it reflects at once the conservative and radical nature of ideas connected with the early feminist movement. While its proposals for equal rights for women were clearly revolutionary in the nineteenth century, it had not broken with the notion that men and women are essentially different, and hence with stereotypes of women. Emerson's "woman" is still on a pedestal—she has great magnanimity, she is the educator of humanity through the care of her children, she is the civilizer of mankind. He agrees that intuition and sentiment are primary in women's life whereas logic and will are primary in men's. Yet Emerson offers precisely this image of women as his chief argument for their suffrage, since these qualities are far from being liabilities.

WOMAN'S SUFFRAGE*

Among those movements which seem to be, now and then, endemic in the public mind,—perhaps we should say, sporadic,— rather than the single inspiration of one mind, is that which has urged on society the benefits of action having for its object a benefit to the position of Woman. And none is more seriously interesting to every healthful and thoughtful mind.

In that race which is now predominant over all the other races of men, it was a cherished belief that women had an oracular nature. They are more delicate than men,—delicate as iodine to light,—and thus more impressionable. They are the best index of the coming hour. I share this belief. I think their words are to be weighed; but it is their inconsiderate word,—according to the rule, "take their first advice, not their second": as Coleridge was wont to apply to a lady for her judgment in questions of taste, and accept it; but when

* From Ralph Waldo Emerson, "Woman," A lecture read before the Woman's Rights Convention, Boston, September 20, 1855, reprinted in *Miscellanies* (Boston: Houghton, Mifflin and Company, 1884).

she added—"I think so, because"—"Pardon me, madam," he said, "leave me to find out the reasons for myself." In this sense, as more delicate mercuries of the imponderable and immaterial influences, what they say and think is the shadow of coming events. Their very dolls are indicative. Among our Norse ancestors, Frigga was worshipped as the goddess of women. "Weirdes all," said the Edda, "Frigga knoweth, though she telleth them never." That is to say, all wisdoms Woman knows; though she takes them for granted, and does not explain them as discoveries, like the understanding of man. Men remark figure: women always catch the expression. They inspire by a look, and pass with us not so much by what they say or do, as by their presence. They learn so fast and convey the result so fast as to outrun the logic of their slow brother and make his acquisitions poor. 'Tis their mood and tone that is important. Does their mind misgive them, or are they firm and cheerful? 'Tis a true report that things are going ill or well. And any remarkable opinion or movement shared by woman will be the first sign of revolution.

Plato said, Women are the same as men in faculty, only less in degree. But the general voice of mankind has agreed that they have their own strength; that women are strong by sentiment; that the same mental height which their husbands attain by toil, they attain by sympathy with their husbands. Man is the will, and Woman the sentiment. In this ship of humanity, Will is the rudder, and Sentiment the sail: when Woman affects to steer, the rudder is only a masked sail. When women engage in any art or trade, it is usually as a resource, not as a primary object. The life of the affections is primary to them, so that there is usually no employment or career which they will not with their own applause and that of society quit for a suitable marriage. And they give entirely to their affections, set their whole fortune on the die, lose themselves eagerly in the glory of their husbands and children. Man stands astonished at a magnanimity he cannot pretend to. Mrs. Lucy Hutchinson, one of the heroines of the English Commonwealth, who wrote the life of her husband, the Governor of Nottingham, says, "If he esteemed her at a higher rate than she in herself could have deserved, he was the author of that virtue he doted on, while she only reflected his own glories upon him. All that she was, was *him,* while he was hers, and all that she is now, at best, but his pale shade."

As for Plato's opinion, it is true that, up to recent times, in no art or science, not in painting, poetry, or music, have they produced a master-piece. Till the new education and larger opportunities of very modern times, this position, with the fewest possible exceptions, has always been true. Sappho, to be sure, in the Olympic Games, gained the crown over Pindar. But, in general, no mastery in either of the fine arts—which should, one would say, be the arts of women—has yet been obtained by them, equal to the mastery of men in the same. The part they play in education, in the care of the young and the tuition of older children, is their organic office in the world. So much sympathy as they have, makes them inestimable as the mediators between those who have knowledge and those who want it: besides, their fine organization, their taste, and love of details, makes the knowledge they give better in their hands.

But there is an art which is better than painting, poetry, music, or architecture,—better than botany, geology, or any science; namely, Conversation. Wise, cultivated, genial conversation is the last flower of civilization and the best result which life has to offer us,—a cup for gods, which has no repentance. Conversation is our account of ourselves. All we have, all we can, all we know, is brought into play, and as the reproduction, in finer form, of all our havings.

Women, are, by this and their social influence, the civilizers of mankind. What is civilization? I answer, the power of good women. It was Burns's remark when he first came to Edinburgh that between the men of rustic life and the polite world he observed little difference; that in the former, though unpolished by fashion and unenlightened by science, he had found much observation and much intelligence; but a refined and accomplished woman was a being almost new to him, and of which he had formed a very inadequate idea. "I like women," said a clear-headed man of the world, "they are so finished." They finish society, manners, language. Form and ceremony are their realm. They embellish trifles. All these ceremonies that hedge our life around are not to be despised, and when we have become habituated to them cannot be dispensed with. No woman can despise them with impunity. Their genius delights in ceremonies, in forms, in decorating life with manners, with proprieties, order and grace. They are, in their nature, more relative; the circumstance must always be fit; out of place they lose half their weight, out of place they are disfranchised. Position, Wren said, is essential to the perfecting of beauty;—a fine building is lost in a dark lane; a statue should stand in the air; much more true is it of woman.

We commonly say that easy circumstances seem somehow necessary to the finish of the female character: but then it is to be remembered that they create these with all their might. They are always making that civilization which they require; that state of art, of decoration, that ornamental life in which they best appear.

The spiritual force of man is as much shown in taste, in his fancy and imagination—attaching deep meanings to things and to arbitrary inventions of no real value,—as in his perception of truth. He is as much raised above the beast by this creative faculty as by any other. The horse and ox use no delays; they run to the river when thirsty, to the corn when hungry, and say no thanks but fight down whatever opposes their appetite. But man invents and adorns all he does with delays and degrees, paints it all over with forms, to please himself better; he invented majesty and the etiquette of courts and drawing-rooms; architecture, curtains, dress, all luxuries and adornments, and the elegance of privacy, to increase the joys of society. He invented marriage; and surrounded by religion, by comeliness, by all manner of dignities and renunciations, the union of the sexes.

And how should we better measure the gulf between the best intercourse of men in old Athens, in London, or in our American capitals,—between this and the hedgehog existence of diggers of worms, and the eaters of clay and offal,—than by signalizing just this department of taste or comeliness? Herein woman is the prime genius and ordainer. There is no grace that is taught by the dancing-master, no style adopted into the etiquette of courts, but was first the whim and mere action of some brilliant woman, who charmed beholders by this new expression, and made it remembered and copied. And I think they should magnify their ritual of manners. Society, conversation, decorum, flowers, dances, colors, forms, are their homes and attendants. They should be found in fit surroundings—with fair approaches, with agreeable architecture, and with all advantages which the means of man collect:—

> The far-fetched diamond finds its home
>   Flashing and smouldering in her hair.
> For her the seas their pearls reveal,
>   Art and strange lands her pomp supply
> With purple, chrome and cochineal,
>   Ochre and lapis lazuli.
> The worm its golden woof presents.
>   Whatever runs, flies, dives or delves
> All doff for her their ornaments,
>   Which suit her better than themselves.

There is no gift of nature without some drawback. So, to women, this exquisite structure could not exist without its own penalty. More vulnerable, more infirm, more mortal than men, they could not be such excellent artists in this element of fancy if they did not lend and give themselves to it. They are poets who believe their own poetry. They emit from their pores a colored atmosphere, one would say, wave upon wave of rosy light, in which they walk evermore, and see all objects through this warm-tinted mist that envelops them.

But the starry crown of woman is in the power of her affection and sentiment, and the infinite enlargements to which they lead. Beautiful is the passion of love, painter and adorner of youth and early life: but who suspects, in its blushes and tremors, what tragedies, heroisms and immortalities are beyond it? The passion, with all its grace and poetry, is profane to that which follows it. All these affections are only introductory to that which is beyond, and to that which is sublime.

We men have no right to say it, but the omnipotence of Eve is in humility. The instincts of mankind have drawn the Virgin Mother—

> Created beings all in lowliness
> Surpassing, as in height above them all.

This is the Divine Person whom Dante and Milton saw in vision. This is the victory of Griselda, her supreme humility. And it is when love has reached this height that all our pretty rhetoric begins to have meaning. When we see that, it adds to the soul a new soul, it is honey in the mouth, music in the ear and balsam in the heart.

> Far have I clambered in my mind,
> But nought so great as Love I find.
> What is thy tent, where dost thou dwell?
>
> "My mansion is humility,
> Heaven's vastest capability."
> The further it doth downward tend,
> The higher up it doth ascend.

The first thing men think of, when they love, is to exhibit their usefulness and advantages to the object of their affection. Women make light of these, asking only love. They wish it to be an exchange of nobleness.

There is much in their nature, much in their social position which gives them a certain power of divination. And women know, at first sight, the characters of those with whom they converse. There is much that tends to give them a religious height which men do not attain. Their sequestration from affairs and from the injury to the moral sense which affairs often inflict, aids this. And in every remarkable religious development in the world, women have taken a leading part. It is very curious that in the East, where Woman occupies, nationally, a lower sphere, where the laws resist the education and emancipation of women,—in the Mohammedan faith, Woman yet occupies the same leading position, as a prophetess, that she has among the ancient Greeks, or among the Hebrews, or among the Saxons. This power, this religious character, is everywhere to be remarked in them.

The action of society is progressive. In barbarous society the position of women is always low—in the Eastern nations lower than in the West. "When a daughter is born," says the Shiking, the old Sacred Book of China, "she sleeps on the ground, she is clothed with a wrapper, she plays with a tile; she is incapable of evil or of good." And something like that position, in all low society, is the position of woman; because, as before remarked, she is herself its civilizer. With the advancements of society the position and influence of woman bring her strength or her faults into light. In modern times, three or four conspicuous instrumentalities may be marked. After the deification of Woman in the Catholic Church, in the sixteenth or seventeeth century,—when her religious nature gave her, of course, new importance,—the Quakers have the honor of having first established, in their discipline, the equality in the sexes. It is even more perfect in the later sect of the Shakers, wherein no business is broached or counselled without the intervention of one elder and one elderess.

A second epoch for Woman was in France,—entirely civil; the change of sentiment from a rude to a polite character, in the age of Louis XIV.,—commonly dated from the building of the Hôtel de Rambouillet. I think another important step was made by the doctrine of Swedenborg, a sublime genius who gave a scientific exposition of the part played severally by man and woman in the world, and showed the difference of sex to run through nature and through thought. Of all Christian sects this is at this moment the most vital and aggressive.

Another step was the effect of the action of the age in the

antagonism to Slavery. It was easy to enlist Woman in this; it was impossible not to enlist her. But that Cause turned out to be a great scholar. He was a terrible metaphysican. He was a jurist, a poet, a divine. Was never a University of Oxford or Göttingen that made such students. It took a man from the plough and made him acute, eloquent, and wise, to the silencing of the doctors. There was nothing it did not pry into, no right it did not explore, no wrong it did not expose. And it has, among its other effects given Woman a feeling of public duty and an added self-respect.

One truth leads in another by the hand; one right is an accession of strength to take more. And the times are marked by the new attitude of Woman; urging, by argument and by association, her rights of all kinds,—in short, to one-half of the world;—as the right to education, to avenues of employment, to equal rights of property, to equal rights in marriage, to the exercise of the professions and of suffrage.

Of course, this conspicuousness had its inconveniences. But it is cheap wit that has been spent on this subject; from Aristophanes, in whose comedies I confess my dulness to find good joke, to Rabelais, in whom it is monstrous exaggeration of temperament, and not borne out by anything in nature,—down to English Comedy, and, in our day, to Tennyson, and the American newspapers. In all, the body of the joke is one, namely, to charge women with temperament; to describe them as victims of temperament; and is identical with Mahomet's opinion that women have not a sufficient moral or intellectual force to control the perturbations of their physical structure. These were all drawings of morbid anatomy, and such satire as might be written on the tenants of a hospital or on an asylum for idiots. Of course it would be easy for women to retaliate in kind, by painting men from the dogs and gorillas that have worn our shape. That they have not, is an eulogy on their taste and self-respect. The good easy world took the joke which it liked. There is always the want of thought; there is always credulity. There are plenty of people who believe women to be incapable of anything but to cook, incapable of interest in affairs. There are plenty of people who believe that the world is governed by men of dark complexions, that affairs are only directed by such, and do not see the use of contemplative men, or how ignoble would be the world that wanted them. And so without the affection of women.

But for the general charge: no doubt it is well founded. They are victims of the finer temperament. They have tears, and gaieties, and faintings, and glooms, and devotion to trifles. Nature's end, of maternity for twenty years, was of so supreme importance that it was to be secured at all events, even to the sacrifice of the highest beauty. They are more personal. Men taunt them that, whatever they do, say, read or write, they are thinking of themselves and their set. Men are not to the same degree temperamented, for there are multitudes of men who live to objects quite out of them, as to politics, to trade, to letters or an art, unhindered by any influence of constitution.

The answer that lies, silent or spoken, in the minds of well-meaning persons, to the new claims, is this: that, though their mathematical justice is not to be denied, yet the best women do not wish these things; they are asked for by people who intellectually seek them, but who have not the support or sympathy of the truest women; and that, if the laws and customs were modified in the manner proposed, it would embarrass and pain gentle and lovely persons with duties which they would find irksome and distasteful. Very likely. Providence is always surprising us with new and unlikely instruments. But perhaps it is because these people have been deprived of education, fine companions, opportunities, such as they wished,—because they feel the same rudeness and disadvantage which offends you,—that they have been stung to say, "It is too late for us to be polished and fashioned into beauty, but, at least, we will see that the whole race of women shall not suffer as we have suffered."

They have an unquestionable right to their own property. And if a woman demand votes, offices and political equality with men, as among the Shakers an Elder and Elderess are of equal power,—and among the Quakers,—it must not be refused. It is very cheap wit that finds it so droll that a woman should vote. Educate and refine society to the highest point,—bring together a cultivated society of both sexes, in a drawing-room, and consult and decide by voices on a question of taste or on a question of right, and is there any absurdity or any practical difficulty in obtaining their authentic opinions? If not, then there need be none in a hundred companies, if you educate them and accustom them to judge. And, for the effect of it, I can say, for one, that all my points would sooner be carried in the state if women voted. On the questions that are important;—whether the government shall be in one person, or whether representative, or whether democratic; whether men shall be holden in bondage, or shall be roasted alive and eaten, as in Typee, or shall be hunted with bloodhounds, as in this country; whether men shall be hanged for stealing, or hanged at all; whether the unlimited sale of cheap liquors shall be allowed;—they would give, I suppose, as intelligent a vote as the voters of Boston or New York.

We may ask, to be sure,—Why need you vote? If new power is here, of a character which solves old tough questions, which puts me and all the rest in the wrong, tries and condemns our religion, customs, laws, and opens new careers to our young receptive men and women, you can well leave voting to the old dead people. Those whom you teach, and those whom you half teach, will fast enough make themselves considered and strong with their new insight, and votes will follow from all the dull.

The objection to their voting is the same as is urged, in the lobbies of legislatures, against clergymen who take an active part in politics;—that if they are good clergymen they are unacquainted with the expediencies of politics, and if they become good politicians they are worse clergymen. So of women, that they cannot enter this arena without being contaminated and unsexed.

Here are two or three objections; first, a want of practical wisdom; second, a too purely ideal view; and, third, danger of contamination. For their want of intimate knowledge of affairs, I do not think this ought to disqualify them from voting at any town-meeting which I ever attended. I could heartily wish the objection were sound. But if any man will take the trouble to see how our people vote,—how many gentlemen are willing to take on themselves the trouble of thinking and determining for you, and, standing at the door of the polls, give every innocent citizen his ticket as he comes in, informing him that this is the vote of his party; and how the innocent citizen, without further demur, goes and drops it in the ballot-box,—I cannot but think he will agree that most women might vote as wisely.

For the other point, of their not knowing the world, and aiming at abstract right without allowance for circumstances,—that is not a disqualification, but a qualification. Human society is made up of partialities. Each citizen has an interest and a view of his own, which, if followed out to the extreme, would leave no room for any other citizen. One man is timid and another rash; one would change nothing, and the other is pleased with nothing; one wishes schools, another armies, one gunboats, another public gardens. Bring all these biases together and something is done in favor of them all.

Every one is a half vote, but the next elector behind him brings the other or corresponding half in his hand: a reasonable result is had. Now there is no lack, I am sure, of the expediency, or of the interests of trade or of imperative class-interests being neglected. There is no lack of votes representing the physical wants; and if in your city the uneducated emigrant vote numbers thousands, representing a brutal ignorance and mere animal wants, it is to be corrected by an educated and religious vote, representing the wants and desires of honest and refined persons. If the wants, the passions, the vices, are allowed a full vote through the hands of a half-brutal intemperate population, I think it but fair that the virtues, the aspirations should be allowed a full vote, as an offset, through the purest part of the people.

As for the unsexing and contamination,—that only accuses our existing politics, shows how barbarous we are,—that our policies are so crooked, made up of things not to be spoken, to be understood only by wink and nudge; this man to be coaxed, that man to be bought, and that other to be duped. It is easy to see that there is contamination enough, but it rots the men now, and fills the air with stench. Come out of that: it is like a dance-cellar. The fairest names in this country in literature, in law, have gone into Congress and come out dishonored. And when I read the list of men of intellect, of refined pursuits, giants in law, or eminent scholars, or of social distinction, leading men of wealth and enterprise in the commercial community, and see what they have voted for and suffered to be voted for, I think no community was ever so politely and elegantly betrayed.

I do not think it yet appears that women wish this equal share in public affairs. But it is they and not we that are to determine it. Let the laws be purged of every barbarous remainder, every barbarous impediment to women. Let the public donations for education be equally shared by them, let them enter a school as freely as a church, let them have and hold and give their property as men do theirs;—and in a few years it will easily appear whether they wish a voice in making the laws that are to govern them.If you do refuse them a vote, you will also refuse to tax them,—according to our Teutonic principle, No representation, no tax.

All events of history are to be regarded as growths and offshoots of the expanding mind of the race, and this appearance of new opinions, their currency and force in many minds, is itself the wonderful fact. For whatever is popular is important, shows the spontaneous sense of the hour. The aspiration of this century will be the code of the next. It holds of high and distant causes, of the same influences that make the sun and moon. When new opinions appear, they will be entertained and respected, by every fair mind, according to their reasonableness, and not according to their convenience, or their fitness to shock our customs. But let us deal with them greatly; let them make their way by the upper road, and not by the way of manufacturing public opinion, which lapses continually into expediency, and makes charlatans. All that is spontaneous is irresistible, and forever it is individual force that interests. I need not repeat to you,—your own solitude will suggest it,—that a masculine woman is not strong, but a lady is. The loneliest thought, the purest prayer, is rushing to be the history of a thousand years.

Let us have the true woman, the adorner, the hospitable, the religious heart, and no lawyer need be called in to write stipulations, the cunning clauses of provision, the strong investitures;—for woman moulds the lawgiver and writes the law. But I ought to say, I think it impossible to separate the interests and education of the sexes. Improve and refine the men, and you do the same by the women, whether you will or no. Every woman being the wife or the daughter of a man,—wife, daughter, sister, mother, of a man, she can never be very far from his ear, never not of his counsel, if she has really something to urge that is good in itself and agreeable to nature. Slavery it is that makes slavery; freedom, freedom. The slavery of women happened when the men were slaves of kings. The melioration of manners brought their melioration of course. It could not be otherwise, and hence the new desire of better laws. For there are always a certain number of passionately loving fathers, brothers, husbands and sons who put their might into the endeavor to make a daughter, a wife, or a mother happy in the way that suits best. Woman should find in man her guardian. Silently she looks for that, and when she finds that he is not, as she instantly does, she betakes her to her own defences, and does the best she can. But when he is her guardian, fulfilled with all nobleness, knows and accepts his duties as her brother, all goes well for both.

The new movement is only a tide shared by the spirits of man and woman; and you may proceed in the faith that whatever the woman's heart is prompted to desire, the man's mind is simultaneously prompted to accomplish.

John Stuart Mill

If Schopenhauer's essay is the classic misogynist piece, Mill's *The Subjection of Women* (1869) is the classic feminist piece. Written in England during the early years of the nineteenth-century feminist movement, it provided theoretical foundations for the argument in favor of equality between the sexes. Mill supported the drive for recognition of women's rights by consistently applying egalitarian principles, both as a utilitarian and as a committed advocate of civil liberties. On utilitarian grounds, he argued that no society could hope to approach justice so long as half its people were in a state of subjection. As a civil libertarian Mill lamented that women were deprived of freedom and dignity. Fully congnizant of the prejudices and customs that militate against reason and fair play on the issue of women's rights, Mill makes in *The Subjection of Women* a penetrating analysis of the historical subjection of women. His analysis of the physical, psychological, legal, and practical grounds of this subjection provides the evidence for his thesis that the subordination of women is wrong in itself. Ultimately, Mill argues, woman's smaller degree of muscular strength has rendered her subject to the principle of force, which expressed itself in barbaric cultures as "might makes right" and in civilized cultures as paternalism. The latter is subtle and puts the best face on force, since control by the male sex is based on chivalry and generosity, and uses bribery and intimidation instead of brutality to secure obedience, deference, and gratitude for protection. This bribery and intimidation is effected by rendering women economically and morally dependent on men. The law completes the intimidation by its discriminatory statutes. It is because of this subjection that Mill makes his famous analogy of the position of women with slavery.

THE SUBJECTION OF WOMEN*

The object of this Essay is to explain as clearly as I am able, the grounds of an opinion which I have held from the very earliest period when I had formed any opinions at all on social or political matters, and which, instead of being weakened or modified, has been constantly growing stronger by the progress of reflection and the experience of life. That the principle which regulates the existing social relations between the two sexes—the legal subordination of one sex to the other—is wrong in itself, and now one of the chief hindrances to human improvement; and that it ought to be replaced by a principle of perfect equality, admitting no power or privilege on the one side, nor disability on the other.

The very words necessary to express the task I have undertaken, show how arduous it is. But it would be a mistake to suppose that the difficulty of the case must lie in the insufficiency or obscurity of the grounds of reason on which my conviction rests. The difficulty

* From John Stuart Mill, *The Subjection of Women* (Bungay, Suffolk: Richard Clay, Ltd., 1869), Chaps. 1, 3.

is that which exists in all cases in which there is a mass of feeling to be contended against. So long as an opinion is strongly rooted in the feelings, it gains rather than loses in stability by having a preponderating weight of argument against it. For if it were accepted as a result of argument, the refutation of the argument might shake the solidity of the conviction; but when it rests solely on feeling, the worse it fares in argumentative contest, the more persuaded its adherents are that their feeling must have some deeper ground, which the arguments do not reach; and while the feeling remains, it is always throwing up fresh intrenchments of argument to repair any breach made in the old. And there are so many causes tending to make the feelings connected with this subject the most intense and most deeply-rooted of all those which gather round and protect old institutions and customs, that we need not wonder to find them as yet less undermined and loosened than any of the rest by the progress of the great modern spiritual and social transition; nor suppose that the barbarisms to which men cling longest must be less barbarisms than those which they earlier shake off.

In every respect the burden is hard on those who attack an almost universal opinion. They must be very fortunate as well as unusually capable if they obtain a hearing at all. They have more difficulty in obtaining a trial, than any other litigants have in getting a verdict. If they do extort a hearing, they are subjected to a set of logical requirements totally different from those exacted from other people. In all other cases, the burthen of proof is supposed to lie with the affirmative. If a person is charged with a murder, it rests with those who accuse him to give proof of his guilt, not with himself to prove his innocence. If there is a difference of opinion about the reality of an alleged historical event, in which the feelings of men in general are not much interested, as the Siege of Troy for example, those who maintain that the event took place are expected to produce their proofs, before those who take the other side can be required to say anything; and at no time are these required to do more than show that the evidence produced by the others is of no value. Again, in practical matters, the burden of proof is supposed to be with those who are against liberty; who contend for any restriction or prohibition; either any limitation of the general freedom of human action, or any disqualification or disparity of privilege affecting one person or kind of persons, as compared with others. The *a priori* presumption is in favour of freedom and impartiality. It is held that there should be no restraint not required by the general good, and that the law should be no respecter of persons, but should treat all alike, save where dissimilarity of treatment is required by positive reasons, either of justice or of policy. But of none of these rules of evidence will the benefit be allowed to those who maintain the opinion I profess. It is useless for me to say that those who maintain the doctrine that men have a right to command and women are under an obligation to obey, or that men are fit for government and women unfit, are on the affirmative side of the question, and that they are bound to show positive evidence for the assertions, or submit to their rejection. It is equally unavailing for me to say that those who deny to women any freedom or privilege rightly allowed to men, having the double presumption against them that they are opposing freedom and recommending partiality, must be held to the strictest proof of their case, and unless their success be such as to exclude all doubt, the judgment ought to go against them. These would be thought good pleas in any common case; but they will not be thought so in this instance. Before I could hope to make any impression, I should be expected not only to answer all that has ever been said by those who take the other side of the question, but to imagine all that could be said by them—to find them in reasons, as well as answer all I find: and besides refuting all arguments for the affirmative, I shall be called upon for invincible positive arguments to prove a negative. And even if I could do all this, and leave the opposite party with a host of unanswered arguments against them, and not a single unrefuted one on their side, I should be thought to have done little; for a cause supported on the one hand by universal usage, and on the other by so great a preponderance of popular sentiment, is supposed to have a presumption in its favour, superior to any conviction which any appeal to reason has power to produce in any intellects but those of a high class.

I do not mention these difficulties to complain of them; first, because it would be useless; they are inseparable from having to contend through people's understandings against the hostility of their feelings and practical tendencies: and truly the understandings of the majority of mankind would need to be much better cultivated than has ever yet been the case, before they can be asked to place such reliance in their own power of estimating arguments, as to give up practical principles in which they have been born and bred and which are the basis of much of the existing order of the world, at the first argumentative attack which they are not capable of logically resisting. I do not therefore quarrel with them for having too little faith in argument, but for having too much faith in custom and the general feeling. It is one of the characteristic prejudices of the reaction of the nineteenth century against the eighteenth, to accord to the unreasoning elements in human nature the infallibility which the eighteenth century is supposed to have ascribed to the reasoning elements. For the apotheosis of Reason we have substituted that of Instinct; and we call everything instinct which we find in ourselves and for which we cannot trace any rational foundation. This idolatry, infinitely more degrading than the other, and the most pernicious of the false worships of the present day, of all of which it is now the main support, will probably hold its ground until it gives way before a sound psychology laying bare the real root of much that is bowed down to as the intention of Nature and the ordinance of God. As regards the present question, I am willing to accept the unfavourable conditions which the prejudice assigns to me. I consent that established custom, and the general feeling, should be deemed conclusive against me, unless that custom and feeling from age to age can be shown to have owed their existence to other causes than their soundness, and to have derived their power from the worse rather than the better parts of human nature. I am willing that judgment should go against me, unless I can show that my judge has been tampered with. The concession is not so great as it might appear; for to prove this, is by far the easiest portion of my task.

The generality of a practice is in some cases a strong presumption that it is, or at all events once was, conductive to laudable ends. This is the case, when the practice was first adopted, or afterwards kept up, as a means to such ends, and was grounded on experience of the mode in which they could be most effectually attained. If the authority of men over women, when first established, had been the result of a conscientious comparison between different modes of constituting the government of society; if, after trying various other modes of social organisation—the government of women over men, equality between the two, and such mixed and divided modes of government as might be invented—it had been decided, on the testimony of experience, that the mode in which women are wholly under the rule of men, having no share at all in public concerns, and each in private being under the legal obligation of obedience to the man with whom she has associated her destiny, was the arrangement most conducive to the happiness and well-being of both; its general adoption might then be fairly thought to be some evidence that, at the time when it was adopted, it was the best: though even then the considerations which recommended it may, like so many other primeval social facts of the greatest importance, have subsequently, in the course of ages, ceased to exist. But the state of the case is in every respect the reverse of this. In the first place, the opinion in favour of the present system, which entirely subordinates the weaker sex to the stronger, rests upon theory only; for there never has been trial made of any other: so the experience, in the sense in which it is vulgarly opposed to theory, cannot be pretended to have pronounced any verdict. And in the second place, the adoption of this system of inequality never was the result of deliberation, or forethought, or any social ideas, or any notion whatever of what conduced to the benefit of humanity or the good order of society. It arose simply from the fact that from the very earliest twilight of human society, every woman (owing to the value attached to her by men, combined with her inferiority in muscular strength) was found in a state of bondage to some man. Laws and systems of polity always begin by recognising the relations they find already existing between individuals. They convert what was a mere physical fact into a legal right, give it the sanction of society, and principally aim at the substitution of public and organised means of asserting and protecting these rights, instead of the irregular and lawless conflict of physical strength. Those who had already been compelled to obedience became in this manner legally bound to it. Slavery, from being a mere affair of force between the master and the slave, became regularised and a matter of compact among the masters, who, binding themselves to one another for common protection, guaranteed by their collective strength the private possessions of each, including his slaves. In early times, the great majority of the male sex were slaves as well as the whole of the female. And many ages elapsed, some of them ages of high cultivation, before any thinker was bold enough to question the rightfulness, and the absolute social necessity, either of the one slavery or of the other. By degrees such thinkers did arise; and (the general progress of society assisting) the slavery of the male sex has, in all the countries of Christian Europe at least (though, in one of them, only within the last few years) been at length abolished, and that of the female sex has been gradually changed into a milder form of dependence. But this dependence, as it exists at present, is not an original institution, taking a fresh start from considerations of justice and social expediency—it is the primitive state of slavery lasting on, through successive mitigations and modifications occasioned by the same causes which have softened the general manners, and brought all human relations more under the control of justice and the influence of humanity. It has not lost the taint of its brutal origin. No presumption in its favour, therefore, can be drawn from the fact of its existence. The only such presumption which it could be supposed to have, must be grounded on its having lasted till now, when so many other things which came down from the same odious source have been done away with. And this, indeed, is what makes it strange to ordinary ears, to hear it asserted that the inequality of rights between men and women has no other source than the law of the strongest.

That this statement should have the effect of a paradox, is in some respects creditable to the progress of civilisation, and the improvement of the moral sentiments of mankind. We now live— that is to say, one or two of the most advanced nations of the world now live—in a state in which the law of the strongest seems to be entirely abandoned as the regulating principle of the world's affairs: nobody professes it, and, as regards most of the relations between human beings, nobody is permitted to practise it. When anyone succeeds in doing so, it is under cover of some pretext which gives him the semblance of having some general social interest on his side. This being the ostensible state of things, people flatter themselves that the rule of mere force is ended; that the law of the strongest cannot be the reason of existence of anything which has remained in full operation down to the present time. However, any of our present institutions may have begun, it can only, they think, have been preserved to this period of advanced civilisation by a well-grounded feeling of its adapatation to human nature, and conduciveness to the general good. They do not understand the great vitality and durability of institutions which place right on the side of might; how intensely they are clung to; how the good as well as the bad propensities and sentiments of those who have power in their hands, become identified with retaining it; how slowly these bad institutions give way, one at a time, the weakest first, beginning with those which are least interwoven with the daily habits of life; and how very rarely those who have obtained legal power because they first had physical, have ever lost their hold of it until the physical power has passed over to the other side. Such shifting of the physical force not having taken place in the case of women; this fact, combined with all the peculiar and characteristic features of the particular case, made it certain from the first that this branch of the system of right founded on might, though softened in its most atrocious features at an earlier period than several of the others, would be the very last to disappear. It was inevitable that this one case of a social relation grounded on force, would survive through generations of institutions grounded on equal justice, an almost solitary exception to the general character of their laws and customs; but which, so long as it does not proclaim its own origin, and as discussion has not brought out its true character, is not felt to jar with modern civilisation, any more than domestic slavery among the Greeks jarred with their notion of themselves as a free people. . . .

In this case, too, the possessor of the undue power, the person directly interested in it, is only one person, while those who are subject to it and suffer from it are literally all the rest. The yoke is naturally and necessarily humiliating to all persons, except the one who is on the throne, together with, at most, the one who expects to succeed to it. How different are these cases from that of the power of men over women! I am not now prejudging the question of its justifiableness. I am showing how vastly more permanent it could not but be, even if not justifiable, than these other dominations which have nevertheless lasted down to our own time. Whatever gratification of pride there is in the possession of power, and whatever personal interest in its exercise, is in this case not confined to a limited class, but common to the whole male sex. Instead of being, to most of its supporters a thing desirable chiefly in the abstract, or, like the political ends usually contended for by factions, of little private importance to any but the leaders; it comes home to the person and hearth of every male head of a family, and of everyone who looks forward to being so. The clodhopper exercises, or is to exercise, his share of the power equally with the highest nobleman. And the case is that in which the desire of power is the strongest for everyone who desires power, desires it most over those who are nearest to him, with whom his life is passed, with whom he has most concerns in common, and in whom any independence of his authority is oftenest likely to interfere with his individual preferences. If, in the other cases specified, powers manifestly grounded only on force and having so much less to support them, are so slowly and with so much difficulty got rid of, much more must be so with this, even if it rests on no better foundation than those. We must consider too, that the possessors of the power have facilities in this case, greater than in any other, to prevent any uprising against it. Everyone of the subjects lives under the very eye, and almost, it may be said, in the hands, of one of the masters—in closer intimacy with him than with any of her fellow-subjects; with no means of combining against him, no power of even locally overmastering him, and, on the other hand, with the strongest motives for seeking his favour and avoiding to give him offence. In struggles for political emancipation, everybody knows how often its champions are bought off by bribes, or daunted by terrors. In the case of women, each individual of the subject-class is in a chronic state of bribery and intimidation combined. In setting up the standard of resistance, a large number of the leaders, and still more of the followers, must make an almost complete sacrifice of the pleasures or the alleviations of their own individual lot. If ever any system of privilege and enforced subjection had its yoke tightly riveted on the necks of those who are kept down by it, this has. I have not yet shown that it is a wrong system: but everyone who is capable of thinking on the subject must see that even if it is, it was certain to outlast all other forms of unjust authority. And when some of the grossest of the other forms still exist in many civilised countries, and have only recently been got rid of in others, it would be strange if that which is so much the deepest rooted had yet been perceptibly shaken anywhere. There is more reason to wonder that the protests and testimonies against it should have been so numerous and so weighty as they are. . . .

All causes, social and natural, combine to make it unlikely that women should be collectively rebellious to the power of men. They are so far in a position different from all other subject classes, that their masters require something more from them than actual service. Men do not want solely the obedience of women, they want their sentiments. All men, except the most brutish, desire to have, in the woman most nearly connected with them, not a forced slave but a willing one, not a slave merely, but a favourite. They have therefore put everything in practice to enslave their minds. The masters of all other slaves rely, for maintaining obedience, on fear; either fear of themselves, or religious fears. The masters of women wanted more than simple obedience, and they turned the whole force of education to effect their purpose. All women are brought up from the very earliest years in the belief that their ideal of character is the very opposite to that of men; not self-will, and government by self-control, but submission, and yielding to the control of others. All the moralities tell them that it is the duty of women, and all the current sentimentalities that it is their nature, to live for others; to make complete abnegation of themselves, and to have no life but in their affections. And by their affections are meant the only ones they are allowed to have—those to the men with whom they are connected, or to the children who constitute an additional and indefeasible tie between them and a man. When we put together three things—first, the natural attraction between opposite sexes; secondly, the wife's entire dependence on the husband, every privilege or pleasure she has being either his gift, or depending entirely on his will; and lastly, that the principal object of human pursuit, consideration, and all objects of social ambition, can in general be sought or obtained by her only through him, it would be a miracle if the object of being attractive to men had not become the polar star of feminine education and formation of character. And, this great means of influence over the minds of women having been acquired, an instinct of selfishness made men avail themselves of it to the utmost as a means of holding women in subjection, by representing to them meekness, submissiveness, and resignation of all individual will into the hands of a man, as an essential part of sexual attractivenss. Can it be doubted that any of the other yokes which mankind have succeeded in breaking, would have subsisted till now if the same means had existed, and had been so sedulously used, to bow down their minds to it? If it had been made the object of the life of every young plebeian to find personal favour in the eyes of some patrician, of every young serf with some seigneur; if domestication with him, and a share of his personal affections, had been held out as the prize which they all should look out for, the most gifted and aspiring being able to reckon on the most desirable prizes; and if, when this prize had been obtained, they had been shut out by a wall of brass from all interests not centring in him, all feelings and desires but those which he shared or inculcated; would not serfs and seigneurs, plebeians and patricians, have been as broadly distinguished at this day as men and women are? and would not all but a thinker here and there, have believed the distinction to be a fundamental and unalterable fact in human nature?

The preceding considerations are amply sufficient to show that custom, however universal it may be, affords in this case no presumption, and ought not to create any prejudice, in favour of the arrangements which place women in social and political subjection to men. But I may go farther, and maintain that the course of history, and the tendencies of progressive human society, afford not only no presumption in favour of this system of inequality of rights, but a strong one against it; and that so far as the whole course of human improvement up to the time, the whole stream of modern tendencies, warrants any inference on the subject, it is, that this relic of the past is discordant with the future, and must necessarily disappear.

For, what is the peculiar character of the modern world—the difference which chiefly distinguishes modern institutions, modern social ideas, modern life itself, from those of times long past? It is, that human beings are no longer born to their place in life, and chained down by an inexorable bond to the place they are born to, but are free to employ their faculties, and such favourable chances as offer, to achieve the lot which may appear to them most desirable. . . .

If this general principle of social and economical science is not true; if individuals, with such help as they can derive from the opinion of those who know them, are not better judges than the law and the government, of their own capacities and vocation; the world cannot too soon abandon this principle, and return to the old system of regulations and disabilities. But if the principle is true, we ought to act as if we believed it, and not to ordain that to be born a girl instead of a boy, any more than to be born black instead of white, or a commoner instead of a nobleman, shall decide the person's position through all life—shall interdict people from all the more elevated social positions, and from all, except a few respectable occupations. Even were we to admit the utmost that is ever pretended as to the superior fitness of men for all the functions now reserved to them, the same argument applies which forbids a legal qualification for Members of Parliament. If only once in a dozen years the conditions of eligibility exclude a fit person, there is a real loss, while the exclusion of thousands of unfit persons is no gain; for if the constitution of the electoral body disposes them to choose unfit persons, there are always plenty of such persons to choose from. In all things of any difficulty and importance, those who can do them well are fewer than the need, even with the most unrestricted latitude of choice: and any limitation of the field of selection deprives society of some chances of being served by the competent, without ever saying it from the incompetent.

At present, in the more improved countries, the disabilities of women are the only case, save one, in which laws and institutions take persons at their birth, and ordain that they shall never in all their lives be allowed to compete for certain things. The one exception is that of royalty. Persons still are born to the throne; no one, not of the reigning family, can ever occupy it, and no one even of that family can, by any means but the course of hereditary succession, attain it. All other dignities and social advantages are open to the whole male sex: many indeed are only attainable by wealth, but wealth may be striven for by anyone, and is actually obtained by many men of the very humblest origin. The difficulties, to the majority, are indeed insuperable without the aid of fortunate accidents; but no male human being is under any legal ban: neither law nor opinion superadd artificial obstacles to the natural ones. Royalty, as I have said, is excepted: but in this case everyone feels

sexes adapts them to their present functions and position, and renders these appropriate to them. Standing on the ground of common sense and the constitution of the human mind, I deny that anyone knows, or can know, the nature of the two sexes, as long as they have only been seen in their present relation to one another. If men had ever been found in society without women, or women without men, or if there had been a society of men and women in which the women were not under the control of the men, something might have been positively known about the mental and moral difference which may be inherent in the nature of each. What is now called the nature of women is an eminently artificial thing—the result of forced repression in some directions, unnatural stimulation in others. It may be asserted without scruple, that no other class of dependents have had their character so entirely distorted from its natural proportions by their relation with their masters; for, if conquered and slave races have been, in some respects, more forcibly repressed, whatever in them has not been crushed down by an iron heel has generally been let alone, and if left with any liberty of development, it has developed itself according to its own laws; but in the case of women, a hot-house and stove cultivation has always been carried on of some of the capabilities of their nature, for the benefit and pleasure of their masters. Then, because certain products of the general vital force sprout luxuriantly and reach a great development in this heated atmosphere and under this active nurture and watering, while other shoots from the same root, which are left outside in the wintry air, with ice purposely heaped all round them, have stunted growth, and some are burnt off with fire and disappear; men, with that inability to recognise their own work which distinguishes the unanalytic mind, indolently believe that the tree grows of itself in the way they have made it grow, and that it would die if one half of it were not kept in a vapour bath and the other half in the snow.

Of all difficulties which impede the progress of thought, and the formation of well-grounded opinions on life, and social arrange-ments, the greatest is now the unspeakable ignorance and inattention of mankind in respect to the influences which form human character. Whatever any portion of the human species now are, or seem to be, such, it is supposed, they have a natural tendency to be: even when the most elementary knowledge of the circumstances in which they have been placed, clearly points out the causes that made them what they are. Because a cottier deeply in arrears to his landlord is not industrious, there are people who think that the Irish are naturally idle. Because constitutions can be overthrown when the authorities appointed to execute them turn their arms against them, there are people who think the French incapable of free government. Because the Greeks cheated the Turks, and the Turks only plundered the Greeks, there are persons who think that the Turks are naturally more sincere: and because women, as is often said, care nothing about politics except their personalities, it is supposed that the general good is naturally less interesting to women than to men. History, which is now so much better understood than formerly, teaches another lesson: if only by showing the extraordinary susceptibility of human nature to external influences, and the extreme variableness of those of its manifestations which are supposed to be most universal and uniform. But in history, as in travelling, men usually see only what they already had in their own minds; and few learn much from history, who do not bring much with them to its study.

Hence, in regard to that most difficult question, what are the natural differences between the two sexes—a subject on which it is impossible in the present state of society to obtain complete and correct knowledge—while almost everybody dogmatises upon it, almost all neglect and make light of the only means by which any partial insight can be obtained into it. This is, an analytic study of the most important department of psychology, the laws of the influence of circumstances on character. For, however great and apparently ineradicable the moral and intellectual differences between men and women might be, the evidence of there being natural differences could only be negative. Those only could be inferred to be natural which could not possibly be artificial—the residuum, after deducting every characteristic of either sex which can admit of being explained from education or external circumstances. The profoundest knowledge of the laws of the formation of character is indispensable to entitle anyone to affirm even that there is any difference, much more what the difference is, between the two sexes considered as moral and rational beings; and since no one, as yet, has that knowledge (for there is hardly any subject which, in proportion to its importance, has been so little studied), no one is thus far entitled to any positive opinion on the subject. Conjectures are all that can at present be made; conjectures more or less probable, according as more or less authorised by such knowledge as we yet have of the laws of psychology, as applied to the formation of character. . . .

The general opinion of men is supposed to be, that the natural vocation of a woman is that of a wife and mother. I say, is supposed to be, because, judging from acts—from the whole of the present constitution of society—one might infer that their opinion was the direct contrary. They might be supposed to think that the alleged natural vocation of women was of all things the most repugnant to their nature; insomuch that if they are free to do anything else—if any other means of living or occupation of their time and faculties, is open, which has any chance of appearing desirable to them—there will not be enough of them who will be willing to accept the condition said to be natural to them. If this is the real opinion of men in general, it would be well that it should be spoken out. I should like to hear somebody openly enunciating the doctrine (it is already implied in much that is written on the subject)—"It is necessary to society that women should marry and produce children. They will not do so unless they are compelled. Therefore it is necessary to compel them." The merits of the case would then be clearly defined. It would be exactly that of the slave-holders of South Carolina and Louisiana. "It is necessary that cotton and sugar should be grown. White men cannot produce them. Negroes will not, for any wages which we choose to give. *Ergo* they must be compelled." An illustration still closer to the point is that of impressment. Sailors must absolutely be had to defend the country. It often happens that they will not voluntarily enlist. Therefore there must be the power of forcing them. How often has this logic been used! and, but for one flaw in it, without doubt it would have been successful up to this day. But it is open to the retort—First pay the sailors the honest value of the labour. When you have made it as well worth their while to serve you, as to work for other employers, you will have no more difficulty than others have in obtaining their services. To this there is no logical answer except "I will not": and as people are now not only ashamed, but are not desirous, to rob the labourer of his hire, impressment is no longer advocated. Those who attempt to force women into marriage by closing all other doors against them, lay themselves open to a similar retort. If they mean what they say, their opinion must evidently be, that men do not render the married condition so desirable to women, as to induce them to accept it for its own recommendations. It is not a sign of one's thinking the boon one offers very attractive, when one allows only Hobson's choice, "that or none." And here, I believe, is the clue to the feelings of those men, who have a real antipathy to the equal freedom of women. I believe they are afraid, not lest women should be unwilling to marry, for I do not think that anyone in reality has that apprehension; but lest they should insist that marriage should be on equal conditions; lest all women of spirit and capacity should prefer doing almost anything else, not in their own eyes degrading, rather than marry, when marrying is giving themselves a master, and a master too of all their earthly possessions. And truly, if this conseqence were necessarily incident to marriage, I think that the apprehension would be very well founded. I agree in thinking it probable that few women, capable of anything else, would, unless under an irresistible *entrainement*, rendering them for the time insensible to anything but itself, choose such a lot, when any other means were open to them of filling a conventionally honourable place in life and if men are determined that the law of marriage shall be a law of despotism, they are quite right, in point of mere policy, in leaving to women only Hobson's choice. But, in that case, all that has been done in the modern world to relax the chain on the minds of women has been a mistake. They never should have been allowed to receive a literary education. Women who read, much more women who write, are, in the existing constitution of things, a contradiction and a disturbing element: and it was wrong to bring women up with any acquirements but those of an odalisque, or of a domestic servant. . . .

As for moral differences, considered as distinguished from intellectual, the distinction commonly drawn is to the advantage of women. They are declared to be better than men; an empty compliment, which must provoke a bitter smile from every woman of spirit, since there is no other situation in life in which it is the established order and considered quite natural and suitable, that the better should obey the worse. If this piece of idle talk is good for anything, it is only as an admission by men, of the corrupting influence of power; for that is certainly the only truth which the fact, if it be a fact, either proves or illustrates. And it *is* true that servitude, except when it actually brutalises, though corrupting to both, is less so to the slaves than to the slave-masters. It is wholesomer for the moral nature to be restrained, even by arbitrary power, than to be allowed to exercise arbitrary power without restraint. Women, it is said, seldomer fall under the penal law— contribute a much smaller number of offenders to the criminal calendar, than men. I doubt not that the same thing may be said, with the same truth, of Negro slaves. Those who are under the control of others cannot often commit crimes, unless at the command and for the purposes of their masters. I do not know a more signal instance of the blindness with which the world, including the herd of studious men, ignore and pass over all the influences of social circumstances, than their silly depreciation of the intellectual, and silly panegyrics on the moral nature of women. . . .

There remains a question, not of less importance than those already discussed, and which will be asked the most importunately by those opponents whose conviction is somewhat shaken on the main point. What good are we to expect from the changes proposed in our customs and institutions? Would mankind be at all better off if women were free? If not, why disturb their minds, and attempt to make a social revolution in the name of an abstract right?

It is hardly to be expected that this question will be asked in respect to the change proposed in the condition of women in marriage. The sufferings, immoralities, evils of all sorts, produced in innumerable cases by the subjection of individual women to individual men, are far too terrible to be overlooked. Unthinking or uncandid persons, counting those cases alone which are extreme, or which attain publicity, may say that the evils are exceptional; but no one can be blind to their existence, nor, in many cases, to their intensity. And it is perfectly obvious that the abuse of the power cannot be very much checked while the power remains. It is a power given, or offered, not to good men, or to decently respectable men, but to all men; the most brutal, and the most criminal. There is no check but that of opinion, and such men are in general within the reach of no opinion but that of men like themselves. If such men did not brutally tyrannise over the one human being whom the law compels to bear everything from them, society must already have reached a paradisiacal state. There could be no need any longer of laws to curb men's vicious propensities. Astraea must not only have returned to earth, but the heart of the worst man must have become her temple. The law of servitude in marriage is a monstrous contradiction to all the principles of the modern world, and to all the experience through which those principles have been slowly and painfully worked out. It is the sole case, now that Negro slavery has been abolished, in which a human being in the plenitude of every faculty is delivered up to the tender mercies of another human being, in the hope forsooth that this other will use the power solely for the good of the person subjected to it. Marriage is the only actual bondage known to our law. There remain no legal slaves, except the mistress of every house.

It is not, therefore, on this part of the subject, that the question is likely to be asked, *Cui bono?* We may be told that the evil would outweigh the good, but the reality of the good admits no dispute. In regard, however, to the larger question, the removal of women's disabilities—their recognition as the equals of men in all that belongs to citizenship—the opening to them of all honourable employments, and of the training and education which qualifies for those employments—there are many persons for whom it is not enough that the inequality has no just or legitimate defence; they require to be told what express advantage would be obtained by abolishing it.

To which let me first answer, the advantage of having the most universal and pervading of all human relations regulated by justice instead of injustice. The vast amount of this gain to human nature, it is hardly possible, by any explanation or illustration, to place in a stronger light than it is placed by the bare statement, to anyone who attaches a moral meaning to words. All the selfish propensities, the self-worship, the unjust self-preference, which exist among mankind, have their source and root in, and derive their principal nourishment from, the present constitution of the relation between men and women. Think what it is to a boy, to grow up to manhood in the belief that without any merit or any exertion of his own, though he may be the most frivolous and empty or the most ignorant and stolid of mankind, by the mere fact of being born a male he is by right the superior of all and every one of an entire half of the human race; including probably some whose real superiority to himself he has daily or hourly occasion to feel; but even if in his whole conduct he habitually follows a woman's guidance, still, if he is a fool, she thinks that of course she is not, and cannot be, equal in ability and judgment to himself; and if he is not a fool, he does worse—he sees that she is superior to him, and believes that, notwithstanding her superiority, he is entitled to command and she is bound to obey. What must be the effect on his character, of this lesson? And men of the cultivated classes are often not aware how deeply it sinks into the immense majority of male minds. For, among right-feeling and well-bred people, the inequality is kept as much as possible out of sight; above all, out of sight of the children. As much obedience is required from boys to their mother as to their father: they are not permitted to domineer over their sisters, nor are they accustomed to see these postponed to them, but the contrary; the compensations of the chivalrous feeling being made prominent, while the servitude which requires them is kept in the background. Well brought-up youths in the higher classes thus often escape the bad influences of the situation in their early years, and only experience them when, arrived at manhood, they fall under the dominion of facts as they really exist. Such people are little aware, when a boy is differently brought up, how early the notion of his inherent superiority to a girl arises in his mind; how it grows with his growth and strengthens with his strength; how it is inoculated by one schoolboy upon another; how early the youth thinks himself superior to his mother, owing her perhaps forbearance, but no real respect; and how sublime and sultan-like a sense of superiority he feels, above all, over the woman whom he honours by admitting her to a partnership of his life. Is it imagined that all this does not pervert the whole manner of existence of the man, both as an individual and as a social being? It is an exact parallel to the feeling of a hereditary king that he is excellent above others by being born a king, or a noble by being born a noble. The relation between husband and wife is very like that between lord and vassal, except that the wife is held to more unlimited obedience than the vassal was. However, the vassal's character may have been affected, for better and for worse, by his subordination, who can help seeing that the lord's was affected greatly for the worse? whether he was led to believe that his vassals were really superior to himself, or to feel that he was placed in command over people as good as himself, for no merits or labours of his own, but merely for having, as Figaro says, taken the trouble to be born. The self-worship of the monarch, or of the feudal superior, is matched by the self-worship of the male. Human beings do not grow up from childhood in the possession of unearned distinctions, without pluming themselves upon them. Those whom privileges not acquired by their merit, and which they feel to be disproportioned to it, inspire with additional humility, are always the few, and the best few. The rest are only inspired with pride, and the worst sort of pride, that which values itself upon accidental advantages, not of its own achieving. Above all, when the feeling of being raised above the whole of the other sex is combined with personal authority over one individual among them; the situation, if a school of conscientious and affectionate forbearance to those whose strongest points of character are conscience and affection, is to men of another quality a regularly constituted academy or gymnasium for training them in arrogance and overbearingness; which vices, if curbed by the certainty of resistance in their intercourse with other men, their equals, break out towards all who are in a position to be obliged to tolerate them, and often revenge themselves upon the unfortunate wife for the involuntary restraint which they are obliged to submit to elsewhere.

The example afforded, and the education given to the sentiments, by laying the foundation of domestic existence upon a relation contradictory to the first principles of social justice, must, from the very nature of man, have a perverting influence of such magnitude, that it is hardly possible with our present experience to raise our imaginations to the conception of so great a change for the better as would be made by its removal. All that education and civilisation are doing to efface the influences on character of the law of force, and replace them by those of justice, remains merely on the surface, as long as the citadel of the enemy is not attacked. The principle of the modern movement in morals and politics, is that conduct, and conduct alone, entitles to respect: that not what men are, but what they do, constitutes their claim to deference; that, above all, merit, and not birth, is the only rightful claim to power and authority. . . .

When we consider the positive evil caused to the disqualified half of the human race by their disqualification—first in the loss of the most inspiriting and elevating kind of personal enjoyment, and next in the weariness, disappointment, and profound dissatisfaction with life, which are so often the substitute for it; one feels that among all the lessons which men require for carrying on the struggle against the inevitable imperfections of their lot on earth, there is no lesson which they more need, than not to add to the evils which nature inflicts, by their jealous and prejudiced restrictions on one another. Their vain fears only substitute other and worse evils for those which they are idly apprehensive of: while every restraint on the freedom of conduct of any of their human fellow-creatures (otherwise than by making them responsible for any evil actually caused by it), dries up *pro tanto* the principal fountain of human happiness, and leaves the species less rich, to an inappreciable degree, in all that makes life valuable to the individual human being.

Charles Darwin

Darwin's theory of evolution *(Origin of the Species,* 1859) exploded upon the intellectual commmunity of the mid-nineteenth century, supported as it was by a mass of evidence. In 1871 he published the companion piece to *Origin, The Descent of Man.* Together these two pieces describe the mechanisms whereby evolution is effected—natural selection, sexual selection, and inheritance of acquired characteristics. By natural selection, variations in plants and animals that are advantageous in the struggle to survive are passed on to offspring, while disadvantageous variations do not last. Natural selection has produced new varieties and new species. By sexual selection, which is more directly relevant to the Woman Question, when either male or female possesses a characteristic that increases the ability to produce offspring, that characteristic will be passed on to descendants even though it has no other use (for example, the bright colored plumage of birds). Darwin's theory of evolution had one salutary effect for women. It undermined the biblical tradition by which man's existence is due to a special creative act of God and woman is merely a derived being. But what Darwin gave with one hand he took away with the other. Sexual selection purported to demonstrate a biological basis for the traditional differences between the sexes, and so it seemed that science supported the idea that women are inferior to men. Darwin maintained that as a result of sexual selection women are more self-sacrificing, affectionate, gentle and, in a classic bit of circular reasoning, maternal. Men, on the other hand, are more intelligent, pugnacious, competitive, courageous, and energetic than women and have greater physical strength.

THE ORIGIN OF SEXUAL DIFFERENCES *

With mankind the differences between the sexes are greater than in most of the Quadrumana, but not so great as in some, for instance, the mandrill. Man on an average is considerably taller, heavier, and stronger than woman, with squarer shoulders and more plainly-pronounced muscles. Owing to the relation which exists between muscular development and the projection of the brows,[1] the superciliary ridge is generally more marked in man than in woman. His body, and especially his face, is more hairy, and his voice has a different and more powerful tone. In certain races the women are said to differ slightly in tint from the men. For instance, Schweinfurth, in speaking of a negress belonging to the Monbut-toos, who inhabit the interior of Africa a few degrees north of the Equator, says, "Like all her race, she had a skin several shades

---

* From Charles Darwin, *The Descent of Man,* 2nd ed. rev. (London: John Murray, 1874), Part 3, Chap. 19.

[1] Schaaffhausen, translation in "Anthropological Review," Oct. 1868, pp. 419, 420, 427.

lighter than her husband's being something of the colour of half-roasted coffee."[2] As the women labour in the fields and are quite unclothed, it is not likely that they differ in colour from the men owing to less exposure to the weather. European women are perhaps the brighter coloured of the two sexes, as may be seen when both have been equally exposed.

Man is more courageous, pugnacious and energetic than woman, and has a more inventive genius. His brain is absolutely larger, but whether or not proportionately to his larger body, has not, I believe, been fully ascertained. In woman the face is rounder; the jaws and the base of the skull smaller; the outlines of the body rounder, in parts more prominent; and her pelvis is broader than in man;[3] but this latter character may perhaps be considered rather as a primary than a secondary sexual character. She comes to maturity at an earlier age than man.

As with animals of all classes, so with man, the distinctive characters of the male sex are not fully developed until he is nearly mature; and if emasculated they never appear. The beard, for instance, is a secondary sexual character, and male children are beardless, though at an early age they have abundant hair on the head. It is probably due to the rather late appearance in life of the successive variations whereby man has acquired his masculine characters, that they are transmitted to the male sex alone. Male and female children resemble each other closely, like the young of so many other animals in which the adult sexes differ widely; they likewise resemble the mature female much more closely than the mature male. The female, however, ultimately assumes certain distinctive characters, and in the formation of her skull, is said to be intermediate between the child and the man.[4]

[2] "The Heart of Africa," Eng. translat. 1873, vol. i, p. 544.

[3] Ecker, translation in "Anthropological Review," Oct. 1868, pp. 351-356. The comparison of the form of the skull in men and women has been followed out with much care by Welcker.

[4] Ecker and Welcker, "Anthropological Review," Oct. 1868, pp. 352, 355; Vogt, "Lectures on Man," Eng. translat. p. 81.

Again, as the young of closely allied though distinct species do not differ nearly so much from each other as do the adults, so it is with the children of the different races of man. Some have even maintained that race-differences cannot be detected in the infantile skull.[5] In regard to colour, the new-born negro child is reddish nut-brown, which soon becomes slaty-grey; the black colour being fully developed within a year in the Soudan, but not until three years in Egypt. The eyes of the negro are at first blue, and the hair chestnut-brown rather than black, being curled only at the ends. The children of the Australians immediately after birth are yellowish-brown, and become dark at a later age. Those of the Guaranys of Paraguay are whitish-yellow, but they acquire in the course of a few weeks, the yellowish-brown tint of their parents. Similar observations have been made in other parts of America.[6]

I have specified the foregoing differences between the male and female sex in mankind, because they are curiously like those of the Quadrumana. With these animals the female is mature at an earlier age than the male; at least this is certainly the case in the *Cebus azaroe*.[7] The males of most species are larger and stronger than the females, of which fact the gorilla affords a well-known instance. Even in so trifling a character as the greater prominence of the superciliary ridge, the males of certain monkeys differ from the females,[8] and agree in this respect with mankind. In the gorilla and certain other monkeys, the cranium of the adult male presents a strongly-marked sagittal crest, which is absent in the female; and

[5] Schaaffhausen, "Anthropological Review," Oct. 1868, p. 429.

[6] Prunner-Bey, on negro infants as quoted by Vogt, "Lectures on Man," Eng. translat. 1864, p. 189: for further facts on negro infants, as quoted from Winterbottom and Camper, see Lawrence, "Lectures on Physiology," &c. 1822, p. 451. For the infants of the Guaranys, see Rengger, "Säugethiere," &c. s. 3. See also Godron, "De l'Espece," tom. ii. 1859, p. 253. For the Australians, Waitz, "Introduct. to Anthropology" Eng. translat. 1863, p. 99.

[7] Rengger, "Säugethiere," &c. 1830, s. 49.

[8] As in *Macacus cynomolgus* (Desmarest, "Mammalogie," p. 65), and in *Hylobates agilis* (Geoffroy St. Hilaire and F. Cuvier, "Hist. Nat. des Mamm." 1824, tom. i. p. 2).

Ecker found a trace of a similar difference between the two sexes in the Australians.[9] With monkeys when there is a difference in the voice, that of the male is the more powerful. We have seen that certain male monkeys have a well-developed beard, which is quite deficient, or much less developed in the female. No instance is known of the beard, whiskers, or moustache being larger in the female than in the male monkey. Even in the colour of the beard there is a curious parallelism between man and the Quadrumana, for with man when the beard differs in colour from the hair on the head, as is commonly the case, it is, I believe, almost always of a lighter tint, being often reddish. I have repeatedly observed this fact in England; but two gentlemen have lately written to me, saying that they form an exception to the rule. One of these gentlemen accounts for the fact by the wide difference in colour of the hair on the paternal and maternal sides of his family. Both had been long aware of this peculiarity (one of them having often been accused of dyeing his beard), and had thus led to observe other men, and were convinced that the exceptions were very rare. Dr. Hooker attended to this little point for me in Russia, and found no exception to the rule. In Calcutta, Mr. J. Scott, of the Botanic Gardens, was so kind as to observe the many races of men to be seen there, as well as in some other parts of India, namely, two races in Sikhim, the Bhoteas, Hindoos, Burmese, and Chinese, most of which races have very little hair on the face; and he always found that when there was any difference in colour between the hair on the head and the beard, the latter was invariably lighter. Now with monkeys, as has already been stated, the beard frequently differs strikingly in colour from the hair on the head, and in such cases it is always of a lighter hue, being often pure white, sometimes yellow or reddish.[10]

9 "Anthropological Review," Oct. 1868, p. 353.

10 Mr. Blyth informs me that he has only seen one instance of the beard, whiskers, &c., in a monkey becoming white with old age, as is so commonly the case with us. This, however, occurred in an aged *Macacus cynomolgus,* kept in confinement, whose moustaches were "remarkably long and human-like." Al-

In regard to the general hairiness of the body, the women in all races are less hairy than the men; and in some few Quadrumana the under side of the body of the female is less hairy than that of the male.[11] Lastly, male monkeys, like men, are bolder and fiercer than the females. They lead the troop, and when there is danger, come to the front. We thus see how close is the parallelism between the sexual differences of man and the Quadrumana. With some few species, however, as with certain baboons, the orang and the gorilla, there is a considerably greater difference between the sexes, as in the size of the canine teeth, in the development and colour of the hair, and especially in the colour of the naked parts of the skin, than in mankind.

All the secondary sexual characters of man are highly variable, even within the limits of the same race; and they differ much in the several races. These two rules hold good generally throughout the animal kingdom. In the excellent observations made on board the *Novara*,[12] the male Australians were found to exceed the females by only 65 millim. in height, whilst with the Javans the average excess was 218 millim.; so that in this latter race the difference in height between the sexes is more than thrice as great as with the Australians. Numerous measurements were carefully made of the stature, the circumference of the neck and chest, the length of the back-bone and of the arms, in various races; and nearly all these measurements shew that the males differ much more from one another than do the females. This fact indicates that, as far as these

---

together this old monkey presented a ludicrous resemblance to one of the reigning monarchs of Europe, after whom he was universally nick-named. In certain races of man the hair on the head hardly ever becomes grey; thus Mr. D. Forbes has never, as he informs me, seen an instance with the Aymaras and Quichaus of S. America.

[11] This is the case with the females of several species of Hylobates, see Geoffroy St.-Hiliare and F. Cuvier, "Hist. Nat. des Mamm." tom. i. See, also, on H. lar. "Penny Cyclopedia," vol. ii. pp. 149, 150.

[12] The results were deduced by Dr. Weisbach from the measurements made by Drs. K. Scherzer and Schwarz, see "Reise der Novara: Anthropolog. Theil," 1867, ss. 216, 231, 234, 236, 239, 269.

characters are concerned, it is the male which has been chiefly modified, since the several races diverged from their common stock.

The development of the beard and the hairiness of the body differ remarkably in the men of distinct races, and even in different tribes or families of the same race. We Europeans see this amongst ourselves. In the Island of St. Kilda, according to Martin,[13] the men do not acquire beards until the age of thirty or upwards, and even then the beards are very thin. On the Europaeo-Asiatic continent, beards prevail until we pass beyond India; though with the natives of Ceylon they are often absent, as was noticed in ancient times by Diodorus.[14] Eastward of India beards disappear, as with the Siamese, Malays, Kalmucks, Chinese, and Japanese; nevertheless the Ainos,[15] who inhabit the northernmost islands of the Japan Archipelago are the hairiest men in the world. With negroes the beard is scanty or wanting, and they rarely have whiskers; in both sexes the body is frequently almost destitute of fine down.[16] On the other hand, the Papuans of the Malay Archipelago, who are nearly as black as negroes, possess well-developed beards.[17] In the Pacific Ocean the inhabitants of the Fiji Archipelago have large bushy beards, whilst those of the not distant archipelagoes of Tonga and Samoa are beardless; but these men belong to distinct races. In the Ellice group all the inhabitants belong to the same race; yet on one island alone, namely Nunemaya, "the men have splendid beards;" whilst on the other islands "they have, as a rule, a dozen straggling hairs for a beard." [18]

[13] "Voyage to St. Kilda" (3rd edit. 1753), p. 37.

[14] Sir J. E. Tennent, "Ceylon," vol. ii. 1859, p. 107.

[15] Quatrefages, "Revue des Cours Scientifiques," Aug. 29, 1868, p. 630; Vogt, "Lectures on Man," Eng. translat. p. 127.

[16] On the beards of negroes, Vogt, "Lectures," &c. p. 127; Waitz, "Introduct. to Anthropology," Engl. translat. 1863, vol. i. p. 96. It is remarkable that in the United States ("Investigations in Military and Anthropological Statistics of American Soldiers," 1869, p. 569) the pure negroes and their crossed offspring seem to have bodies almost as hairy as Europeans.

[17] Wallace, "The Malay Arch." vol. ii. 1869, p. 178.

[18] Dr. J. Barnard Davis On Oceanic Races, in "Anthropolog. Review," April, 1870, pp. 185, 191.

Throughout the great American continent the men may be said to be beardless; but in almost all the tribes a few short hairs are apt to appear on the face, especially in old age. With the tribes of North America, Catlin estimates that eighteen out of twenty men are completely destitute by nature of a beard; but occasionally there may be seen a man, who has neglected to pluck out the hairs at puberty, with a soft beard an inch or two in length. The Guaranys of Paraguay differ from all the surrounding tribes in having a small beard, and even some hair on the body, but no whiskers.[19] I am informed by Mr. D. Forbes, who particularly attended to this point, that the Aymaras and Quichuas of the Cordillera are remarkably hairless, yet in old age a few straggling hairs occasionally appear on the chin. The men of these two tribes have very little hair on the various parts of the body where hair grows abundantly in Europeans, and the women have none on the corresponding parts. The hair on the head, however, attains an extraordinary length in both sexes, often reaching almost to the ground; and this is likewise the case with some of the N. American tribes. In the amount of hair, and in the general shape of the body, the sexes of the American aborigines do not differ so much from each other, as in most other races.[20] This fact is analogous with what occurs with some closely allied monkeys; thus the sexes of the chimpanzee are not as different as those of the orang or gorilla.[21]

In the previous chapters we have seen that with mammals, birds, fishes, insects, &c., many characters, which there is every reason to believe were primarily gained through sexual selection by one sex, have been transferred to the other. As this same form of transmission has apparently prevailed much with mankind, it will save

[19] Catlin, "North American Indians," 3rd ed. 1842, vol. ii. p. 227. On the Guaranys, see Azara, "Voyages dans l'Amérique Mérid." tom. ii. 1809, p. 58; also Rengger, "Säugethiere von Paraguay," s. 3.

[20] Prof. and Mrs. Agassiz ("Journey in Brazil," p. 530) remark that the sexes of the American Indians differ less than those of the negroes and of the higher races. See also Rengger, ibid. p. 3, on the Guaranys.

[21] Rütimeyer, "Die Grenzen der Thierwelt; eine Betrachtung zu Darwin's Lehre," 1868, s. 54.

useless repetition if we discuss the origin of characters peculiar to the male sex together with certain other characters common to both sexes.

Law of Battle. — With savages, for instance the Australians, the women are the constant cause of war both between members of the same tribe and between distinct tribes. So no doubt it was in ancient times; "nam fuit ante Helenam mulier teterrima belli causa." With some of the North American Indians, the contest is reduced to a system. That excellent observer, Hearne,[22] says: —

> It has ever been the custom among these people for the men to wrestle for any woman to whom they are attached; and of course, the strongest party always carries off the prize. A weak man, unless he be a good hunter, and well-beloved, is seldom permitted to keep a wife that a stronger man thinks worth his notice. This custom prevails throughout all the tribes, and causes a great spirit of emulation among their youth, who are upon all occasions, from their childhood, trying their strength and skill in wrestling.

With the Guanas of South America, Azara states that the men rarely marry till twenty years old or more, as before that age they cannot conquer their rivals.

Other similar facts could be given; but even if we had no evidence on this head, we might feel almost sure, from the analogy of the higher Quadrumana,[23] that the law of battle had prevailed with man during the early stages of his development. The occasional appearance at the present day of canine teeth which project above the others, with traces of a diastema or open space for the reception of the opposite canines, is in all probability a case of

22 "A Journey from Prince of Wales Fort." 8vo. edit. Dublin, 1796, p. 104. Sir J. Lubbock ("Origin of Civilisation," 1870, p. 69) gives other and similar cases in North America. For the Guanas of S. America see Azara, "Voyages," &c. tom. ii, p. 94.

23 On the fighting of the male gorillas, see Dr. Savage, in "Boston Journal of Nat. Hist." vol. v. 1847, p. 423. On *Prebytis entellus,* see the "Indian Field," 1859, p. 146.

reversion to a former state, when the progenitors of man were provided with these weapons, like so many existing male Quadrumana. It was remarked in a former chapter that as man gradually became erect, and continually used his hands and arms for fighting with sticks and stones, as well as for the other purposes of life, he would have used his jaws and teeth less and less. The jaws, together with their muscles, would then have been reduced through disuse, as would the teeth through the not well understood principles of correlation and economy of growth; for we everywhere see that parts, which are no longer of service, are reduced in size. By such steps the original inequality between the jaws and teeth in the two sexes of mankind would ultimately have been obliterated. The case is almost parallel with that of many male Ruminants, in which the canine teeth have been reduced to mere rudiments, or have disappeared, apparently in consequence of the development of horns. As the prodigious difference between the skulls of the two sexes in the orang and gorilla stands in close relation with the development of the immense canine teeth in the males, we may infer that the reduction of the jaws and teeth in the early male progenitors of man must have led to a most striking and favourable change in his appearance.

There can be little doubt that the greater size and strength of man, in comparison with woman, together with his broader shoulders, more developed muscles, rugged outline of body, his greater courage and pugnacity, are all due in chief part to inheritance from his half-human male ancestors. These characters would, however, have been preserved or even augmented during the long ages of man's savagery, by the success of the strongest and boldest men, both in the general struggle for life and in their contests for wives; a success which would have ensured their leaving a more numerous progeny than their less favoured brethren. It is not probable that the greater strength of man was primarily acquired through the inherited effects of his having worked harder than woman for his own subsistence and that of his family; for the women in all barbarous nations are compelled to work at least as hard as the men. With civilised people the arbitrament of battle for the possession of the women has long ceased; on the other hand, the men, as a general rule, have to work harder than the women for their joint subsistence, and thus their greater strength will have been kept up.

Difference in the Mental Powers of the two Sexes. — With respect to differences of this nature between man and woman, it is probable that sexual selection has played a highly important part. I am aware that some writers doubt whether there is any such inherent difference; but this is at least probable from the analogy of the lower animals which present other secondary sexual characters. No one disputes that the bull differs in disposition from the cow, the wild-boar from the sow, the stallion from the mare, and, as is well known to the keepers of menageries the males of the larger apes from the females. Woman seems to differ from man in mental disposition, chiefly in her greater tenderness and less selfishness; and this holds good even with savages, as shewn by a well-known passage in Mungo Park's Travels, and by statements made by many other travellers. Woman, owing to her maternal instincts, displays these qualities towards her infants in an eminent degree; therefore it is likely that she would often extend them towards her fellow-creatures. Man is the rival of other men; he delights in competition, and this leads to ambition which passes too easily into selfishness. These latter qualities seem to be his natural and unfortunate birthright. It is generally admitted that with woman the powers of intuition, of rapid perception, and perhaps of imitation, are more strongly marked than in man; but some, at least, of these faculties are characteristic of the lower races, and therefore of a past and lower state of civilisation.

The chief distinction in the intellectual powers of the two sexes is shewn by man's attaining to a higher eminence, in whatever he takes up, than can woman—whether requiring deep thought, reason, or imagination, or merely the use of senses and hands. If two lists were made of the most eminent men and women in poetry, painting, sculpture, music (inclusive both of composition and performance), history, science, and philosophy with half-a-dozen names under each subject, the two lists would not bear comparison. We may also infer, from the law of the deviation from averages, so well illustrated by Mr. Galton, in his work on "Hereditary Genius," that if men are capable of a decided pre-eminence over women in many subjects, the average of mental power in man must be above that of woman.

Amongst the half-human progenitors of man, and amongst savages, there have been struggles between the males during many generations for the possession of the females. But mere bodily strength and size would do little for victory, unless associated with courage, perseverance, and determined energy. With social animals, the young males have to pass through many a contest before they win a female, and the older males have to retain their females by renewed battles. They have, also, in the case of mankind, to defend their females, as well as their young, from enemies of all kinds, and to hunt for their joint subsistence. But to avoid enemies or to attack them with success, to capture wild animals, and to fashion weapons, requires the aid of the higher mental faculties, namely, observation, reason, invention, or imagination. These various faculties will thus have been continually put to the test and selected during manhood; they will, moreover, have been strengthened by use during this same period of life. Consequently, in accordance with the principle often alluded to, we might expect that they would at least tend to be transmitted chiefly to the male offspring at the corresponding period of manhood.

Now, when two men are put into competition, or a man with a woman, both possessed of every mental quality in equal perfection, save that one has higher energy, perseverance, and courage, the latter will generally become more eminent in every pursuit, and will gain the ascendancy.[24] He may be said to possess genius—for genius

[24] J. Stuart Mill remarks ("The Subjection of Women," 1869, p. 122), "The things in which man most excels woman are those which require most plodding, and long hammering at single thoughts." What is this but energy and perseverance?

has been declared by a great authority to be patience; and patience, in this sense, means unflinching, undaunted perseverance. But this view of genius is perhaps deficient; for without the higher powers of the imagination and reason, no eminent success can be gained in many subjects. These latter faculties, as well as the former, will have been developed in man, partly through sexual selection,—that is, through the contest of rival males, and partly through natural selection,—that is, from success in the general struggle for life; and as in both cases the struggle will have been during maturity, the characters gained will have been transmitted more fully to the male than to the female offspring. It accords in a striking manner with this view of the modification and re-inforcement of many of our mental faculties by sexual selection, that, firstly they notoriously undergo a considerable change at puberty,[25] and, secondly, that eunuchs remain throughout life inferior in these same qualities. Thus man has ultimately become superior to woman. It is, indeed, fortunate that the law of the equal transmission of characters to both sexes prevails with mammals; otherwise it is probable that man would have become as superior in mental endowment to woman, as the peacock is in ornamental plumage to the peahen.

It must be borne in mind that the tendency in characters acquired by either sex late in life, to be transmitted to the same sex at the same age, and of early acquired characters to be transmitted to both sexes, are rules which, though general, do not always hold. If they always held good, we might conclude (but I here exceed my proper bounds) that the inherited effects of the early education of boys and girls would be transmitted equally to both sexes; so that the present inequality in mental power between the sexes would not be effaced by a similar course of early training; nor can it have been caused by their dissimilar early training. In order that woman should reach the same standard as man, she ought, when nearly adult, to be trained to energy and perseverance, and to have her reason and imagination exercised to the highest point; and then she

[25] Maudsley, "Mind and Body," p. 31.

would probably transmit these qualities chiefly to her adult daughters. All women, however, could not be thus raised, unless during many generations those who excelled in the above robust virtues were married, and produced offspring in larger numbers than other women. As before remarked of bodily strength, although men do not now fight for their wives, and this form of selection has passed away, yet during manhood, they generally undergo a severe struggle in order to maintain themselves and their families; and this will tend to keep up or even increase their mental powers and, as a consequence, the present inequality between the sexes.[26]

[26] An observation by Vogt bears on this subject: he says, "It is a remarkable circumstance, that the difference between the sexes, as "regards the cranial cavity, increases with the development of the race, so that the male European excels much more the female, than the negro the negress. Welcker confirms this statement of Huschke from his measurements of negro and German skulls." But Vogt admits ("Lectures on Man," Eng. translat. 1864, p. 81) that more observations are requisite on this point.

Friedrich Nietzsche

Unlike Mill, who argued for a perfect equality between the sexes, Nietzsche lashed out at every turn against the growing movement for women's rights. Most of his works are peppered with attacks against women and those who supported their cause. In this regard Nietzsche is more typical than Mill, for he expressed the prevailing ideas about women's place in life. Nietzsche, who was influenced by his contemporary Charles Darwin, saw man as part of the natural world and rejected the Christian interpretation of life, which, in principle if not in fact, values death and eternal life over this world. For Nietzsche, God is dead—man is the creator of values. In his classic distinction between the master and slave mentalities, woman emerges as characterizing the slave. The master mentality legislates its own value, has a creative vision of the possible, understands its own power, has pride and courage, welcomes risk and danger, and wars against conventional values. The slave, on the other hand, passively adjusts, is humble and practical, acts out a prescribed role, avoids risk, accepts values "out there," has limited vision, and, above all, values security and stability. It is a great irony that while the revolutionary women engaged in the pursuit of freedom exemplified his master mentality in every way, Nietzsche nonetheless condemns them out of hand. In *Thus Spake Zarathustra* (1883), he presents a caricature of woman that repeats the negative aspects of the traditional ideas on woman. Women exist as the instruments of men; they should be raised for the relaxation of men, who as warriors particularly enjoy women's dangerous qualities. On the other hand, women use men for their single goal in life—pregnancy and children; Therefore their only hope in life is to produce Supermen, that is, those with a master mentality.

WOMAN AS DANGEROUS PLAYTHING *

"Why ever do you sneak around so warily through the twilight, Zarathustra? And what do you cover up so defensively under your coat?

"Is it a treasure which has been given to you? Or a child which has been born to you? Or do you at the present time go the way of robbers, you friend of evil men?"

"Truly, my brother!" Zarathustra said. "It is a treasure which has been given to me: it is a small truth which I bear.

"However, it is unruly like a small child; and when I do not hold its mouth, then it shrieks very noisily.

"Today as I went my way by myself, during the time when the sun sets, a small old woman approached me and addressed my soul in the following way:

" 'Zarathustra has said many things to us women, however he has never said anything to us about women.'

* From Friedrich Nietzsche, "Vom Alten und Jungen Weiblein," in *Also Sprach Zarathustra* (1883), newly translated by Rosemary Agonito.

"And I responded to her: 'Man should speak only to men about women.'

" 'Speak to me about women also,' she said; 'I am old enough so that I will forget it again.'

"And I proceeded to accommodate the small old woman and said the following to her:

" 'Everything concerning woman is a puzzle, and everything concerning woman has one solution: it is named pregnancy.

" 'For woman man is a means, the goal is always the child. However what is a woman for man?

" 'The real man wishes for two things: danger and recreation. Hence man wants woman as the most dangerous plaything. Man should be brought up for the purpose of war and woman for the relaxation of the soldier: everything else is foolish.

" 'The soldier does not enjoy fruit that is too sweet. Hence he enjoys woman; even the sweetest woman is bitter.

" 'Woman comprehends children better than a man, but a man is even more childish than a woman.

" 'A child is bound up in a real man who wishes to play. Get up, you ladies, find me the child in man!

" 'Let woman be a plaything, pure and simple as a priceless gem reflecting the virtues of a world which is not yet here.

" 'Let the brilliance of a star reflect in your love! Let your hope ask: "May I give birth to a Superman!"

" ' Let there be bravery in your love! You should go toward him who frightens you with your love.

" 'In your love let there be dignity! Woman comprehends little else about dignity! However, let this be your dignity: that at all times you love more than you are loved, and that you never be second in this.

" 'Let man be afraid of woman when she loves: for then she brings every offering, and every other thing appears worthless to her.

" 'Let man be afraid of woman when she hates: for man in the depth of his soul is only evil, but a woman is base in her soul.

" 'Who does woman hate the most? The following is what the iron said to the magnet: "I hate you the most since you attract me but you are not powerful enough to drag me to you."

" 'The joy of man says: "I will." The joy of woman says: "he will."

" ' "Look, at this moment the world became perfect!" This is the way every woman thinks when she obeys from all her love.

" 'And a woman must obey and must find a depth for her superficiality. Superficiality is the character of woman, a moving, tempestuous membrane on shallow water.

" 'But the soul of man is deep; his stream thunders through underground caverns: woman guesses his power but is unable to understand it.'

"Then the small old woman responded to me: 'Zarathustra has spoken many nice things and particularly for those who are young enough for them.

" 'How strange it is that Zarathustra knows very little concerning women, and still he has the right idea about them! Has this come about because nothing is impossible regarding women?

" 'And now take a small truth in thanks. Certainly I am old enough for it!

" 'Cover it and hold its mouth or else this small truth will shriek very noisily.'

" 'Give me your small truth, Woman!' I said. And the old woman said the following:

" 'Do you go to women? Do not forget the whip!' "

Thus spake Zarathustra.

Friedrich Engels

In the midst of the Industrial Revolution, with its appalling abuse of the laboring class, emerged a political philosopher, Karl Marx, whose influence has survived to present times. Together with Engels he expounded the philosophy of historical materialism, which held that (1) all social and intellectual relations are ultimately explained by the material conditions of human life, and (2) the most basic material condition is the economic structure (i.e., the modes of production and distribution of goods). Since the most fundamental social relation is that between men and women, the position of women is ultimately explained by economic conditions. It was Engels who attempted a systematic exposition of this thesis in *Origin of the Family* (1884), using as his basis the anthropological evidence of Lewis Morgan. He employs Morgan's threefold classi-fication of the stages of history—savagery, marked by gathering and hunting; barbarism, marked by animal breeding and agriculture; civilization, marked by art and industry—to demonstrate how women's position deteriorates outside the communist structure. In savagery, group marriage or unrestricted sexual freedom prevailed, paternity was unknown, and only the female line, or Mother Right, was recognized. The child-bearing function, and hence woman, was held in high esteem. In this communist structure everyone contributed to the economy, no one was dependent, and there was no distinction between the public and the domestic. With barbarism the pairing family emerged, and to insure paternity, women were held to strict fidelity. The division of labor became segregated, since, without the need to hunt, men turned to flocks and crops. Thus private property and paternity effected the overthrow of Mother Right, and women were rendered economically dependent. With civilization monogamy prevailed, and the patriarchal family solidified male supremacy. Hence emerged the first class struggle, the antagonism between the sexes—in the family, man is bourgeois and woman is proletarian.

THE ORIGIN OF THE OPPRESSION
OF WOMEN *

The development of the family, then, is founded on the continual contraction of the circle, originally comprising the whole tribe, within which marital intercourse between both sexes was general. By the continual exclusion, first of near, then of ever remoter relatives, including finally even those who were simply related legally, all group marriage becomes practically impossible. At last only one couple, temporarily and loosely united, remains; that molecule, the dissolution of which absolutely puts an end to marriage. Even from this we may infer how little the sexual love of the individual in the modern sense of the word had to do with the origin of monogamy. The practice of all nations of that stage still more proves this. While in the previous form of the family the men were never embarrassed for women, but rather had more than enough of them, women now became scarce and were sought after.

* From Friedrich Engels, *The Origin of the Family, Private Property and the State,* trans. Ernest Untermann (Chicago: C.H. Kerr and Company, 1902), Chap. 2: Sects. 3, 4.

With the pairing family, therefore, the abduction and barter of women began—widespread symptoms, and nothing but that, of a new and much more profound change. The pedantic Scot, McLennan, however, transmuted these symptoms, mere methods of obtaining women, into separate classes of the family under the head of "marriage by capture" and "marriage by barter." Moreover among American Indians and other nations in the same stage, the marriage agreement is not the business of the parties most concerned, who often are not even asked, but of their mothers. Frequently two persons entirely unknown to one another are thus engaged to be married and receive no information of the closing of the bargain, until the time for the marriage ceremony approaches. Before the wedding, the bridegroom brings gifts to the maternal relatives of the bride (not to her father or his relatives) as an equivalent for ceding the girl to him. Either of the married parties may dissolve the marriage at will. But among many tribes, as, e.g., the Iroquois, public opinion has gradually become averse to such separations. In case of domestic differences the gentile relatives of both parties endeavor to bring about a reconciliation, and not until they are unsuccessful a separation takes place. In this case the woman keeps the children, and both parties are free to marry again.

The pairing family, being too weak and too unstable to make an independent household necessary or even desirable, in no way dissolves the traditional communistic way of housekeeping. But household communism implies supremacy of women in the house as surely as exclusive recognition of a natural mother and the consequent impossibility of identifying the natural father signify high esteem for women, i.e., mothers. It is one of the most absurd notions derived from eighteenth century enlightenment, that in the beginning of society woman was the slave of man. Among all savages and barbarians of the lower and middle stages, sometimes even of the higher stage, women not only have freedom, but are held in high esteem. What they were even in the pairing family, let Arthur Wright, for many years a missionary among the Seneca Iroquois, testify:

As to their families, at a time when they still lived in their old long houses (communistic households of several families) ... a certain clan (gens) always reigned, so that the women choose their husbands from other clans (gentes).... The female part generally ruled the house; the provisions were held in common; but woe to the luckless husband or lover who was too indolent or too clumsy to contribute his share to the common stock. No matter how many children or how much private property he had in the house, he was liable at any moment to receive a hint to gather up his belongings and get out. And he could not dare to venture any resistance; the house was made too hot for him and he had no other choice, but to return to his own clan (gens) or, as was mostly the case, to look for another wife in some other clan. The women were the dominating power in the clans (gentes) and everywhere else. Occasionally they did not hesitate to dethrone a chief and degrade him to a common warrior.

The communistic household, in which most or all the women belong to one and the same gens, while the husbands come from different gentes, is the cause and foundation of the general and widespread supremacy of women in primeval times. The discovery of this fact is the third merit of Bachofen....

Bachofen, furthermore, is perfectly right in contending that the transition from what he calls "hetaerism" or "incestuous generation" to monogamy was brought about mainly by women. The more in the course of economic development, undermining the old communism and increasing the density of population, the traditional sexual relations lost their innocent character suited to the primitive forest, the more debasing and oppressive they naturally appeared to women; and the more they consequently longed for relief by the right of chastity, of temporary or permanent marriage with one man. This progress could not be due to men for the simple reason that they never, even to this day, had the least intention of renouncing the pleasures of actual group marriage. Not until the women had accomplished the transition to the pairing family could the men introduce strict monogamy—true, only for women.

The pairing family arose on the boundary line between savagery and barbarism, generally in the higher stage of savagery, here and there in the lower stage of barbarism. It is the form of the family characteristic for barbarism, as group marriage is for savagery and monogamy for civilization. In order to develop it into established monogamy, other causes than those active hitherto were required. In the pairing family the group was already reduced to its last unit, its biatomic molecule: one man and one woman. Natural selection had accomplished its purpose by a continually increasing restriction of sexual intercourse. Nothing remained to be done in this direction. Unless new social forces became active, there was no reason why a new form of the family should develop out of the pairing family. But these forces did become active.

We now leave America, the classic soil of the pairing family. No sign permits the conclusion that a higher form of the family was developed here, that any established form of monogamy ever existed anywhere in the New World before the discovery and conquest. Not so in the Old World.

In the latter, the domestication of animals and the breeding of flocks had developed hitherto unknown source of wealth and created entirely new social conditions. Up to the lower stage of barbarism, fixed wealth was almost exclusively represented by houses, clothing, rough ornaments and the tools for obtaining and preparing food: boats, weapons and household articles of the simplest kind. Nourishment had to be secured afresh day by day. But now, with their herds of horses, camels, donkeys, cattle, sheep, goats and hogs, the advancing nomadic nations—the Aryans in the Indian Punjab, in the region of the Ganges and the steppes of the Oxus and Jaxartes, then still more rich in water-veins than now; the Semites on the Euphrates and Tigris—had acquired possessions demanding only the most crude attention and care in order to propagate themselves in ever increasing numbers and yield the most abundant store of milk and meat. All former means of obtaining food were now forced to the background. Hunting, once a necessity, now became a sport.

But who was the owner of this new wealth? Doubtless it was

originally the gens. However, private ownership of flocks must have had an early beginning. It is difficult to say whether to the author of the so-called first book of Moses Father Abraham appeared as the owner of his flocks by virtue of his privilege as head of a communistic family or of his capacity as gentle chief by actual descent. So much is certain: we must not regard him as a proprietor in the modern sense of the word. It is furthermore certain that everywhere on the threshold of documentary history we find the flocks in the separate possession of chiefs of families, exactly like the productions of barbarian art, such as metal ware, articles of luxury and, finally, the human cattle—the slaves.

For now slavery was also invented. To the barbarian of the lower stage a slave was of no use. The American Indians, therefore, treated their vanquished enemies in quite a different way from nations of a higher stage. The men were tortured or adopted as brothers into the tribe of the victors. The women were married or likewise adopted with their surviving children. The human labor power at this stage does not yet produce a considerable amount over and above its cost of subsistence. But the introduction of cattle raising, metal industry, weaving and finally agriculture wrought a change. Just as the once easily obtainable wives now had an exchange value and were bought so labor power was now procured, especially since the flocks had definitely become private property. The family did not increase as rapidly as the cattle. More people were needed for superintending; for this purpose the captured enemy was available and, besides, he could be increased by breeding like the cattle.

Such riches, once they had become the private property of certain families and augmented rapidly, gave a powerful impulse to society founded on the pairing family and the maternal gens. The pairing family had introduced a new element. By the side of the natural mother it had placed the authentic natural father who probably was better authenticated than many a "father" of our day. According to the division of labor in those times, the task of obtaining food and the tools necessary for this purpose fell to the share of the man; hence he owned the latter and kept them in case of a separation, as the women did the household goods. According to the social custom of that time, the man was also the owner of the new source of existence, the cattle, and later on of the new labor power, the slaves. But according to the same custom, his children could not inherit his property, for the following reasons: By maternal law, i.e., while descent was traced only along the female line, and by the original custom of inheriting in the gens, the gentile relatives inherited the property of their deceased gentile relative. The wealth had to remain in the gens. In view of the insignificance of the objects, the property may have gone in practice to the closest gentile relatives, i.e., the consanguine relatives on the mother's side. The children of the dead man, however, did not belong to his gens, but to that of their mother. They inherited first together with the other consanguine relatives of the mother, later on perhaps in preference to the others. But they could not inherit from their father, because they did not belong to his gens, where his property had to remain. Hence, after the death of a cattle owner, the cattle would fall to his brothers, sisters and the children of his sisters, or to the offspring of the sisters of his mother. His own children were disinherited.

In the measure of the increasing wealth man's position in the family became superior to that of woman, and the desire arose to use this fortified position for the purpose of overthrowing the traditional law of inheritance in favor of his children. But this was not feasible as long as maternal law was valid. This law had to be abolished, and it was. This was by no means as difficult as it appears to us to-day. For this revolution—one of the most radical ever experienced by humanity—did not have to touch a single living member of the gens. All its members could remain what they had always been. The simple resolution was sufficient, that henceforth the offspring of the male members should belong to the gens, while the children of the female members should be excluded by transferring them to the gens of their father. This abolished the tracing of descent by female lineage and the maternal right of inheritance, and instituted descent by male-lineage and the paternal right of inheritance. How and when this revolution was accomplished by the nations of the earth, we do not know. It belongs entirely to prehistoric times. That it was accomplished is proven more than satisfactorily by the copious traces of maternal law collected especially by Bachofen. . . .

The downfall of maternal law was the historic defeat of the female sex. The men seized the reins also in the house, the women were stripped of their dignity, enslaved, tools of men's lust and mere machines for the generation of children. This degrading position of women, especially conspicuous among the Greeks of heroic and still more of classic times, was gradually glossed over and disguised or even clad in a milder form. But it is by no means obliterated.

The first effect of the established supremacy of men became now visible in the reappearance of the intermediate form of the patriarchal family. Its most significant feature is not polygamy, of which more anon, but

> the organization of a certain number of free and unfree persons into one family under the paternal authority of the head of the family. In the Semitic form this head of the family lives in polygamy, the unfree members have wife and children, and the purpose of the whole organization is the tending of herds in a limited territory.

The essential points are the assimilation of the unfree element and the paternal authority. Hence the ideal type of this form of the family is the Roman family. The word familia did not originally signify the composite ideal of sentimentality and domestic strife in the present day philistine mind. Among the Romans it did not even apply in the beginning to the leading couple and its children, but to the slaves alone. Famulus means domestic slave, and familia is the aggregate number of slaves belonging to one man. At the time of Gajus, the familia, id est patrimonium (i.e., paternal legacy), was still bequeathed by testament. The expression was invented by the

Romans in order to designate a new social organism, the head of which had a wife, children and a number of slaves under his paternal authority and according to Roman law the right of life and death over all of them.

> The word is, therefore, not older than the ironclad family system of the Latin tribes, which arose after the introduction of agriculture and of lawful slavery, and after the separation of the Aryan Itali from the Greeks.

Marx adds:

> The modern family contains the germ not only of slavery (servitus), but also of serfdom, because it has from the start a relation to agricultural service. It comprises in miniature all those contrasts that later on develop more broadly in society and the state.

Such a form of the family shows the transition from the pairing family to monogamy. In order to secure the faithfulness of the wife, and hence the reliability of paternal lineage, the women are delivered absolutely into the power of the men; in killing his wife, the husband simply exercises his right.

With the patriarchal family we enter the domain of written history. . . .

The whole severity of this new form of the family confronts us among the Greeks. While, as Marx observes, the position of the female gods in mythology shows an earlier period, when women still occupied a freer and more respected plane, we find woman already degraded by the supremacy of man and the competition of slaves during the time of the heroes. Read in the Odysseia how Telemachos reproves and silences his mother. The captured young women, according to Homer, are delivered to the sensual lust of the victors. The leaders in the order of their rank select the most beautiful captives. The whole Iliad notoriously revolves around the quarrel between Achilles and Agamemnon about such a captured woman. In mentioning any hero of importance, the captured girl sharing his tent and bed is never omitted. These girls are also taken into the hero's home country and his house, as Kassandra by Agamemnon in Aeschylus. Boys born by these female slaves receive a small share of the paternal heirloom and are regarded as free men. Teukros is such an illegitimate son and may use his father's name. The wife is expected to put up with everything, while herself remaining chaste and faithful. Although the Greek woman of heroic times is more highly respected than she of the civilized period, still she is for her husband only the mother of his legal heirs, his first housekeeper and the superintendent of the female slaves, whom he can and does make his concubines at will.

It is this practice of slavery by the side of monogamy, the existence of young and beautiful female slaves belonging without any restriction to their master, which from the very beginning gives to monogamy the specific character of being monogamy for women only, but not for men. And this character remains to this day. . . .

Monogamy, then, does by no means enter history as a reconciliation of man and wife and still less as the highest form of marriage. On the contrary, it enters as the subjugation of one sex by the other, as the proclamation of an antagonism between the sexes unknown in all preceding history. In an old unpublished manuscript written by Marx and myself in 1846, I find the following passage: "The first division of labor is that of man and wife in breeding children." And to-day I may add: The first class antagonism appearing in history coincides with the development of the antagonism of man and wife in monogamy, and the first class oppression with that of the female by the male sex. Monogamy was a great historical progress. But by the side of slavery and private property it marks at the same time that epoch which, reaching down to our days, takes with all progress also a step backwards, relatively speaking, and develops the welfare and advancement of one by the woe and submission of the other. It is the cellular form of civilized society which enables us to study the nature of its now fully-developed contrasts and contradictions. . . .

The marriage is influenced by the class environment of the participants and in this respect it always remains conventional. This conventionalism often enough results in the most pronounced prostitution—sometimes of both parties, more commonly of the women. She is distinguished from a courtisane only in that she does not offer her body for money by the hour like a commodity, but sells it into slavery for once and all. Fourier's words hold good with respect to all conventional marriages: "As in grammar two negatives make one affirmative, so in matrimonial ethics, two prostitutions are considered as one virtue." Sexual love in man's relation to woman becomes and can become the rule among the oppressed classes alone, among the proletarians of our day—no matter whether this relation is officially sanctioned or not.

Here all the fundamental conditions of classic monogamy have been abolished. Here all property is missing and it was precisely for the protection and inheritance of this that monogamy and man rule were established. Hence all incentive to make this rule felt is wanting here. More still, the funds are missing. Civil law protecting male rule applies only to the possessing classes and their intercourse with proletarians. Law is expensive and therefore the poverty of the laborer makes it meaningless for his relation to his wife. Entirely different personal and social conditions decide in this case. And finally, since the great industries have removed women from the home to the labor market and to the factory, the last remnant of man rule in the proletarian home has lost its ground—except, perhaps, a part of the brutality against women that has become general since the advent of monogamy. Thus the family of the proletarian is no longer strictly monogamous, even with all the most passionate love and the most unalterable loyalty of both parties, and in spite of any possible clerical or secular sanction. Consequently the eternal companions of monogamy, hetaerism and adultery, play an almost insignificant role here. The woman has practically regained the right of separation, and if a couple cannot agree, they rather separate. In short, the proletarian marriage is monogamous in the etymological sense of the word, but by no means in a historical sense.

True, our jurists hold that the progress of legislation continually lessens all cause of complaint for women. The modern systems of civil law recognize, first, that marriage, in order to be legal, must be a contract based on voluntary consent of both parties, and secondly that during marriage the relations of both parties shall be founded on equal rights and duties. These two demands logically enforced will, so they claim, give to women everything they could possibly ask.

This genuinely juridical argumentation is exactly the same as that used by the radical republican bourgeois to cut short and dismiss the proletarian. The labor contract is said to be voluntarily made by both parties. But it is considered as voluntary when the law places both parties on equal terms on paper. The power conferred on one party by the division of classes, the pressure thereby exerted on the other party, the actual economic relation of the two—all this does not concern the law. Again, during the term of the contract both parties are held to have equal rights, unless one has expressly renounced his right. That the economic situation forces the laborer to give up even the last semblance of equality, that is not the fault of the law.

In regard to marriage, even the most advanced law is completely satisfied after both parties have formally declared their willingness. What passes behind the juridical scenes where the actual process of living is going on, and how this willingness is brought about, that cannot be the business of the law and the jurist. Yet the simplest legal comparison should show to the jurist what this willingness really means. In those countries where a legitimate portion of the parental wealth is assured to children and where these cannot be disinherited—in Germany, in countries with French law, etc.—the children are bound to secure the consent of their parents for marrying. In countries with English law, where the consent of the parents is by no means a legal qualification of marriage, the parents have full liberty to bequeath their wealth to anyone and may disinherit their children at will. Hence it is clear that among classes having any property to bequeath the freedom to marry is not a particle greater in England and America than in France and Germany.

The legal equality of man and woman in marriage is by no means better founded. Their legal inequality inherited from earlier stages of society is not the cause, but the effect of the economic oppression of women. In the ancient communistic household comprising many married couples and their children, the administration of the household entrusted to women was just as much a public function, a socially necessary industry, as the procuring of food by men. In the patriarchal and still more in the monogamous family this was changed. The administration of the household lost its public character. It was no longer a concern of society. It became a private service. The woman became the first servant of the house, excluded from participation in social production. Only by the great industries of our time the access to social production was again opened for women—for proletarian women alone, however. This is done in such a manner that they remain excluded from public production and cannot earn anything, if they fulfill their duties in the private service of the family; or that they are unable to attend to their family duties, if they wish to participate in public industries and earn a living independently. As in the factory, so women are situated in all business departments up to the medical and legal professions. The modern monogamous family is founded on the open or disguised domestic slavery of women, and modern society is a mass composed of molecules in the form of monogamous families. In the great majority of cases the man has to earn a living and to support his family, at least among the possessing classes. He thereby obtains a superior position that has no need of any legal special privilege. In the family, he is the bourgeois, the woman represents the proletariat. In the industrial world, however, the specific character of the economic oppression weighing on the proletariat appears in its sharpest outlines only after all special privileges of the capitalist class are abolished and the full legal equality of both classes is established. A democratic republic does not abolish the distinction between the two classes. On the contrary, it offers the battleground on which this distinction can be fought out. Likewise the peculiar character of man's rule over woman in the modern family, the necessity and the manner of accomplishing the real social equality of the two, will appear in broad daylight only then, when both of them will enjoy complete legal equality. It will then be seen that the emancipation of women is primarily dependent on the re-introduction of the whole female sex into the public industries. To accomplish this, the monogamous family must cease to be the industrial unit of society.

We have, then, three main forms of the family, corresponding in general to the three main stages of human development. For savagery group marriage, for barbarism the pairing family, for civilization monogamy supplemented by adultery and prostitution. Between the pairing family and monogamy, in the higher stage of barbarism, the rule of men over female slaves and polygamy is inserted.

As we proved by our whole argument, the progress visible in this chain of phenomena is connected with the peculiarity of more and more curtailing the sexual freedom of the group marriage for women, but not for men. And group marriage is actually practised by men to this day. What is considered a crime for women and entails grave legal and social consequences for them, is considered honorable for men or in the worst case a slight moral blemish born with pleasure. But the more traditional hetaerism is changed in our day by capitalistic production and conforms to it, the more hetaerism is transformed into undisguised prostitution, the more demoralizing are its effects. And it demoralizes men far more than women. Prostitution does not degrade the whole female sex, but only the luckless women that become its victims, and even those not to the extent generally assumed. But it degrades the character of the entire male world. Especially a long engagement is in nine cases out of ten a perfect training school of adultery.

We are now approaching a social revolution, in which the old economic foundations of monogamy will disappear just as surely as those of its complement, prostitution. Monogamy arose through the concentration of considerable wealth in one hand—a man's hand—and from the endeavor to bequeath this wealth to the children of this man to the exclusion of all others. This necessitated monogamy on the woman's, but not on the man's part. Hence this monogamy of women in no way hindered open or secret polygamy of men. Now, the impending social revolution will reduce this whole care of inheritance to a minimum by changing at least the overwhelming part of permanent and inheritable wealth—the means of production—into social property. Since monogamy was caused by economic conditions, will it disappear when these causes are abolished?

One might reply, not without reason: not only will it not disappear, but it will rather be perfectly realized. For with the transformation of the means of production into collective property, wagelabor will also disappear, and with it the proletariat and the necessity for a certain, statistically ascertainable number of women to surrender for money. Prostitution disappears and monogamy, instead of going out of existence, at last become a reality—for men also.

At all events, the situation will be very much changed for men. But also that of women and of all women, will be considerably altered. With the transformation of the means of production into collective property the monogamous family ceases to be the economic unit of society. The private household changes to a social industry. The care and education of children becomes a public matter. Society cares equally well for all children, legal or illegal. This removes the care about the "consequences" which now forms the essential social factor—moral and economic—hindering a girl to surrender unconditionally to the beloved man. Will not this be sufficient cause for a gradual rise of a more unconventional intercourse of the sexes and a more lenient public opinion regarding virgin honor and female shame? And finally, did we not see that in the modern world monogamy and prostitution, though antitheses, are inseparable and poles of the same social condition? Can prostitution disappear without engulfing at the same time monogomy? . . .

Hence the full freedom of marriage can become general only after all minor economic considerations, that still exert such a powerful influence on the choice of a mate for life, have been removed by the abolition of capitalistic production and of the property relations created by it. Then no other motive will remain but mutual fondness.

Since sexlove is exclusive by its very nature—although this exclusiveness is at present realized for women alone—marriage founded on sexlove must be monogamous. We have seen that Bachofen was perfectly right in regarding the progress from group marriage to monogamy mainly as the work of women. Only the advance from the pairing family to monogamy must be charged to the account of men. This advance inplied, historically, a deterioration in the position of women and a greater opportunity for men to be faithless. Remove the economic considerations that now force women to submit to the customary disloyalty of men, and you will place women on an equal footing with men. All present experiences prove that this will tend much more strongly to make men truly monogamous, than to make women polyandrous.

However, those peculiarities that were stamped upon the face of monogamy by its rise through property relations, will decidedly vanish, namely the supremacy of men and the indissolubility of marriage. The supremacy of man in marriage is simply the consequence of his economic superiority and will fall with the abolition of the latter.

The indissolubility of marriage is partly the consequence of economic conditions, under which monogamy arose, partly tradition from the time where the connection between this economic situation and monogamy, not yet clearly understood, was carried to extremes by religion. To-day, it has been perforated a thousand times. If marriage founded on love is alone moral, then it follows that marriage is moral only as long as love lasts. The duration of an attack of individual sexlove varies considerably according to individual disposition, especially in men. A positive cessation of fondness or its replacement by a new passionate love makes a separation a blessing for both parties and for society. But humanity will be spared the useless wading through the mire of a divorce case.

What we may anticipate about the adjustment of sexual relations after the impending downfall of capitalist production is mainly of a negative nature and mostly confined to elements that will disappear. But what will be added? That will be decided after a new generation has come to maturity: a race of men who never in their lives have had any occasion for buying with money or other economic means of power the surrender of a woman; a race of women who have never had any occasion for surrendering to any man for any other reason but love, or for refusing to surrender to their lover from fear of economic consequences. Once such people are in the world, they will not give a moment's thought to what we today believe should be their course. They will follow their own practice and fashion their own public opinion about the individual practice of every person—only this and nothing more.

Bertrand Russell

It was in the context of a discussion of sexual ethics in *Marriage and Morals* (1929) that Russell raised the question of women's liberation. Russell picked up a theme that Hume sounded almost two hundred years before, that women's virtue is prized because men want to be sure that they have fathered their wives' children. Russell stresses the psychological aspect: a legitimate child expresses a man's ego—his achievements are continued and his immortality insured. Man thereby gives vent to his urge for survival and power, at the same time effecting the physical and mental subjection of women, a subjection virtually unknown during prehistory when it was not yet understood that males had anything to do with producing offspring. Russell believes that Christianity, with its repressive views of sex and marriage, went very far in further degrading the position of women. A great admirer of Mary Wollstonecraft's liberal views on sex, he regrets that women's rights pioneers did not challenge Christian sexual ethics but were themselves rigid moralists. With characteristic wit, Russell points out the logical implications of equality between the sexes, including the abandonment of traditional sexual morality together with its double standard. On the other hand, if the old morality is to be reaffirmed, it will be necessary to educate girls to be stupid and superstitious, institute rigid censorship, keep women in the home, forbid females under fifty from owning motorcars, jail unmarried women who lose their virginity, and castrate all men.

SEXUAL ETHICS AND WOMEN *

As soon as the physiological fact of paternity is recognized, a quite new element enters into paternal feelings, an element which has led almost everywhere to the creation of patriarchal societies. As soon as a father recognizes that the child is, as the Bible says, his "seed," his sentiment towards the child is reinforced by two factors, the love of power and the desire to survive death. The achievements of a man's descendants are in a sense his achievements, and their life is a continuation of his life. Ambition no longer finds its termination at the grave, but can be indefinitely extended through the careers of descendants. Consider, for example, the satisfaction of Abraham when he is informed that his seed shall possess the land of Canaan. In a matrilineal society family ambition would have to be confined to women, and as women do not do the fighting, such family ambition as they may have has less effect than that of men. One must suppose, therefore, that the

* From Bertrand Russell, *Marriage and Morals* (New York: Horace Liveright Inc., 1929).

discovery of fatherhood would make human society more competitive, more energetic, more dynamic and hustling than it had been in
the matrilineal stage. Apart from this effect, which is to some
extent hypothetical, there was a new and all-important reason for
insisting upon the virtue of wives. The purely instinctive element in
jealousy is not nearly so strong as most moderns imagine. The
extreme strength of jealousy in patriarchal societies is due to the
fear of falsification of descent. This may be seen in the fact that a
man who is tired of his wife and passionately devoted to his mistress
will nevertheless be more jealous where his wife is concerned than
when he finds a rival to the affections of his mistress. A legitimate
child is a continuation of a man's ego, and his affection for the child
is a form of egoism. If, on the other hand, the child is not
legitimate, the putative father is tricked into lavishing care upon a
child with whom he has no biological connection. Hence the
discovery of fatherhood led to the subjection of women as the only
means of securing their virtue—a subjection first physical and then
mental. . . .

"Marriage," says Westermarck, "is rooted in family rather than
family in marriage." This view would have been a truism in pre-
Christian times, but since the advent of Christianity it has become
an important proposition needing to be stated with emphasis.
Christianity, and more particularly St. Paul, introduced an entirely
novel view of marriage, that it existed not primarily for the
procreation of children, but to prevent the sin of fornication. . . .

St. Paul's views were emphasized and exaggerated by the early
Church; celibacy was considered holy and men retired into the
desert to wrestle with Satan while he filled their imaginations with
lustful visions. . . .

The Christian ethics inevitably, through the emphasis laid upon
sexual virtue, did a great deal to degrade the position of women.
Since the moralists were men, woman appeared as the temptress; if
they had been women, man would have had this role. Since woman
was the temptress, it was desirable to curtail her opportunities for
leading men into temptation; consequently respectable women were

more and more hedged about with restrictions, while the women who were not respectable, being regarded as sinful, were treated with the utmost contumely. It is only in quite modern times that women have regained the degree of freedom which they enjoyed in the Roman Empire. The patriarchal system, as we saw, did much to enslave women, but a great deal of this was undone just before the rise of Christianity. After Constantine, women's freedom was again curtailed under the pretence of protecting them from sin. It is only with the decay of the notion of sin in modern times that women have begun to regain their freedom. . . .

Let us, however, pause a moment to consider the logical implications of the demand that women should be the equals of men. Men have from time immemorial been allowed in practice, if not in theory, to indulge in illicit sexual relations. It has not been expected of a man that he should be a virgin on entering marriage, and even after marriage, infidelities are not viewed very gravely if they never come to the knowledge of a man's wife and neighbours. The possibility of this system has depended upon prostitution. This institution, however, is one which it is difficult for a modern to defend, and few will suggest that women should acquire the same rights as men through the establishment of a class of male prostitutes for the satisfaction of women who wish, like their husbands, to seem virtuous without being so. Yet it is quite certain that in these days of late marriage only a small percentage of men will remain continent until they can afford to set up house with a woman of their own class. And if unmarried men are not going to be continent, unmarried women, on the ground of equal rights, will claim that they also need not be continent. To the moralists this situation is no doubt regrettable. Every conventional moralist who takes the trouble to think it out will see that he is committed in practice to what is called the double standard, that is to say, the view that sexual virtue is more essential in a woman than in a man. It is all very well to argue that his theoretical ethic demands continence of men also. To this there is the obvious retort that the demand cannot be enforced on the men since it is easy for them to sin secretly. The conventional moralist is thus committed against his will not only to an inequality as between men and women, but also to the view that it is better for a young man to have intercourse with prostitutes than with girls of his own class, in spite of the fact that with the latter, though not with the former, his relations are not mercenary and may be affectionate and altogether delightful. Moralists, of course, do not think out the consequences of advocating a morality which they know will not be obeyed; they think that so long as they do not advocate prostitution they are not responsible for the fact that prostitution is the inevitable outcome of their teaching. This, however, is only another illustration of the well-known fact that the professional moralist in our day is a man of less than average intelligence.

In view of the above circumstances, it is evident that so long as many men for economic reasons find early marriage impossible, while many women cannot marry at all, equality as between men and women demands a relaxation in the traditional standards of feminine virtue. If men are allowed prenuptial intercourse (as in fact they are), women must be allowed it also. And in all countries where there is an excess of women it is an obvious injustice that those women who by arithmetical necessity must remain unmarried should be wholly debarred from sexual experience. Doubtless the pioneers of the women's movement had no such consequences in view but their modern followers perceive them clearly, and whoever opposes these deductions must face the fact that he or she is not in favour of justice to the female sex.

A very clear-cut issue is raised by this question of the new morality versus the old. If the chastity of girls and the faithfulness of wives is no longer to be demanded, it becomes necessary either to have new methods of safeguarding the family or else to acquiesce in the breakup of the family. It may be suggested that the procreation of children should only occur within marriage, and that all extra-marital sexual intercourse should be rendered sterile by the use of contraceptives. In that case husbands might learn to be as tolerant of lovers as Orientals are of eunuchs. The difficulty of such a scheme as yet is that it requires us to place more reliance on the efficacy of contraceptives and the truthfulness of wives than seems rational; this difficulty may, however, be diminished before long. The other alternative compatible with the new morality is the decay of fatherhood as an important social institution, and the taking over of the duties of the father by the State. In particular cases where a man felt sure of his paternity and fond of the child, he might, of course, voluntarily undertake to do what fathers now normally do in the way of financial support for the mother and child; but he would not be obliged to do so by law. Indeed all children would be in the position in which illegitimate children of unknown paternity are now, except that the State, regarding this as the normal case, would take more trouble with their nurture than it does at present.

If, on the other hand, the old morality is to be reestablished, certain things are essential; some of them are already done, but experience shows that these alone are not effective. The first essential is that the education of girls should be such as to make them stupid and superstitious and ignorant; this requisite is already fulfilled in schools over which the churches have any control. The next requisite is a very severe censorship upon all books giving information on sex subjects; this condition also is coming to be fulfilled in England and in America, since the censorship, without change in the law, is being tightened up by the increasing zeal of the police. These conditions, however, since they exist already, are clearly insufficient. The only thing that will suffice is to remove from young women all opportunity of being alone with men: girls must be forbidden to earn their living by work outside the home; they must never be allowed an outing unless accompanied by their mother or an aunt; the regrettable practice of going to dances without a chaperon must be sternly stamped out. It must be illegal for an unmarried woman under fifty to possess a motor-car, and perhaps it would be wise to subject all unmarried women once a month to medical examination by police doctors, and to send to a penitentiary all such as were found to be not virgins. The use of contraceptives must, of course, be eradicated, and it must be illegal in conversation with unmarried women to throw doubt upon the dogma of eternal damnation. These measures, if carried out vigorously for a hundred years or more, may perhaps do something to stem the rising tide of immorality. I think, however, that in order to avoid the risk of certain abuses, it would be necessary that all policemen and all medical men should be castrated. Perhaps it would be wise to carry this policy a step further, in view of the inherent depravity of the male character. I am inclined to think that moralists would be well advised to advocate that all men should be castrated, with the exception of ministers of religion.

It will be seen that there are difficulties and objections whichever course we adopt. If we are to allow the new morality to take its course, it is bound to go further than it has done and to raise difficulties hardly as yet appreciated. If, on the other hand, we attempt in the modern world to enforce restrictions which were possible in a former age, we are led into an impossible stringency of regulation, against which human nature would soon rebel. This is so clear that, whatever the dangers or difficulties, we must be content to let the world go forward rather than back. For this purpose we shall need a genuinely new morality. I mean by this that obligations and duties will still have to be recognized, though they may be very different from the obligations and duties recognized in the past. So long as all the moralists content themselves with preaching a return to a system which is as dead as the Dodo, they can do nothing whatever to moralize the new freedom or to point out the new duties which it brings with it. I do not think that the new system any more than the old should involve an unbridled yielding to impulse, but I think the occasions for restraining impulse and the motives for doing so will have to be different from what they have been in the past. In fact, the whole problem of sexual morality needs thinking out afresh.

Sigmund Freud

Freud's theories on women have had a tremendous impact in the twentieth century. His view that anatomy is destiny is still being expounded by prominent psychologists, though in altered forms. Freud's theories center on a concept of his own invention: "penis envy." He held that during the phallic stage of childhood, a girl's interest turns to her clitoris, but when she sees male genitals the male organ appears superior to her own, the castration complex sets in, and the girl develops an envious desire to be a boy. Concurrent with this, the girl's attachment to her mother suffers a serious reversal, since she concludes that her mother is responsible for her castration, that she has been punished for some unknown crime. This in turn leads to the Oedipus complex, attachment to her father. Acceptance of femininity entails reconciliation with her castration and even when the reality is intellectually accepted, the wish to be a man continues in the unconscious, expressing itself in various sublimated forms. Indeed, Freud argues, a female's development subsequent to discovery of castration may lead to neurosis, or to a masculinity complex, in which case she rebels against castration and continues to identify herself as male, to behave as though she were a man (for example, by pursuing intellectual and professional goals). The following piece, "Femininity," was published in 1933 and brings together Freud's previous papers on the subject.

WOMAN AS CASTRATED MAN *

To-day's lecture, too, should have no place in an introduction; but it may serve to give you an example of a detailed piece of analytic work, and I can say two things to recommend it. It brings forward nothing but observed facts, almost without any speculative additions, and it deals with a subject which has a claim on your interest second almost to no other. Throughout history people have knocked their heads against the riddle of the nature of femininity—

> Häupter in Hieroglyphenmützen,
> Häupter in Turban und schwarzem Barett,
> Perückenhäupter und tausend andre
> Arme, schwitzende Menschenhäupter. . . .[1]

---

* From Sigmund Freud, *New Introductory Lectures on Psychoanalysis,* trans. James Strachey (New York: W. W. Norton and Company, Inc., 1965), Lecture 33.

[1] Heads in hieroglyphic bonnets,
Heads in turbans and black birettas,
Heads in wigs and thousand other
Wretched, sweating heads of humans. . . .
  (Heine, *Nordsee* [Second Cycle, VII, "Fragen"].)

Nor will *you* have escaped worrying over this problem—those of
you who are men; to those of you who are women this will not
apply—you are yourselves the problem. When you meet a human
being, the first distinction you make is "male or female?" and you
are accustomed to make the distinction with unhesitating certainty.
Anatomical science shares your certainty at one point and not much
further. The male sexual product, the spermatozoon, and its vehicle
are male; the ovum and the organism that harbours it are female. In
both sexes organs have been formed which serve exclusively for the
sexual functions; they were probably developed from the same
[innate] disposition into two different forms. Besides this, in both
sexes the other organs, the bodily shapes and tissues, show the
influence of the individual's sex, but this is inconstant and its
amount variable; these are what are known as the secondary sexual
characters. Science next tells you something that runs counter to
your expectations and is probably calculated to confuse your
feelings. It draws your attention to the fact that portions of the
male sexual apparatus also appear in women's bodies, though in an
atrophied state, and vice versa in the alternative case. It regards
their occurrence as indications of *bisexuality, as though an individual*
is not a man or a woman but always both—merely a certain amount
more the one than the other. You will then be asked to make
yourselves familiar with the idea that the proportion in which
masculine and feminine are mixed in an individual is subject to quite
considerable fluctuations. Since, however, apart from the very rarest
cases, only one kind of sexual product—ova or semen—is nevertheless present in one person, you are bound to have doubts as to the
decisive significance of those elements and must conclude that what
constitutes masculinity or femininity is an unknown characteristic
which anatomy cannot lay hold of.

Can psychology do so perhaps? We are accustomed to employ
"masculine" and "feminine" as mental qualities as well, and have in
the same way transferred the notion of bisexuality to mental life.
Thus we speak of a person, whether male or female, as behaving in

a masculine way in one connection and in a feminine way in another. But you will soon perceive that this is only giving way to anatomy or to convention. You cannot give the concepts of "masculine" and "feminine" *any* new connotation. The distinction is not a psychological one; when you say "masculine," you usually mean "active," and when you say "feminine," you usually mean "passive." Now it is true that a relation of the kind exists. The male sex-cell is actively mobile and searches out the female one, and the latter, the ovum, is immobile and waits passively. This behaviour of the elementary sexual organisms is indeed a model for the conduct of sexual individuals during intercourse. The male pursues the female for the purpose of sexual union, seizes hold of her and penetrates into her. But by this you have precisely reduced the characteristic of masculinity to the factor of aggressiveness so far as psychology is concerned. You may well doubt whether you have gained any real advantage from this when you reflect that in some classes of animals the females are the stronger and more aggressive and the male is active only in the single act of sexual union. This is so, for instance, with the spiders. Even the functions of rearing and caring for the young, which strike us as feminine *par excellence,* are not invariably attached to the female sex in animals. In quite high species we find that the sexes share the task of caring for the young between them or even that the male alone devotes himself to it. Even in the sphere of human sexual life you soon see how inadequate it is to make masculine behaviour coincide with activity and feminine with passivity. A mother is active in every sense towards her child; the act of lactation itself may equally be described as the mother suckling the baby or as her being sucked by it. The further you go from the narrow sexual sphere the more obvious will the "error of superimposition" become. Women can display great activity in various directions, men are not able to live in company with their own kind unless they develop a large amount of passive adaptability. If you now tell me that these facts go to prove precisely that both men and women are bisexual in the psychological sense, I shall conclude that you have decided in your own minds to make "active" coincide with "masculine" and "passive" with "feminine." But I advise you against it. It seems to me to serve no useful purpose and adds nothing to our knowledge.

One might consider characterizing femininity psychologically as giving preference to passive aims. This is not, of course, the same thing as passivity; to achieve a passive aim may call for a large amount of activity. It is perhaps the case that in a woman, on the basis of her share in the sexual function, a preference for passive behaviour and passive aims is carried over into her life to a greater or lesser extent, in proportion to the limits, restricted or far-reaching, within which her sexual life thus serves as a model. But we must beware in this of underestimating the influence of social customs, which similarly force women into passive situations. All this is still far from being cleared up. There is one particularly constant relation between femininity and instinctual life which we do not want to overlook. The suppression of women's aggressiveness which is prescribed for them constitutionally and imposed on them socially favours the development of powerful masochistic impulses, which succeed, as we know, in binding erotically the destructive trends which have been diverted inwards. Thus masochism, as people say, is truly feminine. But if, as happens so often, you meet with masochism in men, what is left to you but to say that these men exhibit very plain feminine traits?

And now you are already prepared to hear that psychology too is unable to solve the riddle of femininity. The explanation must no doubt come from elsewhere, and cannot come till we have learnt how in general the differentiation of living organisms into two sexes came about. We know nothing about it, yet the existence of two sexes is a most striking characteristic of organic life which distinguishes it sharply from inanimate nature. However, we find enough to study in those human individuals who, through the possession of female genitals, are characterized as manifestly or predominantly feminine. In conformity with its peculiar nature, psycho-analysis does not try to describe what a woman is—that would be a task it could scarcely perform—but sets about enquiring how she comes into being, how a woman develops out of a child with a bisexual disposition. In recent times we have begun to learn a little about this, thanks to the circumstance that several of our excellent women colleagues in analysis have begun to work at the question. The discussion of this has gained special attractiveness from the distinction between the sexes. For the ladies, whenever some comparison seemed to turn out unfavourable to their sex, were able to utter a suspicion that we, the male analysts, had been unable to overcome certain deeply-rooted prejudices against what was feminine, and that this was being paid for in the partiality of our researches. We, on the other hand, standing on the ground of bisexuality, had no difficulty in avoiding impoliteness. We had only to say: "This doesn't apply to *you*. You're the exception; on this point you're more masculine than feminine."

We approach the investigation of the sexual development of women with two expectations. The first is that here once more the constitution will not adapt itself to its function without a struggle. The second is that the decisive turning-points will already have been prepared for or completed before puberty. Both expectations are promptly confirmed. Furthermore, a comparison with what happens with boys tells us that the development of a little girl into a normal woman is more difficult and more complicated, since it includes two extra tasks, to which there is nothing corresponding in the development of a man. Let us follow the parallel lines from their beginning. Undoubtedly the material is different to start with in boys and girls: it did not need psycho-analysis to establish that. The difference in the structure of the genitals is accompanied by other bodily differences which are too well known to call for mention. Differences emerge too in the instinctual disposition which give a glimpse of the later nature of women. A little girl is as a rule less aggressive, defiant and self-sufficient; she seems to have a greater need for being shown affection and on that account to be more dependent and pliant. It is probably only as a result of this pliancy that she can be taught more easily and quicker to control her excretions: urine and faeces are the first gifts that children make to those who look after them, and controlling them is the first concession to which the instinctual life of children can be induced. One gets an impression, too, that little girls are more intelligent and livelier than boys of the same age; they go out more to meet the external world and at the same time form stronger object-cathexes. I cannot say whether this lead in development has been confirmed by exact observations, but in any case there is no question that girls cannot be described as intellectually backward. These sexual differences are not, however, of great consequence: they can be outweighed by individual variations. For our immediate purposes they can be disregarded.

Both sexes seem to pass through the early phases of libidinal development in the same manner. It might have been expected that in girls there would already have been some lag in aggressiveness in the sadistic-anal phase, but such is not the case. Analysis of children's play has shown our women analysts that the aggressive impulses of little girls leave nothing to be desired in the way of abundance and violence. With their entry into the phallic phase the differences between the sexes are completely eclipsed by their agreements. We are now obliged to recognize that the little girl is a little man. In boys, as we know, this phase is marked by the fact that they have learnt how to derive pleasurable sensations from their small penis and connect its excited state with their ideas of sexual intercourse. Little girls do the same thing with their still smaller clitoris. It seems that with them all their masturbatory acts are carried out on this penis-equivalent, and that the truly feminine vagina is still undiscovered by both sexes. It is true that there are a few isolated reports of early vaginal sensations as well, but it could not be easy to distinguish these from sensations in the anus or vestibulum; in any case they cannot play a great part. We are entitled to keep our view that in the phallic phase of girls the clitoris is the leading erotogenic zone. But it is not, of course, going to remain so. With the change to femininity the clitoris should wholly or in part hand over its sensitivity, and at the same time its importance, to the vagina. This would be one of the two tasks which a woman has to perform in the course of her development, whereas the more fortunate man has only to continue at the time of his sexual maturity the activity that he has previously carried out at the period of the early efflorescence of his sexuality.

We shall return to the part played by the clitoris; let us now turn to the second task with which a girl's development is burdened. A boy's mother is the first object of his love, and she remains so too during the formation of his Oedipus complex and, in essence, all through his life. For a girl too her first object must be her mother (and the figures of wet-nurses and foster-mothers that merge into her). The first object-cathexes occur in attachment to the satisfaction of the major and simple vital needs, and the circumstances of the care of children are the same for both sexes. But in the Oedipus situation the girl's father has become her love-object, and we expect that in the normal course of development she will find her way from this paternal object to her final choice of an object. In the course of time, therefore, a girl has to change her erotogenic zone and her object—both of which a boy retains. The question then arises of how this happens: in particular, how does a girl pass from her mother to an attachment to her father? or, in other words, how does she pass from her masculine phase to the feminine one to which she is biologically destined?

It would be a solution of ideal simplicity if we could suppose that from a particular age onwards the elementary influence of the mutual attraction between the sexes makes itself felt and impels the small woman towards men, while the same law allows the boy to continue with his mother. We might suppose in addition that in this the children are following the pointer given them by the sexual preference of their parents. But we are not going to find things so easy; we scarcely know whether we are to believe seriously in the power of which poets talk so much and with such enthusiasm but which cannot be further dissected analytically. We have found an answer of quite another sort by means of laborious investigations, the material for which at least was easy to arrive at. For you must know that the number of women who remain till a late age tenderly dependent on a paternal object, or indeed on their real father, is very great. We have established some surprising facts about these women with an intense attachment of long duration to their father. We knew, of course, that there had been a preliminary stage of attachment to the mother, but we did not know that it could be so rich in content and so long-lasting, and could leave behind so many opportunities for fixations and dispositions. During this time the girl's father is only a troublesome rival; in some cases the attachment to her mother lasts beyond the fourth year of life. Almost everything that we find later in her relation to her father was already present in this earlier attachment and has been transferred subsequently on to her father. In short, we get an impression that we cannot understand women unless we appreciate this phase of their pre-Oedipus attachment to their mother.

We shall be glad, then, to know the nature of the girl's libidinal relations to her mother. The answer is that they are of very many different kinds. Since they persist through all three phases of infantile sexuality, they also take on the characteristics of the different phases and express themselves by oral, sadistic-anal and phallic wishes. These wishes represent active as well as passive impulses; if we relate them to the differentiation of the sexes which is to appear later—though we should avoid doing so as far as possible—we may call them masculine and feminine. Besides this, they are completely ambivalent, both affectionate and of a hostile and aggressive nature. The later often only come to light after being changed into anxiety ideas. It is not always easy to point to a formulation of these early sexual wishes; what is most clearly expressed is a wish to get the mother with child and the corresponding wish to bear her child—both belonging to the phallic period and sufficiently surprising, but established beyond doubt by analytic observation. The attractiveness of these investigations lies in the surprising detailed findings which they bring us. Thus, for instance, we discover the fear of being murdered or poisoned, which may later form the core of a paranoic illness, already present in this pre-Oedipus period, in relation to the mother. Or another case: you will recall an interesting episode in the history of analytic research which caused me many distressing hours. In the period in which the main interest was directed to discovering infantile sexual traumas, almost all my women patients told me that they had been seduced by their father. I was driven to recognize in the end that these reports were untrue and so came to understand that hysterical symptoms are derived from phantasies and not from real occurrences. It was only later that I was able to recognize in this phantasy of being seduced by the father the expression of the typical Oedipus complex in women. And now we find the phantasy of seduction once more in the pre-Oedipus prehistory of girls; but the seducer is regularly the mother. Here, however, the phantasy touches the ground of reality, for it was really the mother who by her activities over the child's bodily hygiene inevitably stimulated, and perhaps even roused for the first time, pleasurable sensations in her genitals.

I have no doubt you are ready to suspect that this portrayal of the abundance and strength of a little girl's sexual relations with her mother is very much overdrawn. After all, one has opportunities of seeing little girls and notices nothing of the sort. But the objection is not to the point. Enough can be seen in the children if one knows how to look. And besides, you should consider how little of its sexual wishes a child can bring to preconscious expression or communicate at all. Accordingly we are only within our rights if we study the residues and consequences of this emotional world in retrospect, in people in whom these processes of development had attained a specially clear and even excessive degree of expansion. Pathology has always done us the service of making discernible by isolation and exaggeration conditions which would remain concealed in a normal state. And since our investigations have been carried out on people who were by no means seriously abnormal, I think we should regard their outcome as deserving belief.

We will now turn our interest on to the single question of what it is that brings this powerful attachment of the girl to her mother to an end. This, as we know, is its usual fate: it is destined to make room for an attachment to her father. Here we come upon a fact which is a pointer to our further advance. This step in development does not involve only a simple change of object. The turning away from the mother is accompanied by hostility; the attachment to the mother ends in hate. A hate of that kind may become very striking and last all through life; it may be carefully overcompensated later on; as a rule one part of it is overcome while another part persists. Events of later years naturally influence this greatly. We will restrict ourselves, however, to studying it at the time at which the girl turns to her father and to enquiring into the motives for it. We are then given a long list of accusations and grievances against the mother which are supposed to justify the child's hostile feelings; they are of varying validity which we shall not fail to examine. A number of them are obvious rationalizations and the true sources of enmity remain to be found. I hope you will be interested if on this occasion I take you through all the details of a psycho-analytic investigation.

The reproach against the mother which goes back furthest is that she gave the child too little milk—which is construed against her as lack of love. Now there is some justification for this reproach in our families. Mothers often have insufficient nourishment to give their children and are content to suckle them for a few months, for half or three-quarters of a year. Among primitive peoples children are fed at their mother's breast for two or three years. The figure of the wet-nurse who suckles the child is as a rule merged into the mother; when this has not happened, the reproach is turned into another one—that the nurse, who fed the child so willingly, was sent away by the mother too early. But whatever the true state of affairs may have been, it is impossible that the child's reproach can be justified as often as it is met with. It seems, rather, that the child's avidity for its earliest nourishment is altogether insatiable, that it never gets over the pain of losing its mother's breast. I should not be surprised if the analysis of a primitive child, who could still suck at its mother's breast when it was already able to run about and talk, were to bring the same reproach to light. The fear of being poisoned is also probably connected with the withdrawal of the breast. Poison is nourishment that makes one ill. Perhaps children trace back their early illnesses too to this frustration. A fair amount of intellectual education is a prerequisite for believing in chance; primitive people and uneducated ones, and no doubt children as well, are able to assign a ground for everything that happens. Perhaps originally it was a reason on animistic lines. Even to-day in some strata of our population no one can die without having been killed by someone else—preferably by the doctor. And the regular reaction of a neurotic to the death of someone closely connected with him is to put the blame on himself for having caused the death.

The next accusation against the child's mother flares up when the next baby appears in the nursery. If possible the connection with oral frustration is preserved: the mother could not or would not give the child any more milk because she needed the nourishment for the new arrival. In cases in which the two children are so close in age that lactation is prejudiced by the second pregnancy, this reproach acquires a real basis, and it is a remarkable fact that a child, even with an age difference of only 11 months, is not too young to take notice of what is happening. But what the child grudges the unwanted intruder and rival is not only the suckling but all the other signs of maternal care. It feels that it has been dethroned, despoiled, prejudiced in its rights; it casts a jealous hatred upon the new baby and develops a grievance against the faithless mother which often finds expression in a disagreeable change in its behaviour. It becomes "naughty," perhaps, irritable and disobedient and goes back on the advances it has made towards controlling its excretions. All of this has been very long familiar and is accepted as self-evident; but we rarely form a correct idea of the strength of these jealous impulses, of the tenacity with which they persist and of the magnitude of their influence on later development. Especially as this jealousy is constantly receiving fresh nourishment in the later years of childhood and the whole shock is repeated with the birth of each new brother or sister. Nor does it make much difference if the child happens to remain the mother's preferred favourite. A child's demands for love are immoderate, they make exclusive claims and tolerate no sharing.

An abundant source of a child's hostility to its mother is provided by its multifarious sexual wishes, which alter according to the phase of the libido and which cannot for the most part be satisfied. The strongest of these frustrations occur at the phallic period, if the mother forbids pleasurable activity with the genitals—often with severe threats and every sign of displeasure—activity to which, after all, she herself had introduced the child. One would think these were reasons enough to account for a girl's turning away from her mother. One would judge, if so, that the estrangement follows inevitably from the nature of children's sexuality, from the immoderate character of their demand for love and the impossibility of fullfilling their sexual wishes. It might be thought indeed that this first love-relation of the child's is doomed to dissolution for the very reason that it is the first, for these early object-cathexes are regularly ambivalent to a high degree. A powerful tendency to aggressiveness is always present beside a powerful love, and the more passionately a child loves its object the more sensitive does it become to disappointments and frustrations from that object; and in the end the love must succumb to the accumulated hostility. Or the idea that there is an original ambivalence such as this in erotic cathexes may be rejected, and it may be pointed out that it is the special nature of the mother-child relation that leads, with equal inevitability, to the destruction of the child's love; for even the mildest upbringing cannot avoid using compulsion and introducing restrictions, and any such intervention in the child's liberty must provoke as a reaction an inclination to rebelliousness and aggressiveness. A discussion of these possibilities might, I think, be most interesting; but an objection suddenly emerges which forces our interest in another direction. All these factors—the slights, the disappointments in love, the jealousy, the seduction followed by prohibition—are, after all, also in operation in the relation of a *boy* to his mother and are yet unable to alienate him from the maternal object. Unless we can find something that is specific for girls and is not present or not in the same way present in boys, we shall not have explained the termination of the attachment of girls to their mother.

I believe we have found this specific factor, and indeed where we expected to find it, even though in a surprising form. Where we expected to find it, I say, for it lies in the castration complex. After all, the anatomical distinction [between the sexes] must express itself in psychical consequences. It was, however, a surprise to learn from analyses that girls hold their mother responsible for their lack of a penis and do not forgive her for their being thus put at a disadvantage.

As you hear, then, we ascribe a castration complex to women as well. And for good reasons, though its content cannot be the same as with boys. In the latter the castration complex arises after they have learnt from the sight of the female genitals that the organ which they value so highly need not necessarily accompany the body. At this the boy recalls to mind the threats he brought on himself by his doings with that organ, he begins to give credence to them and falls under the influence of fear of castration, which will be the most powerful motive force in his subsequent development. The castration complex of girls is also started by the sight of the genitals of the other sex. They at once notice the difference and, it must be admitted, its significance too. They feel seriously wronged, often declare that they want to "have something like it too," and fall a victim to "envy for the penis," which will leave ineradicable traces on their development and the formation of their character and which will not be surmounted in even the most favourable cases without a severe expenditure of psychical energy. The girl's recognition of the fact of her being without a penis does not by any means imply that she submits to the fact easily. On the contrary, she continues to hold on for a long time to the wish to get something like it herself and she believes in that possibility for improbably long years; and analysis can show that, at a period when knowledge of reality has long since rejected the fulfillment of the wish as unattainable, it persists in the unconscious and retains a considerable cathexis of energy. The wish to get the longed-for penis eventually in spite of everything may contribute to the motives that drive a mature woman to analysis, and what she may reasonably expect from analysis—a capacity, for instance, to carry on an intellectual profession—may often be recognized as a sublimated modification of this repressed wish.

One cannot very well doubt the importance of envy for the penis. You may take it as an instance of male injustice if I assert that envy and jealousy play an even greater part in the mental life of women than of men. It is not that I think these characteristics are absent in men or that I think they have no other roots in women than envy for the penis; but I am inclined to attribute their greater amount in women to this latter influence. Some analysts, however, have shown an inclination to depreciate the importance of this first instalment of penis-envy in the phallic phase. They are of opinion that what we find of this attitude in women is in the main a secondary structure which has come about on the occasion of later conflicts by regression to this early infantile impulse. This, however, is a general problem of depth psychology. In many pathological—or even unusual—instinctual attitudes (for instance, in all sexual perversions) the question arises of how much of their strength is to be attributed to early infantile fixations and how much to the influence of later experiences and developments. In such cases it is almost always a matter of complemental series such as we put forward in our discussion of the aetiology of the neuroses. Both factors play a part in varying amounts in the causation; a less on the one side is balanced by a more on the other. The infantile factor sets the pattern in all cases but does not always determine the issue, though it often does. Precisely in the case of penis-envy I should argue decidedly in favour of the preponderance of the infantile factor.

The discovery that she is castrated is a turning-point in a girl's growth. Three possible lines of development start from it: one leads to sexual inhibition or to neurosis, the second to change of character in the sense of a masculinity complex, the third, finally, to normal femininity. We have learnt a fair amount, though not everything, about all three.

The essential content of the first is as follows: the little girl has hitherto lived in a masculine way, has been able to get pleasure by the excitation of her clitoris and has brought this activity into relation with her sexual wishes directed towards her mother, which are often active ones; now, owing to the influence of her penis-envy, she loses her enjoyment in her phallic sexuality. Her self-love is mortified by the comparison with the boy's far superior equipment and in consequence she renounces her masturbatory satisfaction from her clitoris, repudiates her love for her mother and at the same time not infrequently represses a good part of her sexual trends in general. No doubt her turning away from her mother does not occur all at once, for to begin with the girl regards her castration as an individual misfortune, and only gradually extends it to other females and finally to her mother as well. Her love was directed to her *phallic* mother; with the discovery that her mother is castrated it becomes possible to drop her as an object, so that the motives for hostility, which have long been accumulating, gain the upper hand. This means, therefore, that as a result of the discovery of women's lack of a penis they are debased in value for girls just as they are for boys and later perhaps for men.

You all know the immense aetiological importance attributed by our neurotic patients to their masturbation. They make it responsible for all their troubles and we have the greatest difficulty in persuading them that they are mistaken. In fact, however, we ought to admit to them that they are right, for masturbation is the executive agent of infantile sexuality, from the faulty development of which they are indeed suffering. But what neurotics mostly blame is the masturbation of the period of puberty; they have mostly forgotten that of early infancy, which is what is really in question. I wish I might have an opportunity some time of explaining to you at length how important all the factual details of early masturbation become for the individual's subsequent neurosis or character: whether or not it was discovered, how the parents struggled against it or permitted it, or whether he succeeded in suppressing it himself. All of this leaves permanent traces on his development. But I am on the whole glad that I need not do this. It would be a hard and tedious task and at the end of it you would put me in an embarrassing situation by quite certainly asking me to give you some practical advice as to how a parent or educator should deal with the masturbation of small children. From the development of girls, which is what my present lecture is concerned with, I can give you the example of a child herself trying to get free from masturbating. She does not always succeed in this. If envy for the penis has provoked a powerful impulse against clitoridal masturbation but this nevertheless refuses to give way, a violent struggle for liberation ensues in which the girl, as it were, herself takes over the role of her deposed mother and gives expression to her entire dissatisfaction with her inferior clitoris in her efforts against obtaining satisfaction from it. Many years later, when her masturbatory activity has long since been suppressed, an interest still persists which we must interpret as a defence against a temptation that is still dreaded. It manifests itself in the emergence of sympathy for those to whom similar difficulties are attributed, it plays a part as a motive in contracting a marriage and, indeed, it may determine the choice of a husband or lover. Disposing of early infantile masturbation is truly no easy or indifferent business.

Along with the abandonment of clitoridal masturbation a certain amount of activity is renounced. Passivity now has the upper hand, and the girl's turning to her father is accomplished principally with the help of passive instinctual impulses. You can see that a wave of development like this, which clears the phallic activity out of the way, smooths the ground for femininity. If too much is not lost in the course of it through repression, this femininity may turn out to be normal. The wish with which the girl turns to her father is no doubt originally the wish for the penis which her mother has refused her and which she now expects from her father. The feminine situation is only established, however, if the wish for a penis is replaced by one for a baby, if, that is, a baby takes the place of a penis in accordance with an ancient symbolic equivalence. It has not escaped us that the girl has wished for a baby earlier, in the undisturbed phallic phase: that, of course, was the meaning of her playing with dolls. But that play was not in fact an expression of her femininity; it served as an identification with her mother with the intention of substituting activity for passivity. *She* was playing the part of her mother and the doll was herself: now she could do with the baby everything that her mother used to do with her. Not until the emergence of the wish for a penis does the doll-baby become a baby from the girl's father, and thereafter the aim of the most powerful feminine wish. Her happiness is great if later on this wish for a baby finds fulfillment in reality, and quite especially so if the baby is a little boy who brings the longed-for penis with him. Often enough in her combined picture of "a baby from her father" the emphasis is laid on the baby and her father left unstressed. In this way the ancient masculine wish for the possession of a penis is still faintly visible through the femininity now achieved. But perhaps we ought rather to recognize this wish for a penis as being *par excellence* a feminine one.

With the transference of the wish for a penis-baby on her father, the girl has entered the situation of the Oedipus complex. Her hostility to her mother, which did not need to be freshly created, is now greatly intensified, for she becomes the girl's rival, who receives from her father everything that she desires from him. For a long time the girl's Oedipus complex concealed her pre-Oedipus attachment to her mother from our view, though it is nevertheless so important and leaves such lasting fixations behind it. For girls the Oedipus situation is the outcome of a long and difficult development; it is a kind of preliminary solution, a position of rest which is not soon abandoned, especially as the beginning of the latency period is not far distant. And we are now struck by a difference between the two sexes, which is probably momentous, in regard to the relation of the Oedipus complex to the castration complex. In a boy the Oedipus complex, in which he desires his mother and would like to get rid of his father as being a rival, develops naturally from the phase of his phallic sexuality. The threat of castration compels him, however, to give up that attitude. Under the impression of the danger of losing his penis, the Oedipus complex is abandoned, repressed and, in the most normal cases, entirely destroyed, and a severe super-ego is set up as its heir. What happens with a girl is almost the opposite. The castration complex prepares for the Oedipus complex instead of destroying it; the girl is driven out of her attachment to her mother through the influence of her envy for the penis and she enters the Oedipus situation as though into a haven of refuge. In the absence of fear of castration the chief motive is lacking which leads boys to surmount the Oedipus complex. Girls remain in it for an indeterminate length of time; they demolish it late and, even so, incompletely. In these circumstances the formation of the super-ego must suffer; it cannot attain the strength and independence which gives it its cultural significance, and feminists are not pleased when we point out to them the effects of this factor upon the average feminine character.

To go back a little. We mentioned as the second possible reaction to the discovery of female castration the development of a powerful masculinity complex. By this we mean that the girl refuses, as it were, to recognize the unwelcome fact and, defiantly rebellious, even exaggerates her previous masculinity, clings to her clitoridal activity and takes refuge in an identification with her phallic mother or her father. What can it be that decides in favour of this outcome? We can only suppose that it is a constitutional factor, a greater amount of activity, such as is ordinarily characteristic of a male. However that may be, the essence of this process is that at this point in the development the wave of passivity is avoided which opens the way to the turn towards femininity. The extreme achievement of such a masculinity complex would appear to be the influencing of the choice of an object in the sense of manifest homosexuality. Analytic experience teaches us, to be sure, that female homosexuality is seldom or never a direct continuation of infantile masculinity. Even for a girl of this kind it seems necessary that she should take her father as an object for some time and enter the Oedipus situation. But afterwards, as a result of her inevitable disappointments from her father, she is driven to regress into her early masculinity complex. The significance of these disappointments must not be exaggerated; a girl who is destined to become feminine is not spared them, though they do not have the same effect. The predominance of the constitutional factor seems indisputable; but the two phases in the development of female homosexuality are well mirrored in the practices of homosexuals, who play the parts of mother and baby with each other as often and as clearly as those of husband and wife.

What I have been telling you here may be described as the prehistory of women. It is a product of the very last few years and may have been of interest to you as an example of detailed analytic work. Since its subject is woman, I will venture on this occasion to mention by name a few of the women who have made valuable contributions to this investigation. Dr. Ruth Mack Brunswick [1928] was the first to describe a case of neurosis which went back to a fixation in the pre-Oedipus stage and had never reached the Oedipus situation at all. The case took the form of jealous paranoia and proved accessible to therapy. Dr. Jeanne Lample-de Groot [1927] has established the incredible phallic activity of girls towards their mother by some assured observations, and Dr. Helene Deutsch [1932] has shown that the erotic actions of homosexual women reproduce the relations between mother and baby.

It is not my intention to pursue the further behaviour of femininity through puberty to the period of maturity. Our knowledge, moreover, would be insufficient for the purpose. But I will bring a few features together in what follows. Taking its prehistory as a starting-point, I will only emphasize here that the development of feminity remains exposed to disturbance by the residual phenomena of the early masculine period. Regressions to the fixations of the pre-Oedipus phases very frequently occur; in the course of some women's lives there is a repeated alternation between periods in which masculinity or femininity gains the upper hand. Some portion of what we men call "the enigma of women" may perhaps be derived from this expression of bisexuality in women's lives. But another question seems to have become ripe for judgement in the course of these researches. We have called the motive force of sexual life "the libido." Sexual life is dominated by the polarity of masculine-feminine; thus the notion suggests itself of considering the relation of the libido to this antithesis. It would not be surprising if it were to turn out that each sexuality had its own special libido appropriated to it, so that one sort of libido would pursue the aims of a masculine sexual life and another sort those of a feminine one. But nothing of the kind is true. There is only one libido, which serves both the masculine and the feminine sexual functions. To it itself we cannot assign any sex; if, following the conventional equation of activity and masculinity, we are inclined to describe it as masculine, we must not forget that it also covers trends with a passive aim. Nevertheless the juxtaposition "feminine libido" is without any justification. Furthermore, it is our impression that more constraint has been applied to the libido when it is pressed into the service of the feminine function, and that—to speak teleologically—Nature takes less careful account of its [that function's] demands than in the case of masculinity. And the reason for this may lie—thinking once again teleologically—in the fact that the accomplishment of the aim of biology has been entrusted to the aggressiveness of men and has been made to some extent independent of women's consent.

The sexual frigidity of women, the frequency of which appears to confirm this disregard, is a phenomenon that is still insufficiently understood. Sometimes it is psychogenic and in that case accessible to influence; but in other cases it suggests the hypothesis of its being constitutionally determined and even of there being a contributory anatomical factor.

I have promised to tell you of a few more psychical peculiarities of mature feminity, as we come across them in analytic observation.

We do not lay claim to more than an average validity for these assertions; nor is it always easy to distinguish what should be ascribed to the influence of the sexual function and what to social breeding. Thus, we attribute a larger amount of narcissism to femininity, which also affects women's choice of object, so that to be loved is a stronger need for them than to love. The effect of penis-envy has a share, further, in the physical vanity of women, since they are bound to value their charms more highly as a late compensation for their original sexual inferiority. Shame, which is considered to be a feminine characteristic *par excellence* but is far more a matter of convention than might be supposed, has as its purpose, we believe, concealment of genital deficiency. We are not forgetting that at a later time shame takes on other functions. It seems that women have made few contributions to the discoveries and inventions in the history of civilization; there is, however, one technique which they may have invented—that of plaiting and weaving. If that is so, we should be tempted to guess the unconscious motive for the achievement. Nature herself would seem to have given the model which this achievement imitates by causing the growth at maturity of the pubic hair that conceals the genitals. The step that remained to be taken lay in making the threads adhere to one another, while on the body they stick into the skin and are only matted together. If you reject this idea as fantastic and regard my belief in the influence of lack of a penis on the configuration of femininity as an *idée fixe,* I am of course defenceless.

The determinants of women's choice of an object are often made unrecognizable by social conditions. Where the choice is able to show itself freely, it is often made in accordance with the narcissistic ideal of the man whom the girl had wished to become. If the girl has remained in her attachment to her father—that is, in the Oedipus complex—her choice is made according to the paternal type. Since, when she turned from her mother to her father, the hostility of her ambivalent relation remained with her mother, a choice of this kind should guarantee a happy marriage. But very often the outcome is of a kind that presents a general threat to such a settlement of the conflict due to ambivalence. The hostility that has been left behind follows in the train of the positive attachment and spreads over on the new object. The woman's husband, who to begin with inherited from her father, becomes after a time her mother's heir as well. So it may easily happen that the second half of a woman's life may be filled by the struggle against her husband, just as the shorter first half was filled by her rebellion against her mother. When this reaction has been lived through, a second marriage may easily turn out very much more satisfying. Another alteration in a woman's nature, for which lovers are unprepared, may occur in a marriage after the first child is born. Under the influence of a woman's becoming a mother herself, an identification with her own mother may be revived, against which she had striven up till the time of her marriage, and this may attract all the available libido to itself, so that the compulsion to repeat reproduces an unhappy marriage between her parents. The difference in a mother's reaction to the birth of a son or a daughter shows that the old factor of lack of a penis has even now not lost its strength. A mother is only brought unlimited satisfaction by her relation to a son; this is altogether the most perfect, the most free from ambivalence of all human relationships. A mother can transfer to her son the ambition which she has been obliged to suppress in herself, and she can expect from him the satisfaction of all that has been left over in her of her masculinity complex. Even a marriage is not made secure until the wife has succeeded in making her husband her child as well and in acting as a mother to him.

A woman's identification with her mother allows us to distinguish two strata: the pre-Oedipus one which rests on her affectionate attachment to her mother and takes her as a model, and the later one from the Oedipus complex which seeks to get rid of her mother and take her place with her father. We are no doubt justified in saying that much of both of them is left over for the future and that neither of them is adequately surmounted in the course of development. But the phase of the affectionate pre-Oedipus attachment is the decisive one for a woman's future:

during it preparations are made for the acquisition of the characteristics with which she will later fulfil her role in the sexual function and perform her invaluable social tasks. It is in this identification too that she acquires her attractiveness to a man, whose Oedipus attachment to his mother it kindles into passion. How often it happens, however, that it is only his son who obtains what he himself aspired to! One gets an impression that a man's love and a woman's are a phase apart psychologically.

The fact that women must be regarded as having little sense of justice is no doubt related to the predominance of envy in their mental life; for the demand for justice is a modification of envy and lays down the condition subject to which one can put envy aside. We also regard women as weaker in their social interests and as having less capacity for sublimating their instincts than men. The former is no doubt derived from the dissocial quality which unquestionably characterizes all sexual relations. Lovers find sufficiency in each other, and families too resist inclusion in more comprehensive associations. The aptitude for sublimation is subject to the greatest individual variations. On the other hand I cannot help mentioning an impression that we are constantly receiving during analytic practice. A man of about thirty strikes us as a youthful, somewhat unformed individual, whom we expect to make powerful use of the possibilities for development opened up to him by analysis. A woman of the same age, however, often frightens us by her psychical rigidity and unchangeability. Her libido has taken up final positions and seems incapable of exchanging them for others. There are no paths open to further development; it is as though the whole process had already run its course and remains thenceforward insusceptible to influence—as though, indeed, the difficult development to femininity had exhausted the possibilities of the person concerned. As therapists we lament this state of things, even if we succeed in putting an end to our patient's ailment by doing away with her neurotic conflict.

That is all I had to say to you about femininity. It is certainly incomplete and fragmentary and does not always sound friendly.

But do not forget that I have only been describing women in so far as their nature is determined by their sexual function. It is true that that influence extends very far; but we do not overlook the fact that an individual woman may be a human being in other respects as well. If you want to know more about femininity, enquire from your own experiences of life, or turn to the poets, or wait until science can give you deeper and more coherent information.

Karen Horney

Herself a psychoanalyst, Horney challenged many Freudian assumptions, including the assumption that anatomy is ultimately responsible for the psychological differences between male and female. She rejected Freud's contention that adult attitudes are simply modified versions of childhood attitudes. Instead of Freud's emphasis on heredity and constitutional elements, Horney sought to understand psychology in terms of human relationships and cultural factors. She argued, for example, that the Oedipus complex is neither universal nor innate, but is the result of environmental factors. As for Freud's concept of "penis envy," which is supposed to be rooted in anatomy, Horney argues in *New Ways in Psychoanalysis* (1939) that in fact it contradicts biology. It requires us to accept that though woman is built for female functions, nature has psychically determined her to reject them and desire male functions instead. To Horney it is simplistic to reduce the complex problems of all humans to a single source, the castration complex (men, too, are subject to this, according to Freud, though as a fear rather than as a fact). Given the privileged status of men in our culture, of course women wish for all their privileges, and so in some ways wish to be a man. Ultimately the most serious indictment of Freud's theory of castration complex is its claim to explain every human phenomenon. As later philosophers of science pointed out, this claim renders it utterly vacuous, for there is nothing which can falsify it; no conceivable circumstance can count against it. That which explains everything in the end explains nothing.

RESPONSE TO FREUD *

Freud believes that psychic peculiarities and difficulties in the two sexes are engendered by bisexual trends in both of them. His contention is, briefly, that many psychic difficulties in man are due to his rejection of "feminine" trends in himself, and that many peculiarities in woman are due to her essential wish to be a man. Freud has elaborated this thought in more detail for the psychology of woman than for that of man, and therefore I shall discuss only his views of feminine psychology.

According to Freud the most upsetting occurrence in the development of the little girl is the discovery that other human beings have a penis, while she has none. "The discovery of her castration is the turning point in the life of the girl." [1] She reacts to

* From Karey Horney, *New Ways in Psychoanalysis* (New York: W. W. Norton and Company, Inc., 1939), Chap. 6.

[1] Sigmund Freud, *New Introductory Lectures on Psychoanalysis* (1933), chapter on "The Psychology of Women." The following interpretation of Freud's point of view is based primarily on this source.

this discovery with a definite wish to have a penis too, with the hope that it will still grow, and with an envy of those more fortunate beings who possess one. In the normal development penis-envy does not continue as such; after recognizing her "deficiency" as an unalterable fact, the girl transfers the wish for a penis to a wish for a child. "The hoped-for possession of a child is meant as a compensation for her bodily defect." [2]

Penis-envy is originally a merely narcissistic phenomenon, the girl feeling offended because her body is less completely equipped than the boy's. But it has also a root in object relations. According to Freud the mother is the first sexual object for the girl as well as for the boy. The girl wishes to have a penis not only for the sake of narcissistic pride, but also because of her libidinal desires for the mother, which, in so far as they are genital in nature, have a masculine character. Not recognizing the elemental power of heterosexual attraction, Freud raises the question as to why the girl has any need at all to change her attachment to the father. He gives two reasons for this change in affection: hostility toward the mother, who is held responsible for the lack of a penis, and a wish to obtain this desired organ from the father. "The wish with which girls turn to their father is, no doubt, ultimately the wish for the penis." Thus originally both boys and girls know only one sex: the masculine.

Penis-envy is assumed to leave ineradicable traces in woman's development; even in the most normal development it is overcome only by a great expenditure of energy. Woman's most significant attitudes or wishes derive their energy from her wish for a penis. Some of Freud's principal contentions intended to illustrate this may be briefly enumerated.

Freud considers the wish for a male child to be woman's strongest wish, because the wish for a child is heir to the wish for a penis. The son represents a sort of wish-fulfillment in the sense of his possession. "The only thing that brings a mother undiluted satisfaction is her relation to a son: the mother can transfer to her

Abraham, "Ausserungsformen des weiblichen Kastrationskomplexes" in *ale Zeitschrift für Psychoanalyse* (1921).

son all the ambition which she has had to suppress in herself and she can hope to get from him the satisfaction of all that has remained to her of her masculinity complex."

Happiness during pregnancy, particularly when neurotic disturbances that are otherwise present subside during this time, is referred to as symbolic gratification in the possession of a penis (the penis being the child). When the delivery is delayed for functional reasons, it is suspected that the woman does not want to separate herself from the penis-child. On the other hand, motherhood may be rejected because it is a reminder of femininity. Similarly, depressions and irritations occurring during menstruation are regarded as the result of menstruation being a reminder of femininity. Cramps in menstruation are often interpreted as the result of fantasies in which the father's penis has been swallowed.

Disturbances in the relationship to men are regarded as ultimate results of penis-envy. As women turn to men mainly in the expectation of receiving a gift (penis-child), or in the expectation of having all their ambitions fulfilled, they easily turn against men if they fail to live up to such expectations. Envy of men may show itself also in the tendency to surpass them or in any kind of disparaging or in a striving for independence in so far as it implies disregarding man's help. In the sexual sphere the refutation of the feminine role may appear openly after defloration; the latter may arouse animosity to the partner because it is experienced as a castration.

In fact, there is scarcely any character trait in woman which is not assumed to have an essential root in penis-envy. Feminine inferiority feelings are regarded as an expression of contempt for the woman's own sex because of the lack of a penis. Freud believes that woman is more vain than man and attributes this to her necessity for compensation for the lack of a penis. Woman's physical modesty is born ultimately of a wish to hide the "deficiency" of her genitals. The greater role of envy and jealousy in woman's character is a direct outcome of penis-envy. Her tendency toward envy accounts for woman having "too little sense of justice," as well as for her "preference for mental and occupational interest' belonging to the sphere of men." [3] Practically all of woman's ambitious strivings suggest to Freud her wish for a penis as the ultimate driving force. Also ambitions which are usually regarded as specifically feminine, such as the wish to be the most beautiful woman or the wish to marry the most prominent man, are, according to Abraham, expressions of penis-envy.

Although the concept of penis-envy is related to anatomical differences it is nevertheless contradictory to biological thinking. It would require tremendous evidence to make it plausible that woman, physically built for specifically female functions, should be psychically determined by a wish for attributes of the other sex. But actually the data presented for this contention are scant, consisting of three main observations.

First, it is pointed out that little girls often express the wish to have a penis or the hope that it will still grow. There is no reason, however, to think that this wish is any more significant than their equally frequent wish to have a breast; moreover the wish for a penis may be accompanied by a kind of behavior which in our culture is regarded as feminine.

It is also pointed out that some girls before puberty not only may wish to be a boy, but through their tomboyish behavior may indicate that they really mean it. Again, however, the question is whether we are justified in taking these tendencies at their face value; when they are analyzed we may find good reasons for the apparently masculine wishes: opposition, despair at not being attractive as a girl, and the like. As a matter of fact, since girls have been brought up with greater freedom this kind of behavior has become rare.

Finally, it is pointed out that adult women may express a wish to be a man, sometimes explicitly, sometimes by presenting themselves ᵔ dreams with a penis or penis symbol; they may express contempt women and attribute existing inferiority feelings to being a an; castrative tendencies may be manifest or may be expressed

\braham, *op. cit.*

in dreams, in disguised or undisguised form. These latter data, however, though their occurrence is beyond doubt, are not as frequent as is suggested in some analytical writings. Also they are true only of neurotic women. Finally, they permit of a different interpretation and hence are far from proving the contention beyond dispute. Before discussing them critically let us first try to understand how it is that Freud and many other analysts see such overwhelming evidence for the decisive influence of penis-envy on woman's character.

In my estimation two main factors account for this conviction. On the basis of theoretical biases—which coincide to some extent with existing cultural prejudices—the analyst regards the following trends in women patients as off-hand suggestive of underlying penis-envy: tendencies to boss man, to berate him, to envy his success, to be ambitious themselves, to be self-sufficient, to dislike accepting help. I suspect that these trends are sometimes imputed to underlying penis-envy without further evidence. Further evidence may easily be found, however, in simultaneous complaints about feminine functions (such as menstruation) or frigidity, or in complaints about a brother having been preferred, or in a tendency to point out certain advantages of man's social position, or in dream symbols (a woman carrying a stick, slicing a sausage).

In reviewing these trends, it is obvious that they are characteristic of neurotic men as well as of neurotic women. Tendencies toward dictatorial power, toward egocentric ambition, toward envying and berating others are never-failing elements in present-day neuroses though the role they assume in a neurotic structure varies.

Furthermore, observation of neurotic women shows that all th trends in question appear toward other women or toward childr as well as toward men. It appears dogmatic to assume that th expression in relation to others is merely a radiation from relation to men.

Finally, as to dream symbols, any expression of wish masculinity is taken at its face value instead of being skeptically for a possible deeper meaning. This proc contrary to the customary analytical attitude and can be ascribed only to the determining power of theoretical preconceptions.

Another source feeding the analyst's conviction of the significance of penis-envy lies not in himself but in his women patients. While some women patients are not impressed by interpretations which point to penis-envy as the origin of their troubles, others take them up readily and quickly learn to talk about their difficulties in terms of femininity and masculinity, or even to dream in symbols fitting this kind of thinking. These are not necessarily patients who are particularly gullible. Every experienced analyst will notice whether a patient is docile and suggestible and by analyzing these trends will diminish errors springing from that source. And some patients view their problems in terms of masculinity and femininity without any suggestion from the analyst, for naturally one cannot exclude the influence of literature. But there is a deeper reason why many patients gladly seize upon explanations offered in terms of penis-envy: these explanations present comparatively harmless and simple solutions. It is so much easier for a woman to think that she is nasty to her husband because, unfortunately, she was born without a penis and envies him for having one than to think, for instance, that she has developed an attitude of righteousness and infallibility which makes it impossible to tolerate any questioning or disagreement. It is so much easier for a patient to think that nature ⁀ given her an unfair deal than to realize that she actually makes ⁀ive demands on the environment and is furious whenever they ⁀mplied with. It seems thus that the theoretical bias of the ⁀ coincide with the patient's tendency to leave her real ⁀ched.

⁀sculinity may screen repressed drives, what then ⁀rve in this way?

⁀ cultural factors. The wish to be a man, as ⁀out, may be the expression of a wish for ⁀es which in our culture are regarded as ⁀urage, independence, success, sexual ⁀artner. To avoid misunderstanding let me state explicitly that I do not mean to say that penis-envy is nothing but a symbolic expression of the wish to have the qualities regarded as masculine in our culture. This would not be plausible, because wishes to have these qualities need not be repressed and hence do not require a symbolic expression. A symbolic expression is necessary only for tendencies or feelings shoved out of awareness.

What then are the repressed strivings which are covered up by the wish for masculinity? The answer is not an all-embracing formula but must be discovered from an analysis of each patient and each situation. In order to discover the repressed strivings it is necessary not to take at face value a woman's tendency in one way or another to base her inferiority feelings on the fact that she is a woman; rather it must be pointed out to her that every person belonging to a minority group or to a less privileged group tends to use that status as a cover for inferiority feelings of various sources, and that the important thing is to try to find out these sources. According to my experience, one of the most frequent and effective sources is a failure to live up to certain inflated notions about the self, notions which in turn are necessary because various unrecognized pretenses have to be covered up.

Furthermore, it is necessary to bear in mind the possibility that the wish to be a man may be a screen for repressed ambition. In neurotic persons ambition may be so destructive that it becomes loaded with anxiety and hence has to be repressed. This is true of men as well as of women but as a result of the cultural situation a repressed destructive ambition in a woman may express itself in the comparatively harmless symbol of a wish to be a man. What is required of psychoanalysis is to uncover the egocentric and destructive elements in the ambition and to analyze not only what led up to this kind of ambition but also what consequences it has for the personality in the way of inhibitions to love, inhibitions to work, envy of competitors, self-belittling tendencies, fear of failure and of success.[4] The wish to be a man drops out of the patient's

---

[4] *Cf.* Karen Horney, *The Neurotic Personality of Our Time* (1937) chs. 10-12.

associations as soon as we tackle the underlying problems of her ambition and exalted opinion about what she is or should be. It is then no longer possible for her to hide behind the symbolic screen of masculinity wishes.

In short, interpretations in terms of penis-envy bar the way to an understanding of fundamental difficulties, such as ambition, and of the whole personality structure linked up with them. That such interpretations befog the real issue is my most stringent objection to them, particularly from the therapeutic angle. And I have the same objection to the assumed importance of bisexuality in man's psychology. Freud believes that in man's psychology what corresponds to penis-envy is his "struggle against the passive or feminine attitude toward other men." [5] He calls this fear the "repudiation of femininity" and makes it responsible for various difficulties which in my estimation belong to the structure of types who need to appear perfect and superior.

Freud has made two other suggestions, closely interrelated, concerning inherent feminine characteristics. One is that femininity has "some secret relationship with masochism." [6] The other is that the basic fear in woman is that of losing love, and that this fear corresponds to the fear of castration in man.

Helene Deutsch has elaborated Freud's assumption and generalized it in calling masochism the elemental power in feminine mental life. She contends that what woman ultimately wants in intercourse is to be raped and violated; what she wants in mental life is to be humiliated; menstruation is significant to the woman because it feeds masochistic fantasies; childbirth represents the climax of masochistic satisfaction. The pleasures of motherhood, inasmuch as they include certain sacrifices and a concern for the children, constitute a long drawn out masochistic gratification. Because of these masochistic strivings women, according to Deutsch, are more or less doomed to be frigid unless in intercourse they are

[5] Sigmund Freud, "Analysis Terminable and Interminable," *op. cit.*
[6] Sigmund Freud, *New Introductory Lectures.*

or feel raped, injured or humiliated.[7] Rado holds that woman's preference for masculinity is a defense against feminine masochistic strivings.[8]

Since according to psychoanalytic theory psychic attitudes are molded after sexual attitudes, the contentions concerning a specifically feminine basis of masochism have far-reaching implications. They entail the postulate that women in general, or at least the majority of them, essentially desire to be submissive and dependent. In support of these views is the impression that in our culture masochistic trends are more frequent in women than in men. But it must be remembered that the available data concern only neurotic women.

Many neurotic women have masochistic notions about intercourse, such as that women are prey to man's animal desires, that they have to sacrifice themselves and are debased by the sacrifice. There may be fantasies about being physically injured by intercourse. A few neurotic women have fantasies of masochistic satisfaction in childbirth. The great number of mothers who play the role of martyr and continually emphasize how much they are sacrificing themselves for the children may certainly be proof that motherhood can offer a masochistic satisfaction to neurotic women. There are also neurotic girls who shrink from marriage because they visualize themselves as enslaved and abused by the potential husband. Finally, masochistic fantasies about the sexual role of woman may contribute to a rejection of the female role and a preference for the masculine one.

Assuming that there is indeed a greater frequency of masochistic trends in neurotic women than in neurotic men, how may it be accounted for? Rado and Deutsch try to show that specific factors in feminine development are responsible. I refrain from discussing

[7] Helene Deutsch, "The Significance of Masochism in the Mental Life of Women" (Part I, "Feminine Masochism in Its Relation to Frigidity") in *International Journal of Psychoanalysis* (1930).

[8] Sandor Rado, "Fear of Castration in Women" in *Psychoanalytic Quarterly* (1933).

these attempts because both authors introduce as the basic factor the lack of a penis, or the girl's reaction to the discovery of this fact, and I believe this to be a wrong presupposition. In fact, I do not believe it is possible at all to find specific factors in feminine development which lead to masochism, for all such attempts rest on the premise that masochism is essentially a sexual phenomenon. It is true that the sexual aspect of masochism, as it appears in masochistic fantasies and perversions, is its most conspicuous part and was the first to attract the attention of psychiatrists. I hold, however— and this contention will be elaborated later on—that masochism is not a primarily sexual phenomenon, but is rather the result of certain conflicts in interpersonal relations. When masochistic tendencies are once established they may prevail also in the sexual sphere and here may become the condition for satisfaction. From this point of view masochism cannot be a specifically feminine phenomenon, and the analytical writers who have tried to find specific factors in feminine development accounting for masochistic attitudes in women are not to be blamed for the failure to find them.

In my opinion, one has to look not for biological reasons but for cultural ones. The question then is whether there are cultural factors which are instrumental in developing masochistic trends in women. The answer to this question depends on what one holds to be essential in the dynamics of masochism. My concept, briefly, is that masochistic phenomena represent the attempt to gain safety and satisfaction in life through inconspicuousness and dependency. As will be discussed later on, this fundamental attitude toward life determines the way in which individual problems are dealt with; it leads, for instance, to gaining control over others through weakness and suffering, to expressing hostility through suffering, to seeking in illness an alibi for failure.

If these presuppositions are valid there are indeed cultural factors fostering masochistic attitudes in women. They were more relevant for the past generation than for the present one, but they still throw their shadow today. They are, briefly, the greater dependency of woman; the emphasis on woman's weakness and frailty; the ideology that it is in woman's nature to lean on someone and that her life is given content and meaning only through others: family, husband, children. These factors do not in themselves bring about masochistic attitudes. History has shown that women can be happy, contented and efficient under these conditions. But factors like these, in my judgment, are responsible for the prevalence of masochistic trends in feminine neuroses when neuroses do develop.

Freud's contention that woman's basic fear is that of losing love is in part not separate from, for it is implicitly contained in, the postulate that there are specific factors in feminine development leading to masochism. Inasmuch as masochistic trends, among other characteristics, signify an emotional dependence on others, and inasmuch as one of the predominant masochistic means of reassurance against anxiety is to obtain affection, a fear of losing love is a specific masochistic feature.

It seems to me, however, that in contrast to Freud's other two contentions concerning feminine nature—that of penis-envy and that of a specifically feminine basis for masochism—this last one has some validity also for the healthy woman in our culture. There are no biological reasons but there are significant cultural factors which lead women to overvaluate love and thus to dread losing it.

Woman lived for centuries under conditions in which she was kept away from great economic and political responsibilities and restricted to a private emotional sphere of life. This does not mean that she did not carry responsibility and did not have to work. But her work was done within the confines of the family circle and therefore was based only on emotionalism, in contradistinction to more impersonal, matter of fact relations. Another aspect of the same situation is that love and devotion came to be regarded as specifically feminine ideals and virtues. Still another aspect is that to woman—since her relations to men and children were her only gateway to happiness, security and prestige—love represented a realistic value, which in man's sphere can be compared with his activities relating to earning capacities. Thus not only were pursuits outside the emotional sphere factually discouraged, but in woman's own mind they assumed only secondary importance.

Hence there were, and to some extent still are, realistic reasons in our culture why woman is bound to overrate love and to expect more from it than it can possibly give, and why she is more afraid of losing love than man is.

The cultural situation which has led woman to regard love as the only value that counts in life has implications which may throw light on certain characteristics of modern woman. One of them is the attitude toward aging: woman's age phobia and its implications. Since for such a long time woman's only attainable fulfillments—whether they involved love, sex, home or children—were obtained through men, it necessarily became of paramount importance to please men. The cult of beauty and charm resulting from this necessity might be registered, at least in some respects, as a good effect. But such a concentration on the importance of erotic attractiveness implies an anxiety for the time when it might eventually diminish in value. We should consider it neurotic if men became frightened or depressed when they approached the fifth decade. In a woman this is regarded as natural, and in a way it is natural so long as attractiveness represents a unique value. While age is a problem to everyone it becomes a desperate one if youthfulness is the center of attention.

This fear is not limited to the age which is regarded as ending woman's attractiveness, but throws its shadow over her entire life and is bound to create a great feeling of insecurity toward life. It accounts for the jealousy often existing between mothers and adolescent daughters, and not only helps to spoil their personal relationships but may leave a remnant of hostility toward all women. It prevents woman from evaluating qualities which are outside the erotic sphere, qualities best characterized by the terms maturity, poise, independence, autonomy in judgment, wisdom. Woman can scarcely take the task of the development of her personality as seriously as she does her love life if she constantly entertains a devaluating attitude toward her mature years, and considers them as her declining years.

The all-embracing expectations that are joined to love account to some extent for that discontentment with the female role which Freud ascribed to penis-envy. From this point of view the discontentment has two main reasons. One is that in a culture in which human relationships are so generally disturbed it is difficult to attain happiness in love life (by that I do *not* mean sexual relations). The other is that this situation is likely to create inferiority feelings. Sometimes the question is raised whether in our culture men or women suffer more from inferiority feelings. It is difficult to measure psychic quantities, but there is this difference: as a rule man's feeling of inferiority does not arise from the fact that he is a man; but woman often feels inferior merely because she is a woman. As mentioned before, I believe that feelings of inadequacy have nothing to do with femininity, but use cultural implications of femininity as a disguise for other sources of inferiority feelings which, in essence, are identical in men and women. There remain, however, certain cultural reasons why woman's self-confidence is easily disturbed.

A sound and secure self-confidence draws upon a broad basis of human qualities, such as initiative, courage, independence, talents, erotic values, capacity to master situations. As long as homemaking was a really big task involving many responsibilities, and as long as the number of children was not restricted, woman had the feeling of being a constructive factor in the economic process; thus she was provided with a sound basis for self-esteem. This basis, however, has gradually vanished, and in its departure woman has lost one foundation for feeling herself valuable.

As far as the sexual basis of self-confidence is concerned, certainly the puritanical influences, however one may evaluate them, have contributed toward the debasement of women by giving sexuality the connotation of something sinful and low. In a patriarchal society this attitude was bound to make woman into the symbol of sin; many such allusions may be found in early Christian literature. This is one of the great cultural reasons why woman, even today, considers herself debased and soiled by sexuality and thus lowered in her own self-esteem.

There remains, finally, the emotional basis of self-confidence. If, however, one's self-confidence is dependent on giving or receiving love, then one builds on a foundation which is too small and too shaky—too small because it leaves out too many personality values, and too shaky because it is dependent on too many external factors, such as finding adequate partners. Besides, it very easily leads to an emotional dependence on other people's affection and appreciation, and results in a feeling of unworthiness if one is not loved or appreciated.

As far as the alleged given inferiority of woman is concerned, Freud has, to be sure, made a remark which it is quite a relief to hear from him: "You must not forget, however, that we have only described women in so far as their natures are determined by their sexual function. The influence of this factor is, of course, very far-reaching, but we must remember that *an individual woman may be a human being apart from this*" (italics mine). I am convinced that he really means it, but one would like to have this opinion of his assume a broader place in his theoretical system. Certain sentences in Freud's latest paper on feminine psychology indicate that in comparison with his earlier studies he is giving additional consideration to the influence of cultural factors on women's psychology: "But we must take care not to underestimate the influence of social conventions, which also force women into passive situations. The whole thing is still very obscure. We must not overlook one particularly constant relation between femininity and instinctual life. The repression of their aggressiveness, which is imposed upon women by their constitutions and by society, favors the development of strong masochistic impulses, which have the effect of binding erotically the destructive tendencies which have been turned inwards."

But since he has a primarily biological orientation Freud does not, and on the basis of his premises cannot, see the whole significance of these factors. He cannot see to what extent they mold wishes and attitudes, nor can he evaluate the complexity of interrelations between cultural conditions and feminine psychology.

I suppose everyone agrees with Freud that differences in sexual constitution and functions influence mental life. But it seems unconstructive to speculate on the exact nature of this influence. The American woman is different from the German woman; both are different from certain Pueblo Indian women. The New York society woman is different from the farmer's wife in Idaho. The way specific cultural conditions engender specific qualities and faculties, in women as in men—this is what we may hope to understand.

Simone de Beauvoir

The Second Sex, an existentialist study of woman's status in
Western civilization published in 1949, is the best-known feminist
work of the twentieth century. Its grasp of biology, psychology,
literature, and history, coupled with its analysis and insights, renders
it at once an invaluable critique of the past and a blueprint for
future change. In the following selection De Beauvoir is discussing
woman's life today, her character and situation. She analyzes in
detail the factors that account for woman's qualities, which historically have been deemed natural. It is not necessary to conjure up
the mysteries of nature to account for woman's passivity, mediocrity, servility, selfishness, ignorance, etc., she argues. How could
woman be otherwise given the crushing conditions of her life? "The
totality of her economic, social, and historical conditioning"
provides the answer to the riddle of femininity. Traditional contrasts between the masculine and feminine are predicated either on
the view that context is unimportant or on the view that the
"worlds" of men and women are separate and distinct, each being

what it is because of the nature of its inhabitants. On the contrary, according to De Beauvoir, context is relevant and women form an integral part of a single society, which they inhabit with the men to whom they are subject. Their belonging, paradoxically, is not organic but merely formal. In their group women are outsiders and nonparticipants. Ultimately woman's situation is such that she is without freedom and without responsibility, even for her own life. Woman's dependence is so complete that whatever happens to her is effected through the agency of others. Because she is reduced to servicing men through her sex—whether for pleasure or procreation—woman is exploited.

THE EXISTENTIAL PARALYSIS

OF WOMEN *

We can now understand why there should be so many common features in the indictments drawn up against woman, from the Greeks to our times. Her condition has remained the same through superficial changes, and it is this condition that determines what is called the "character" of woman: she "revels in immanence," she is contrary, she is prudent and petty, she has no sense of fact or accuracy, she lacks morality, she is contemptibly utilitarian, she is false, theatrical, self-seeking, and so on. There is an element of truth in all this. But we must only note that the varieties of behavior reported are not dictated to woman by her hormones nor predetermined in the structure of the female brain: they are shaped as in a mold by her situation. In this perspective we shall endeavor to make a comprehensive survey of woman's situation. This will involve a certain amount of repetition, but it will enable us to apprehend the eternal feminine in the totality of her economic, social, and historical conditioning.

Sometimes the "feminine world" is contrasted with the masculine universe, but we must insist again that women have never con-

* From Simone de Beauvoir, *The Second Sex*, trans. H. M. Parshley (New York: Alfred A. Knopf, 1952), Part 5, Chap. 21.

stituted a closed and independent society; they form an integral part of the group, which is governed by males and in which they have a subordinate place. They are united only in a mechanical solidarity from the mere fact of their similarity, but they lack that organic solidarity on which every unified community is based; they are always compelled—at the time of the mysteries of Eleusis as today in clubs, salons, social-service institutes—to band together in order to establish a counter-universe, but they always set it up within the frame of the masculine universe. Hence the paradox of their situation: they belong at one and the same time to the male world and to a sphere in which that world is challenged; shut up in their world, surrounded by the other, they can settle down nowhere in peace. Their docility must always be matched by a refusal, their refusal by an acceptance. In this respect their attitude approaches that of the young girl, but it is more difficult to maintain, because for the adult woman it is not merely a matter of dreaming her life through symbols, but of living it out in actuality.

Woman herself recognizes that the world is masculine on the whole; those who fashioned it, ruled it, and still dominate it today are men. As for her, she does not consider herself responsible for it; it is understood that she is inferior and dependent; she has not learned the lessons of violence, she had never stood forth as subject before the other members of the group. Shut up in her flesh, her home, she sees herself as passive before these gods with human faces who set goals and establish values. In this sense there is truth in the saying that makes her the "eternal child." Workers, black slaves, colonial natives, have also been called grown-up children—as long as they were not feared; that meant that they were to accept without argument the verities and the laws laid down for them by other men. The lot of woman is a respectful obedience. She has no grasp, even in thought, on the reality around her. It is opaque to her eyes.

And it is true that she lacks the technical training that would permit her to dominate matter. As for her, it is not matter she comes to grips with, but life; and life cannot be mastered through the use of tools: one can only submit to its secret laws. The world does not seem to woman "an assemblage of implements" intermediate between her will and her goals, as Heidegger defines it; it is on the contrary something obstinately resistant, unconquerable; it is dominated by fatality and shot through with mysterious caprices. This mystery of a bloody strawberry that inside the mother is transformed into a human being is one no mathematics can express in an equation, no machine can hasten or delay; she feels the strength of a continuity that the most ingenious instruments are unable to divide or to multiply; she feels it in her body, swayed by the lunar rhythm and first ripened, then corrupted, by the years. Each day the kitchen also teaches her patience and passivity; here is alchemy; one must obey the fire, the water, wait for the sugar to melt, for the dough to rise, and also for the wash to dry, for the fruits to ripen on the shelf. Household activities come close to being technical operations, but they are too rudimentary, too monotonous, to prove to a woman the laws of mechanical causation. Besides, even here things are capricious; there are materials that will stand washing and others that will not, spots that can be removed and others that persist, objects that break all by themselves, dusts that spring up like plants.

Woman's mentality perpetuates that of agricultural civilizations which worshipped the magic powers of the land: she believes in magic. Her passive eroticism makes desire seem to her not will and aggression but an attraction akin to that which causes the divining rod to dip; the mere presence of her flesh swells and erects the male's sex; why should not hidden water make the hazel rod quiver? She feels that she is surrounded by waves, radiations, mystic fluids; she believes in telepathy, astrology, radiotherapy, mesmerism, theosophy, table-tipping, clairvoyants, faithhealers; her religion is full of primitive superstition: wax candles, answered prayers; she believes the saints incarnate the ancient spirits of nature: this one protects travelers, that one women in labor, this other finds lost articles; and, of course, no prodigy can surprise her. Her attitude will be one of conjuration and prayer; to obtain a certain result, she will perform certain well-tested rites.

It is easy to see why woman clings to routine; time has for her no element of novelty, it is not a creative flow; because she is doomed to repetition, she sees in the future only a duplication of the past. If one knows the word and the formula, duration allies itself with the powers of fecundity—but this is itself subject to the rhythm of the months, the seasons; the cycle of each pregnancy, each flowering, exactly reproduces the one that preceded. In this play of cyclical phenomena the sole effect of time is a slow deterioration: it wears out furniture and clothes as it ruins the face; the reproductive powers are gradually destroyed by the passing of years. Thus woman puts no trust in this relentless force for destruction.

Not only is she ignorant of what constitutes a true action, capable of changing the face of the world, but she is lost in the midst of the world as if she were at the heart of an immense, vague nebula. She is not familiar with the use of masculine logic. Stendhal remarked that she could handle it as adroitly as a man if driven to it by necessity. But it is an instrument that she hardly has occasion to use. A syllogism is of no help in making a successful mayonnaise, not in quieting a child in tears; masculine reasoning is quite inadequate to the reality with which she deals. And in the world of men, her thought, not flowing into any project, since she *does* nothing, is indistinguishable from daydreaming. She has no sense of factual truth, for lack of effectiveness; she never comes to grips with anything but words and mental pictures, and that is why the most contradictory assertions give her no uneasiness; she takes little trouble to elucidate the mysteries of a sphere that is in every way beyond her reach. She is content, for her purposes, with extremely vague conceptions, confusing parties, opinions, places, people, events; her head is filled with a strange jumble.

But, after all, to see things clearly is not her business, for she has been taught to accept masculine authority. So she gives up criticizing, investigating, judging for herself, and leaves all this to the superior caste. Therefore the masculine world seems to her a transcendent reality, an absolute. "Men make the gods," says Frazer, "women worship them." Men cannot kneel with complete conviction before the idols they have made; but when women encounter these mighty statues along the roads, they think they are not made with hands, and obediently bow down.[1] In particular they like to have Order and Right embodied in a leader. In every Olympus there is a supreme god; the magic male essence must be concentrated in an archetype of which father, husband, lovers, are only faint reflections. It is rather satirical to say that their worship of this grand totem is of sexual nature; but it is true that in this worship they will fully satisfy their childhood dream of bowing the knee in resignation. In France generals like Boulanger, Pétain, and de Gaulle [2] have always had the support of the women; and one recalls with what fluttering pens the lady journalists on the Communist paper *L'Humanité* formerly celebrated Tito and his splendid uniform. The general, the dictator—eagle-eyed, square-jawed—is the heavenly father demanded by all serious right-thinkers, the absolute guarantor of all values. Women's ineffectiveness and ignorance are what give rise to the respect accorded by them to heroes and to the laws of the masculine world; they accept them not through sound judgment but by an act of faith—and faith gets its fanatical power from the fact that it is not knowledge: it is blind, impassioned, obstinate, stupid; what it declares, it declares unconditionally, against reason, against history, against all denial.

This obstinate reverence can take one of two forms according to circumstances: it may be either the content of the law, or merely its empty form that woman passionately adheres to. If she belongs to the privileged elite that benefits from the established social order, she wants it to be unshakable and she is notably uncompromising in this desire. Man knows that he can develop different institutions, another ethic, a new legal code; aware of his ability to transcend what is, he regards history as a becoming. The most conservative man knows that some evolution is inevitable and realizes that he

[1] See Sartre's play *Les Mains Sales.* "Hoederer: They need props, you understand, they are given ready-made ideas, then they believe in them as they do in God. We're the ones who make these ideas and we know how they are cooked up; we are never quite sure of being right." [An English translation, *Dirty Hands,* is in Jean-Paul Sartre: *Three Plays* (New York: Alfred A. Knopf; 1949).]

[2] "When the general passed through, the public consisted largely of women and children." (Newspaper report of his visit to Savoy.)

must adapt his action and his thinking to it; but as woman takes no part in history, she fails to understand its necessities; she is suspiciously doubtful of the future and wants to arrest the flow of time. If the idols set up by her father, her brothers, her husband, are being torn down, she can offer no way of repopulating the heavens; she rushes wildly to the defense of the old gods.

During the War of Secession no Southerners were more passionate in upholding slavery than the women. In England during the Boer War, in France during the Commune, it was the women who were most belligerently inflamed. They seek to compensate for their inactivity by the intensity of the sentiments they exhibit. With victory won, they rush like hyenas upon the fallen foe; in defeat, they bitterly reject any efforts at conciliation. Their ideas being merely attitudes, they support quite unconcernedly the most outdated causes: they can be legitimists in 1914, czarists in 1953. A man will sometimes smilingly encourage them, for it amuses him to see their fanatical reflections of ideas he expresses in more measured terms; but he may also find it irritating to have his ideas take on such a stupid, stubborn, aspect.

Woman assumes this indomitable attitude only in strongly integrated civilizations and social classes. More generally, she respects the law simply because it is the law, since her faith is blind; if the law changes, it retains its spell. In woman's eyes, might makes right because the rights she recognizes in men depend upon their power. Hence it is that when a society breaks down, women are the first to throw themselves at the feet of the conqueror. On the whole, they accept what is. One of their distinguishing traits is resignation. When the ruins of Pompeii were dug up, it was noticed that the incinerated bodies of the men were fixed in attitudes of rebellion, defying the heavens or trying to escape, while those of the women, bent double, were bowed down with their faces toward the earth. Women feel they are powerless against things: volcanoes, police, patrons, men. "Women are born to suffer," they say; "it's life—nothing can be done about it."

This resignation inspires the patience often admired in women. They can stand physical pain much better than men; they are capable of stoical courage when circumstances demand it; lacking the male's aggressive audacity, many women distinguish themselves by their calm tenacity in passive resistance. They face crises, poverty, misfortune, more energetically than their husbands; respecting duration, which no haste can overcome, they do not ration their time. When they apply their quiet persistence to an enterprise, they are sometimes startlingly successful. "Never underestimate the power of a woman." In a generous woman resignation takes the form of forbearance: she puts up with everything, she condemns no one, because she holds that neither people nor things can be other than they are. A proud woman can make a lofty virtue of resignation, as did the stoical Mme de Charrière. But it also engenders a sterile prudence; women are always trying to conserve, to adapt, to arrange, rather than to destroy and build anew; they prefer compromise and adjustment to revolution.

In the nineteenth century, women were one of the greatest obstacles in the way of the effort to free the workers: for one Flora Tristan, one Louise Michel, how many timid housewives begged their husbands not to take any chances! They were not only afraid of strikes, unemployment, and poverty: they feared that revolt might be a mistake. It is easy to understand that, if they must suffer, they preferred what was familiar to adventuring, for they could achieve a meager welfare more easily at home than in the streets.

Women's fate is bound up with that of perishable things; in losing them they lose all. Only a free subject, asserting himself as above and beyond the duration of things, can check all decay; this supreme recourse has been denied to woman. The real reason why she does not believe in a liberation is that she has never put the powers of liberty to a test; the world seems to her to be ruled by an obscure destiny against which it is presumptuous to rise in protest. She has not herself marked out those dangerous roads she is asked to follow, and so it is natural enough for her not to plunge into them with enthusiasm.[3] Let the future be opened to her and she

---

[3] Compare the passage in *The Journals of André Gide,* Vol. I, p. 301, translated

will no longer cling desperately to the past. When women are called upon for concrete action, when they recognize their interest in the designated goals, they are as bold and courageous as men.[4]

Many of the faults for which women are reproached—mediocrity, laziness, frivolity, servility—simply express the fact that their horizon is closed. It is said that woman is sensual, she wallows in immanence; but she has first been shut up in it. The harem slave feels no morbid passion for rose preserves and perfumed baths: she has to kill time. When woman suffocates in a dull gynaeceum— brothel or middle-class home—she is bound to take refuge in comfort and well-being; besides that, if she eagerly seeks sexual pleasure, it is very often because she is deprived of it. Sexually unsatisfied, doomed to male crudeness, "condemned to masculine ugliness," she finds consolation in creamy sauces, heady wines, velvets, the caress of water, of sunshine, of a woman friend, of a young lover. If she seems to man so "physical" a creature, it is because her situation leads her to attach extreme importance to her animal nature. The call of the flesh is no louder in her than in the male, but she catches its least murmurs and amplifies them. Sexual pleasure, like rending pain, represents the stunning triumph of the

---

by Justin O'Brien (Alfred A. Knopf, 1949): "Creusa or Lot's wife; one tarries and the other looks back, which is a worse way of tarrying. . . . There is no greater cry of passion than this:

> *And Phaedra having braved the Labyrinth with you*
> *Would have been found with you or lost with you.*

But passion blinds her; after a few steps, to tell the truth, she would have sat down, or else would have wanted to go back—or even would have made him carry her."

[The lines quoted are from the *Phèdre* of Racine. The Creusa referred to above was the first wife of Aeneas and mother of Ascanius. As related in Virgil's *Aeneid*, when Troy was taken and burned, they became separated in the confusion, Aeneas escaping and Creusa remaining in the city, to be rescued by Cybele, whose priestess she became. Lot's wife, in the Bible story, looked back at burning Sodom and was punished by being turned into a pillar of salt.—Tr.]

[4] The attitude of proletarian women has changed in just this way after a century; as a particular example, during the recent strikes in mines of northern France, they gave proof of as much passion and energy as the men, demonstrating and fighting beside them.

immediate; in the violence of the instant, the future and the universe are denied; what lies outside the carnal flame is nothing; for the brief moment of this apotheosis, woman is no longer multilated and frustrated. But, once again, she values these triumphs of immanence only because immanence is her lot.

Her frivolity has the same cause as her "sordid materialism"; she considers little things important for lack of any access to great things, and, furthermore, the futilities that fill her days are often of the most serious practical concern to her. She owes her charm and her opportunities to her dress and her beauty. She often appears to be lazy, indolent; but the occupations available to her are as empty as the pure passage of time. If she is a chatterer, a scribbler, it is to divert her idle hours: for impossible action, she substitutes words. The truth is that when a woman is engaged in an enterprise worthy of a human being, she is quite able to show herself as active, efficient, taciturn—and as ascetic—as a man.

She is accused of being servile; she is always ready, it is said, to lie down at her master's feet and kiss the hand that strikes her, and it is true that she is generally lacking in real pride. The counsel dispensed in columns of "advice to the lovelorn," to deceived wives and abandoned lovers, is full of the spirit of abject submission. Woman wears herself out in haughty scenes, and in the end gathers up the crumbs that the male cares to toss to her. But what can be done without masculine support by a woman for whom man is at once the sole means and the sole reason for living? She is bound to suffer every humiliation; a slave cannot have the sense of human dignity; it is enough if a slave gets out of it with a whole skin.

And finally, if woman is earthy, commonplace, basely utilitarian, it is because she is compelled to devote her existence to cooking and washing diapers—no way to acquire a sense of grandeur! It is her duty to assure the monotonous repetition of life in all its mindless factuality. It is natural for woman to repeat, to begin again without ever inventing, for time to seem to her to go round and round without ever leading anywhere. She is occupied without ever *doing* anything, and thus she identifies herself with what she *has*. This dependence on things, a consequence of the dependence in which men keep her, explains her frugality, her avarice. Her life is not directed toward ends: she is absorbed in producing or caring for things that are never more than means, such as food, clothing, and shelter. These things are inessential intermediaries between animal life and free existence. The sole value that appertains to the inessential means is utility; it is at the level of utility that the housekeeper lives, and she does not flatter herself that she is anything more than a person useful to her kindred.

But no existent can be satisfied with an inessential role, for that immediately makes means into ends—as may be observed, for example, in politicians—and the value of the means comes to seem an absolute value. Thus utility reigns in the housekeeper's heaven, above truth, beauty, liberty; and it is in this perspective that she envisages the entire universe. This is why she adopts the Aristotelian morality of the golden mean—that is, of mediocrity. How could one expect her to show audacity, ardor, disinterestedness, grandeur? These qualities appear only when a free being strikes forward through an open future, emerging far beyond all given actuality. Woman is shut up in a kitchen or in a boudoir, and astonishment is expressed that her horizon is limited. Her wings are clipped, and it is found deplorable that she cannot fly. Let but the future be opened to her, and she will no longer be compelled to linger in the present.

The same inconsistency is displayed when, after being enclosed within the limits of her ego or her household, she is reproached for her narcissism, her egotism, with all their train: vanity, touchiness, malice, and so on. She is deprived of all possibility of concrete communication with others; she does not experience either the appeal or the benefits of solidarity, since she is consecrated entirely to her own family, in isolation. She could hardly be expected, then, to transcend herself toward the general welfare. She stays obstinately within the one realm that is familiar to her, where she can control things and in the midst of which she enjoys a precarious sovereignty.

Lock the doors and close the shutters as she will, however, woman fails to find complete security in her home. It is surrounded by that masculine universe which she respects from afar, without daring to venture into it. And precisely because she is incapable of grasping it through technical skill, sound logic, and definite knowledge, she feels, like the child and the savage, that she is surrounded by dangerous mysteries. She projects her magical conception of reality into that male world; the course of events seems to her to be inevitable, and yet anything can happen; she does not clearly distinguish between the possible and the impossible and is ready to believe anything no matter what. She listens to and spreads rumors and starts panics. Even when things are quiet, she feels anxious; lying half asleep at night, her rest is disturbed by the nightmare shapes that reality assumes; and thus for woman condemned to passivity, the inscrutable future is haunted by phantoms of war, revolution, famine, poverty; being unable to act, she worries. Her husband, her son, when undertaking an enterprise or facing an emergency, run their own risks; their plans, the regulations they follow, indicate a sure road through obscurity. But woman flounders in confusion and darkness; she gets used to it because she does nothing; in her imagination all possibilities have equal reality: the train may be derailed, the operation may go wrong, the business may fail. What she is endeavoring to exorcize in her gloomy ruminations is the specter of her own powerlessness.

Her anxiety is the expression of her distrust of the world as given; if it seems threatening, ready to collapse, this is because she is unhappy in it. For most of the time she is not resigned to being resigned; she knows very well that she suffers as she does against her will: she is a woman without having been consulted in the matter. She dares not revolt; she submits unwillingly; her attitude is one of constant reproach. All those in whom women confide— doctors, priests, social workers—know that the usual tone is one of complaint. Among friends, woman groans over her troubles, and they all complain in chorus about the injustice of fate, the world, and men in general.

A free individual blames only himself for his failures, he assumes responsibility for them; but everything happens to women through the agency of others, and therefore these others are responsible for her woes. Her mad despair spurns all remedies; it does not help matters to propose solutions to a woman bent on complaining: she finds none acceptable. She insists on living in her situation precisely as she does—that is, in a state of impotent rage. If some change is proposed she throws up her hands: "That's the last straw!" She knows that her trouble goes deeper than is indicated by the pretexts she advances for it, and she is aware that it will take more than some expedient to deliver her from it. She holds the entire world responsible because it has been made without her, and against her; she has been protesting against her condition since her adolescence, ever since her childhood. She has been promised compensations, she has been assured that if she would place her fortune in man's hands, it would be returned a hundredfold—and she feels she has been swindled. She puts the whole masculine universe under indictment. Resentment is the reverse side of dependence: when one gives all, one never receives enough in return.

Woman is obliged also, however, to regard the male universe with some respect; she would feel in danger without a roof over her head, if she were in total opposition; so she adopts the Manichaeist position—the clear separation of good and evil—which is also suggested by her experience as a housekeeper. The individual who acts considers himself, like others, as responsible for both evil and good, he knows that it is for him to define ends, to bring them to success; he becomes aware, in action, of the ambiguousness of all solutions; justice and injustice, gains and losses, are inextricably mixed. But anyone who is passive is out of the game and declines to pose ethical problems even in thought: the good *should* be realized, and if it is not, there must be some wrongdoing for which those to blame must be punished. Like the child, woman conceives good and evil in simple images, as co-existing, discrete entities; this Manichaeism of hers sets her mind at rest by doing away with the anxiety of making difficult choices. To decide between an evil and a lesser evil, between a present good and a greater good to come, to have to define for herself what is defeat and what is victory—all this involves terrible risks. For the Manichaeist, the good wheat is clearly distinct from the tares, and one has merely to remove the tares; dust stands self-condemned and cleanliness is complete absence of dirt; to clean house is to remove dirt and rubbish.

Thus woman thinks that "it is all the Jews' fault," the Freemasons' or the Bolsheviks', or the government's; she is always *against* someone or something. Among those against Dreyfus the women were even more relentless than the men. They do not always know just where the evil principle may lie, but what they expect of a "good government" is to sweep it out as they sweep dust out of the house. For fervid de Gaullists, de Gaulle is the king of sweepers; they imagine him, feather duster and mop in hand, scrubbing and polishing to make France "nice and clean."

But these hopes are always for the uncertain future; in the meantime evil continues to corrode the good; and since she cannot get her hands on the Jews, the Freemasons, the Bolsheviks, the woman looks about for someone responsible against whom her indignation can find concrete expression. Her husband is the favorite victim. He embodies the masculine universe, through him male society has taken charge of her and swindled her. He bears the weight of the world, and if things go wrong, it is his fault. When he comes in at night, she complains to him about the children, the storekeepers, the cost of living, her rheumatism, the weather—and wants him to feel to blame. She often entertains special grievances against him; but he is guilty in the first place of being a man. He may very well have maladies and cares of his own—"that's different"—but he holds a privilege which she constantly feels as an injustice. It is a remarkable thing that the hostility she feels toward her husband or lover attaches her to him instead of alienating her from him. A man who has begun to detest wife or mistress tries to get away from her; but woman wants to have the man she hates close at hand so she can make him pay. Recrimination is not a way to get rid of her ills but to wallow in them; the wife's supreme consolation is to pose as a martyr. Life, men, have conquered her: she will turn defeat itself into victory. This explains why she will cheerfully abandon herself to frantic tears and scenes, as in her childhood.

Certainly woman's aptitude for facile tears comes largely from the fact that her life is built upon a foundation of impotent revolt; it is also doubtless true that physiologically she has less nervous control than man and that her education has taught her to let herself go more readily. This effect of education, or custom, is indeed evident, since in the past men like Benjamin Constant and Diderot, for instance, used to pour out floods of tears, and then men ceased weeping when it became unfashionable for them. But, above all, the fact is that woman is always prepared to take an attitude of frustration toward the world because she has never frankly accepted it. A man does accept the world; not even misfortune will change his attitude, he will face it, he will not let himself "give up"; whereas it takes only a little trouble to remind a woman of the hostility of the universe and the injustice of her lot. Then she hastily retires to her surest refuge: herself. These warm traces on her cheeks, these reddened eyes, what are they but the visible presence of her grief-stricken soul? . . .

There are many aspects of feminine behavior that should be interpreted as forms of protest. We have seen that a woman often deceives her husband through defiance and not for pleasure; and she may be purposely careless and extravagant because he is methodical and economical. Misogynists who accuse woman of always being late think she lacks a sense of punctuality; but as we have seen, the fact is that she can adjust herself very well to the demands of time. When she is late, she has deliberately planned to be. Some coquettish women think they stimulate the man's desire in this way and make their presence the more highly appreciated; but in making the man wait a few minutes, the woman is above all protesting against that long wait: her life.

In a sense her whole existence is waiting, since she is confined in the limbo of immanence and contingence, and since her justification is always in the hands of others. She awaits the homage, the approval of men, she awaits love, she awaits the gratitude and praise of her husband or her lover. She awaits her support, which comes from man; whether she keeps the checkbook or merely gets a weekly or monthly allowance from her husband, it is necessary for him to have drawn his pay or obtained that raise if she is to be able to pay the grocer or buy a new dress. She waits for man to put in an appearance, since her economic dependence places her at his disposal; she is only one element in masculine life while man is her whole existence. The husband has his occupations outside the home, and the wife has to put up with his absence all day long; the lover—passionate as he may be—is the one who decides on their meetings and separations in accordance with his obligations. In bed, she awaits the male's desire, she awaits—sometimes anxiously—her own pleasure.

All she can do is arrive later at the rendezvous her lover has set, not be ready at the time designated by her husband; in that way she asserts the importance of her own occupations, she insists on her independence; and for the moment she becomes the essential subject to whose will the other passively submits. But these are timid attempts at revenge; however persistent she may be in keeping men waiting, she will never compensate for the interminable hours she has spent in watching and hoping, in awaiting the good pleasure of the male.

Woman is bound in a general way to contest foot by foot the rule of man, though recognizing his over-all supremacy and worshipping his idols. Hence that famous "contrariness" for which she has often been reproached. Having no independent domain, she cannot oppose positive truths and values of her own to those asserted and upheld by males; she can only deny them. Her negation is more or less thoroughgoing, according to the way respect and resentment are proportioned in her nature. But in fact she knows all the faults in the masculine system, and she has no hesitation in exposing them.

Women have no grasp on the world of men because their experience does not teach them to use logic and technique; inversely, masculine apparatus loses its power at the frontiers of the feminine realm. There is a whole region of human experience which the male deliberately chooses to ignore because he fails to *think* it: this experience woman *lives*. The engineer, so precise when he is laying out his diagrams, behaves at home like a minor god: a word, and behold, his meal is served, his shirts starched, his children quieted; procreation is an act as swift as the wave of Moses' wand; he sees nothing astounding in these miracles. The concept of the miracle is different from the idea of magic: it presents, in the midst of a world of rational causation, the radical discontinuity of an event without cause, against which the weapons of thought are shattered; whereas magical phenomena are unified by hidden forces the continuity of which can be accepted—without being understood—by a docile mind. The newborn child is miraculous to the paternal minor god, magical for the mother who has experienced its coming to term within her womb. The experience of the man is intelligible but interrupted by blanks; that of the woman is, within its own limits, mysterious and obscure but complete. This obscurity makes her weighty; in his relations with her, the male seems light: he has the lightness of dictators, generals, judges, bureaucrats, codes of law, and abstract principles. This is doubtless what a housekeeper meant when she said, shrugging her shoulders: "Men, they don't think!" Women say, also: "Men, they don't know, they don't know life." To the myth of the praying mantis, women contrast the symbol of the frivolous and obtrusive drone bee.

It is understandable, in this perspective, that woman takes exception to masculine logic. Not only is it inapplicable to her experience, but in his hands, as she knows, masculine reasoning becomes an underhand form of force; men's undebatable pronouncements are intended to confuse her. The intention is to put her in a dilemma: either you agree or you do not. Out of respect for the whole system of accepted principles she should agree; if she refuses, she rejects the entire system. But she cannot venture to go so far; she lacks the means to reconstruct society in different form. Still, she does not accept it as it is. Halfway between revolt and slavery, she resigns herself reluctantly to masculine authority. On each occasion he has to force her to accept the consequences of her halfhearted yielding. Man pursues that chimera, a companion half slave, half free: in yielding to him, he would have her yield to the convincingness of an argument, but she knows that he has himself chosen the premises on which his rigorous deductions depend. As long as she avoids questioning them, he will easily reduce her to silence; nevertheless he will not convince her, for she senses his arbitrariness. And so, annoyed, he will accuse her of being obstinate and illogical; but she refuses to play the game because she knows the dice are loaded.

Woman does not entertain the positive belief that the truth is something *other* than men claim; she recognizes, rather, that there *is not* any fixed truth. It is not only the changing nature of life that makes her suspicious of the principle of constant identity, nor is it the magic phenomena with which she is surrounded that destroy the notion of causality. It is at the heart of the masculine world itself, it is in herself as belonging to this world that she comes upon the ambiguity of all principle, of all value, of everything that exists. She knows that masculine morality, as it concerns her, is a vast hoax. Man pompously thunders forth his code of virtue and honor; but in secret he invites her to disobey it, and he even counts on this disobedience; without it, all that splendid façade behind which he takes cover would collapse.

Man gladly accepts as his authority Hegel's idea according to which the citizen acquires his ethical dignity in transcending himself toward the universal, but as a private individual he has a right to desire and pleasure. His relations with woman, then, lie in a contingent region, where morality no longer applies, where conduct is a matter of indifference. With other men he has relations in which values are involved; he is a free agent confronting other free agents under laws fully recognized by all; but with woman—she was invented for this purpose—he casts off the responsibility of existence, he abandons himself to the mirage of his *en-soi,* or fixed, lower nature, he puts himself on the plane of inauthenticity. He shows himself tyrannical, sadistic, violent, or puerile, masochistic, querulous; he tries to satisfy his obsessions and whims; he is "at ease," he "relaxes," in view of the rights acquired in his public life.

His wife is often astonished—like Thérèse Desqueyroux—at the contrast between the lofty tone of his public utterances and behavior, and "his persevering inventions in the dark." He preaches the higher bith rate, but he is skillful at begetting no more children than suits his convenience. He lauds chaste and faithful wives, but he asks his neighbor's wife to commit adultery. We have seen how hypocritically men decree that abortion is criminal, when each year in France a million women are put by men in a position to need abortion; often enough the husband or lover demands this solution; often too, they assume tacitly that it will be adopted if necessary. They count openly on the woman's willingness to make herself guilty of a crime: her "immorality" is necessary to the harmony of the moral society respected by men.

The most flagrant example of this duplicity is the male's attitude toward prostitution, for it is his demand that creates the supply. I have told with what disgusted skepticism prostitutes regard the respectable gentlemen who condemn vice in general but view their own personal whims with indulgence; yet they regard the girls who live off their bodies as perverted and debauched, not the males who use them. . . .

Woman plays the part of those secret agents who are left to the firing squad if they get caught, and are loaded with rewards if they succeed; it is for her to shoulder all man's immorality: not the prostitute only, but all women who serve as sewer to the shining, wholesome edifice where respectable people have their abode. When, thereupon, to these women one speaks of dignity, honor, loyalty, of all the lofty masculine virtues, it is not astonishing if they decline to "go along." They laugh in derision particularly when the virtuous males have just reproached them for not being disinterested, for play-acting, for lying.[5] They will know that no other way out is open to them. Man, too, is not "disinterested" regarding money and success, but he has the means for attaining them in his work. Woman has been assigned the role of parasite—and every parasite is an exploiter. Woman has need of the male in order to gain human dignity, to eat, to enjoy life, to procreate; it is through the service of sex that she gets these benefits; because she is confined to that function, she is wholly an instrumentality of exploitation.

[5] "All with that little air of delicacy and touch-me-not prudery, assumed in a long past of slavery, with no other means of salvation and support than that air of unintentional seductiveness biding its time." (Jules Laforgue.)

Ashley Montagu

It is to the traditional belief in woman's inferiority that Montagu addresses his book *The Natural Superiority of Women,* first published in 1952. He maintains that the mass of scientific evidence contradicts this tradition at every turn and proves that women are physically and intellectually superior to men. He suggests that the historical insistence on women's inferiority and their subsequent subjection is caused by men's envy of women's capacity to give birth to children, the great creative act. Man's sense of his own inferiority has expressed itself in debasing and bullying women. His jealousy of woman's power to create life has led him to turn childbirth into a handicap and to assert his superiority at every turn. While history has affirmed that men are physically stronger than women, it has done so by narrowly equating strength with muscle power and ignoring other factors such as longevity, stamina, resistance to disease, and ability to endure pain. Constitutionally, Montagu holds, women are stronger than men. As for intellect, while tradition has insisted that men have greater innate powers of reason, women are in fact superior. Since standards of intelligence are culturally defined, and in our culture verbal ability defines the standard, the available data require the laurels to go to women. As a sequel to his argument, Montagu asserts that their maternal functions have made women more humane than men and that the mother-child relation is the paradigm for all human relationships. Woman, a creator, fosters life; man, a mechanizer, destroys life. Montagu applauds the women's liberation movement because it entails liberation for men as well.

THE INTELLECTUAL AND BODILY
SUPERIORITY OF WOMEN*

The biological differences between the sexes obviously provide
the grounds upon which are based the different social roles the
sexes are expected to play. But the significance of the biological
differences is often interpreted in such a manner as to convey the
appearance of a natural connection between conditions that are, in
fact, only artificially connected, that is, by misinterpretation. For
example, in almost all cultures pregnancy, birth, and nursing are
interpreted by both sexes as handicapping experiences; as a consequence women have been made to feel that by virtue of their
biological functions they have been biologically, naturally, placed in
an inferior position to men. But as we today well know, these
biological functions of women are only minimally, if at all,
handicapping.

It is worth paying some attention to the significance of the fact

* From Ashley Montagu, *The Natural Superiority of Women,* rev. ed. (New
York: Macmillan Co., Inc., 1952).

that in the fundamental role in which one would have thought it all too obviously clear that women were the superiors of men, namely, in their ability to bear and bring up children, women have been made to feel that their roles are handicapping ones. The evidence relating to the conditions of childbirth and child rearing in nonliterate societies is scant enough, but the indications are that, on the whole, women in nonliterate societies seem to have an easier time than they do in more complex ones. Unquestionably, under primitive conditions childbirth and child rearing are to some extent handicapping conditions from the male viewpoint. This is the conscious male viewpoint; the unconscious male viewpoint, there is much factual evidence to show, is of a very different nature. In almost all societies birth seems to have been culturally converted into a very much more complex, difficult, and handicapping process than it in fact is. . . .

I believe the evidence strongly indicates that it has been deliberately, if to some extent unconsciously, done. If one can turn childbirth into a handicapping function, then that makes women so much more inferior to the sex that suffers from no such handicap. Persons who resort to such devices are usually concerned not so much with the inferiorities of others as with their own superiority. If one happens to be lacking in certain capacities with which the opposite sex is naturally endowed, and those capacities happen to be highly, if unacknowledgedly, valued, then one can compensate for one's own deficiency by devaluing the capacities of others. By turning capacities into handicaps, not only can one make their possessors feel inferior, but anyone lacking such capacities can then feel superior for very lack of them.

Ludicrous as the idea may appear to some, the fact is that men have been jealous of women's ability to give birth to children . . .

Man's jealousy of woman's capacity to bear children is nowhere better exhibited than in the Old Testament creation story in which man is caused to give birth (from one of his ribs) to woman . . .

Men project their unconscious wishes upon the screen of their society and make their institutions and their gods in the image of their desires. Their envy of woman's physiological powers causes them to feel weak and inferior, and fear is often added to jealousy. An effective way for men to protect themselves against women, as well as to punish them, is to depreciate their capacities by depreciating their status. One can deny the virtues of women's advantages by treating them as disadvantages and by investing them with mysterious or dangerous properties. By making women objects of fear and something to be avoided as unclean, one can lower the cultural status of women by simple inversion. Their biological advantages are demoted to the status of cultural disadvantages, and as cultural disadvantages they are then converted into biological disadvantages. Once this is achieved, there need be no end to the belief in the cultural and biological disadvantages of these traits. . . .

In all societies women have played a much more important role than their menfolk have been generally inclined to admit. After all, if one is afflicted with feelings of inferiority—as the male is with respect to the female—a strong overcompensatory tendency to play cock o' the roost is likely to develop. It is difficult to admit, even though the dark suspicion may have dawned on one, that women are one's equals, and—perish the thought—they certainly are not one's superiors. After all, is not the evidence, the biological evidence, of male superiority unequivocally clear?

The answer is that it is far from clear that man is biologically superior to woman, and that, on the contrary—as we shall see—the evidence indicates that woman is, on the whole, biologically superior to man. Since we have already used the term "superior" without having defined it, and since it is a significant term for our discussion, we had better define it now. The term is used in its common sense as meaning being of better quality or of higher nature or character.

Of better quality or of higher nature or character in respect to what? The question is a crucial one, and upon its correct answer turns the whole theme of this book. The soundness of the book's argument depends upon the soundness of the answer returned to the question. That answer is: Superiority in any trait, whether biological or social, is measured by the extent to which that trait confers survival benefits upon the person and the group. If you function in such a way as to live longer, be more resistant, healthier, and behave in a manner generally calculated to enable you and your progeny to survive more efficiently than others who do not function as efficiently, then by the measure of our definition of superiority you are superior to the others. The reference here is not simply to immediate survival but to the long-term survival of the group. And by group, for the purposes of this discussion, I mean the immediate family, and then the social group of which the family is a part, and finally the whole group of mankind-humanity. . . .

The myth of female inferiority has been extended not only to the mental functions but also to the physical traits and functions of the female. The lesser muscular power of the female has lent the strongest and most obvious kind of support to this belief. The female is "weaker" than the male. That is all men have known about the "facts," and that is all, they have felt, they needed to know. "The facts, after all, are obvious."

What countless errors, what unspeakable crimes, have been committed in the aura of the "authority" carried by such words as, "The facts, after all, are obvious." But what *is* a fact? And "after all" *what?* And what does "obvious" mean? . . .

The female is generally shorter, slighter, and muscularly less powerful than the male; these facts are obvious to everyone. The male, it is asserted, is clearly superior in these respects to the female. Let us here recall our definition of superiority in terms of the conferral of survival benefits upon the possessors of the particular traits under discussion. Do the greater size and muscular power of the male, from the biological standpoint, confer greater survival benefits upon him? We have already answered this question in the negative in the previous chapter, but let us for a moment continue with question and answer from another point of view. Do the lesser size and muscular power of the female confer lesser survival benefits upon her? The answer to these questions, on the basis of the facts, is a resounding "No!" On the contrary, the facts prove that the biological advantages are with the female. . . .

The greater muscular power of the male has, to a large extent, been an economically valuable trait, especially during the long period of man's history when so much of the labor expended in human societies was in the form of muscle power. Today, when machines do more than 90 percent of the work formerly done by muscle, muscular power has become an outmoded redundancy borne by its possessors at a price that exceeds any return it can yield either to them or to society.

Let us apply another test. What is the answer to the question: Which sex survives the rigors of life, whether normal or extreme, better than the other? The answer is: The female sex.

Women endure all sorts of devitalizing conditions better than men: starvation, exposure, fatigue, shock, illness, and the like. This immediately raises the question of the alleged "weakness" of the female. Is not the female supposed to be "the weaker vessel"? "Weakness" is a misleading word that has, in this connection, confused most people. "Feminine weakness" has generally meant that the female is more fragile and in general less strong than the male. But the fact is that the female is *constitutionally* stronger than the male and only muscularly less powerful; she has greater stamina and lives longer. The male pays heavily for his larger body build and muscular power. Because his expenditure of energy is greater than that of the female, he burns himself out more rapidly and hence dies at an earlier age. The metabolic rate of the male, as I have already stated, is some 6 to 7 percent higher than that of the female.

Where, now, are the much-vaunted advantages of larger size and muscular power? Are they biologically fitter in any way? Are they, any longer, even socially advantageous? The answer is that whatever benefits men may have derived from larger size and muscular power in the past, they have in our own time outlived them. Today the advantages are mostly with the smaller bodied, less muscularly powerful female. . . .

To commence life as a male is to start off with a handicap—a handicap that operates at every stage of life, from conception on.

Even though male-determining sperms are produced in the same numbers as female-determining sperms, between 120 and 150 males are conceived as compared with 100 females. Why this should be so we do not know, but it is a fact. The ratio at birth for American whites is 106 males to 100 females. (The ratios vary for different human groups, depending largely upon their socio-economic or nutritional status.) In India the sex ratio of boys is 98.7 to 100 girls. In other words the poorer the nutritional conditions, the greater the lethality of the males; even fetal females are stronger than fetal males. The records uniformly show that from fertilization on, the mortality rates before birth are higher for the male than for the female fetus and that males after birth continue to have a higher mortality rate than females for every year of age. Within every age range, more males die than females. For example, in 1946-48 three boy babies in the first year of life died for every two girl babies. At about the age of twenty-one, for every female who dies almost two males die. Thereafter, at the age of thirty-five, 1,400 men die for every 1,000 women; at fifty-five 1,800 men die for every 1,000 women; after that the difference in death rate diminishes, though it always remains in favor of the female.

Life expectancy at birth is higher for women than for men all over the world (except certain parts of India), and this fact holds true for females as compared with males for the greater part of the animal kingdom. In the United States in 1965 life expectancy at birth for a white female was 74.1 years, and for a white male 67.4 years; for a nonwhite female 66.3 years, and for a nonwhite male 61.1 years. These facts constitute further evidence that the female is constitutionally stronger than the male. There have been some who have argued that women live longer than men because they don't usually work so hard. Most men, it is urged, work harder, work longer hours, and usually under greater strain and tension than most women. These statements are open to question. I am under the impression that most housewives work at least as hard as their husbands, and under at least as great a strain.

Male fetuses do not work harder than female fetuses in the womb, yet they die more frequently before birth than female fetuses. Newborn males do not work harder than newborn females, yet they die more frequently than newborn girls. One-year-old boys do not work harder than one-year-old girls, but the boys die more frequently than the girls. And so one can go on for every age, with the difference in mortality in favor of the female.

In 1957, Francis C. Madigan, working at the University of North Carolina, published a study on the longevity of Catholic Sisters and Brothers who for many years had been living much the same kinds of lives. The same sort of disparity in their mortality rates was found to obtain as among the rest of the general population. The data were obtained on nearly 30,000 Sisters and more than 10,000 Brothers. The expectation of life at the age of fifty-four was found to be an addtional 34 years for the Sisters, but only 28 years more for the Brothers, a difference in favor of the Sisters of 5-1/2 years.

When we compare the longevity rates of bachelors with jobs with those of spinsters with jobs, we find that the advantage is again with the females. Spinsters with jobs live longer than bachelors with jobs. In 1947 the age-adjusted death rate for single men was one and one-half times that for married men, whereas among single women the death rate was only 10 percent higher than that for the married. It is an interesting fact that both among men and among women, the married have lower death rates than the single, widowed, or divorced.

A 14-nation study of the working mother conducted under the auspices of UNESCO and published in 1967 showed that women in general work longer hours and have less leisure time than men. As Professor Alexander Szalai, the project director, put it, "To summarize our findings, let's say that the last state of human bondage still persists, even if its burdens have been considerably lightened.

"More precisely, both categories of women—the working and the non-working are at a disadvantage compared with men. The working women because they are overburdened with work. The non-working women because their labors are underestimated and their existence is much more drab than that of the men."

Women are healthier than men—if by health one means the capacity to deal with germs and illness. Statistics from the public health services of various countries, and especially the United States, show that while after the age of fifteen the sickness rate is higher among females than among males, females recover from illnesses much more frequently than males do. Death from almost all causes are more frequent in males at all ages. Almost the only disorders from which women die more frequently than men are those subserving the functional systems of reproduction; namely, the reproductive tract and the endocrine glandular system.

Epilepsy has about the same incidence in both sexes, but according to the vital statistics of the Bureau of the Census the death rate from epilepsy is about 30 percent higher for men than for women.

For every female stutterer there are five male stutterers. The "stutter-type personality," who is characterized by a certain jerkiness or "stutter" of movements, as well as of speech, occurs in the ratio of eight males to one female. Word deafness, the inherited inability to understand the meaning of sounds, occurs very much more frequently in the male than in the female, and so do baldness, gout, and ulcers of the stomach. Need one go on?

The evidence is clear: From the constitutional standpoint woman is the stronger sex. . . .

In defining intelligence, the concepts that occur most often in the writings of psychologists are the ability to deal with abstract symbols and relationships, and the ability to adapt oneself to new situations. But these are obviously very general definitions, for there are all sorts of abstract symbols, in mathematics, music, philosophy, logic, and so on. A person may be excellent in one area of abstract symbols and poor in others. Adaptation to new situations will often depend upon a person's previous familiarity with the context of the new situation before he can adjust to it intelligently. A South American Indian from the wilds of the Chaco, however intelligent he might be in adapting himself to new situations in his home environment, would almost certainly behave like an idiot in situations completely new to him in a culture, say, such as ours. Indeed, such behavior has often been misattributed to lack of intelligence, whereas it is usually nothing more than a reflection of the cultural disorientation all of us exhibit in foreign surroundings.

Therefore it should be clear that intelligence is very closely related to experience and that it can be defined only in relation to a definite cultural setting or environmental milieu. Within our own cultural milieu, psychologists are generally agreed, intelligence in large part apparently consists of verbal ability. . . .

Throughout the following presentation of the facts, let us always bear in mind the differences that exist in the social environment for males and females, the differences in what is socially expected of boys and girls, and the differences to which they must adapt themselves. Because the facts are so numerous and because it will be clearer and more helpful to the reader, I shall set those facts out in clear, brief sentences so that the reader may grasp them at a glance. Let the reader also remember that the material that goes into an intelligence test will, to a certain significant extent, determine what is meant by intelligence. Finally, I must make it quite clear that in order to obviate any suspicion of special pleading on my part I have relied entirely for the facts upon the admirable presentation of them by Professor Anne Anastasi of Fordham University and of the Psychological Corporation, in her book *Differential Psychology.*[1] In this volume, the author gives, among many other findings on individual and group differences in behavior, a quite comprehensive survey of the scientific findings relating to the intellectual functions of the sexes.

We may as well be prepared for what we are going to find—the cumulative effect of the repeated shock may in this way, for some males, and perhaps even for some women, be broken—namely, that with the exception of the tests for arithmetic, mathematics, mechan-

[1] Third ed. (New York: The Macmillan Company, 1958).

ics and mazes, females achieve significantly and consistently higher scores on the intelligence tests than males.

At the ages of two, three, and four the average IQ, as tested by the Kuhlmann-Binet test, is higher for girls than for boys.

From school age to adult life females obtain a significantly higher average rank on intelligence tests than men.

On tests designed for testing the intelligence of Army inductees during World War I, the Army Alpha test, New England rural women attained a significantly higher average than the men.

From infancy to adulthood the female superiority in verbal or linguistics functions is consistent and marked.

Girls of preschool age have a larger vocabulary than boys.

Girls on the average begin to talk earlier than boys.

Girls begin to use sentences earlier than boys and tend to use more words in sentences.

Girls learn to read earlier and make more rapid progress in reading than boys.

Girls have few reading difficulties compared with the great number of reading disabilities among boys.

Girls excel in speed of reading, tests of opposites, analogies, sentence completion, and story completion.

Girls do better than boys in code-learning tests.

Girls show a highly significant superiority in handling linguistic relations, as in the test requiring them to construct an artificial language. Here the subject is given a short vocabulary and a few grammatical rules, and is then required to "translate" a brief passage in English into the artificial language.

Girls learn foreign languages much more rapidly and accurately than boys, a difference that is maintained throughout life.

Girls excel in most tests of memory. They do significantly better on tests of picture memories and such tests as copying a bead chain from memory.

Girls tend to excel in logical rather than in rote memory, especially when the content of the test favors neither sex. The suggestion is that logical memory depends more upon verbal comprehension than upon anything else, hence the superior achievement on logical-memory tests of the female.

Women are characterized by a more vivid mental imagery than men.

Girls excel, on the whole, in general school achievement as measured by achievement tests and school grades.

Girls do better than boys, on the whole, in those school subjects that depend largely upon verbal ability, memory, and perceptual speed. Boys do better in those subjects that depend on numerical reasoning and spatial aptitudes, as well as in certain "information" subjects, such as history, geography, and general science.

In so far as school progress in concerned, girls are consistently more successful than boys. Girls are less frequently retarded, more frequently advanced, and promoted in larger numbers than boys.

In school grades girls consistently do better than boys, even in those subjects that favor boys.

Girls obtaining the same achievement-test scores as boys consistently had higher school grades than boys.

At the school ages, but not in the preschool age range, boys do better than girls on spatial and mechanical-aptitude tests. But a cultural factor is suspected as operative here, because boys do no better than girls in the preschool years on such tests, and it seems obvious that they depend upon the special kind of information that helps them in these tests and that is not culturally offered to or encouraged in girls. Furthermore, boys do much better in these tests than they do in the more abstract of spatial relations, upon which both sexes may be equally uninformed.

Boys are found to do better than girls on block counting from pictures, directional orientation, plan of search, tests of form boards, puzzle boxes, assembling objects, pencil-and-paper mazes, mechanical comprehension, arithmetic problems and arithmetic reasoning, ingenuity, and induction.

On the Army Alpha tests boys excel significantly in only three tests: arithmetic reasoning, number-series completion, and information.

In arithmetic computation girls do better than boys, but they do not do as well as boys in solving arithmetic problems and in arithmetic reasoning. . . .

In short, the age-old myth that women are of inferior intelligence to men has, so far as the scientific evidence goes, not a leg to stand upon. Indeed, by present tests and standards of measurement girls, on the whole, do better than boys. At school they make better adjustments to conditions than boys and better satisfy the requirements of the definitions offered at the commencement of this chapter than boys do. The conclusion cannot be avoided that girls of school age are, on the whole, more intelligent than boys of school age. The fact is, whatever it may mean, that on entering school at the age of five years the average girl's mental age is two years ahead of that of the average boy. . . .

The natural superiority of women is a biological fact, and a socially unacknowledged reality. The facts have been available for more than half a century, but in a male-dominated world, in which the inflation of the male ego has been dependent upon the preservation of the myth of male superiority, the significance of those facts has simply been denied attention. When the history of the subject comes to be written, this peculiar omission will no doubt serve as yet another forcible illustration that men see only what and how they want to see.

Betty Friedan

Friedan's book *The Feminine Mystique,* published in 1963, provided the impetus for the new women's liberation movement in the second half of the twentieth century. Friedan sought to explain in her book why American women, after making significant gains during the 1920s and 30s, retreated to their traditional role of wives and mothers following World War II. Despite an apparent growth of opportunities for women, despite the increased time afforded them by technological advances, despite their proven competence in industry and business during the war years, women were returning to or remaining in their domestic world with a zeal bordering on fanaticism. They were marrying younger, having more babies, failing to pursue careers despite their education. To be a suburban housewife appeared to be the goal of most American women. Despite all this, Friedan found evidence at every turn that American women were unhappy and frustrated, having failed to find fulfillment where they sought it. She argued that the "feminine mystique"—a false and dehumanizing ideal to which women were everywhere pressed to conform—was being perpetuated by the media, advertising, business, government, and educators in order to promote every interest except woman's. Like Mill one hundred years previously when he compared woman's state with that of slaves, Friedan made a disturbing analogy: she compared the housewife with a prisoner in a Nazi concentration camp, arguing that both were progressively dehumanized. Both states entailed loss of human identity and destruction of self-respect, both reduced their victims to a concern with simple animal needs, both forced abandonment of individuality and preference for the security of the crowd, both imprisoned their victims, cutting them off from the larger world of ideas and events.

THE FEMININE MYSTIQUE*

Gradually I came to realize that the problem that has no name was shared by countless women in America. As a magazine writer I often interviewed women about problems with their children, or their marriages, or their houses, or their communities. But after a while I began to recognize the telltale signs of this other problem. I saw the same signs in suburban ranch houses and split-levels on Long Island and in New Jersey and Westchester County; in colonial houses in a small Massachusetts town; on patios in Memphis; in suburban and city apartments; in living rooms in the Midwest. Sometimes I sensed the problem, not as a reporter, but as a suburban housewife, for during this time I was also bringing up my own three children in Rockland County, New York. I heard echoes of the problem in college dormitories and semi-private maternity wards, at PTA meetings and luncheons of the League of Women

* From Betty Friedan, *The Feminine Mystique* (New York: W. W. Norton and Company, Inc., 1963), Chaps. 1, 12.

Voters, at suburban cocktail parties, in station wagons waiting for trains, and in snatches of conversation overheard at Schrafft's. The groping words I heard from other women, on quiet afternoons when children were at school or on quiet evenings when husbands worked late, I think I understood first as a woman long before I understood their larger social and psychological implications.

Just what was this problem that has no name? What were the words women used when they tried to express it? Sometimes a woman would say, "I feel empty somehow . . . incomplete." Or she would say, "I feel as if I don't exist." Sometimes she blotted out the feeling with a tranquilizer. Sometimes she thought the problem was with her husband, or her children, or that what she really needed was to redecorate her house, or move to a better neighborhood, or have an affair, or another baby. Sometimes, she went to a doctor with symptoms she could hardly describe: "A tired feeling . . . I get so angry with the children it scares me . . . I feel like crying without any reason." (A Cleveland doctor called it "the housewife's syndrome.") A number of women told me about great bleeding blisters that break out on their hands and arms. "I call it the housewife's blight," said a family doctor in Pennsylvania. "I see it so often lately in these young women with four, five and six children who bury themselves in their dishpans. But it isn't caused by detergent and it isn't cured by cortisone." . . .

It is no longer possible to ignore that voice, to dismiss the desperation of so many American women. This is not what being a woman means, no matter what the experts say. For human suffering there is a reason; perhaps the reason has not been found because the right questions have not been asked, or pressed far enough. I do not accept the answer that there is no problem because American women have luxuries that women in other times and lands never dreamed of; part of the strange newness of the problem is that it cannot be understood in terms of the age-old material problems of man: poverty, sickness, hunger, cold. The women who suffer this problem have a hunger that food cannot fill. It persists in women whose husbands are struggling internes and law clerks, or prosperous doctors and lawyers; in wives of workers and executives who make $5,000 a year or $50,000. It is not caused by lack of material advantages; it may not even be felt by women preoccupied with desperate problems of hunger, poverty or illness. And women who think it will be solved by more money, a bigger house, a second car, moving to a better suburb, often discover it gets worse.

It is no longer possible today to blame the problem on loss of femininity: to say that education and independence and equality with men have made American women unfeminine. I have heard so many women try to deny this dissatisfied voice within themselves because it does not fit the pretty picture of femininity the experts have given them. I think, in fact, that this is the first clue to the mystery: the problem cannot be understood in the generally accepted terms by which scientists have studied women, doctors have treated them, counselors have advised them, and writers have written about them. Women who suffer this problem, in whom this voice is stirring, have lived their whole lives in the pursuit of feminine fulfillment. They are not career women (although career women may have other problems); they are women whose greatest ambition has been marriage and children. For the oldest of these women, these daughters of the American middle class, no other dream was possible. The ones in their forties and fifties who once had other dreams gave them up and threw themselves joyously into life as housewives. For the youngest, the new wives and mothers, this was the only dream. They are the ones who quit high school and college to marry, or marked time in some job in which they had no real interest until they married. These women are very "feminine" in the usual sense, and yet they still suffer the problem. . . .

I think it will not end, as long as the feminine mystique masks the emptiness of the housewife role, encouraging girls to evade their own growth by vicarious living, by non-commitment. We have gone on too long blaming or pitying the mothers who devour their children, who sow the seeds of progressive dehumanization, because they have never grown to full humanity themselves. If the mother is at fault, why isn't it time to break the pattern by urging all these

Sleeping Beauties to grow up and live their own lives? There never will be enough Prince Charmings, or enough therapists to break that pattern now. It is society's job, and finally that of each woman alone. For it is not the strength of the mothers that is at fault but their weakness, their passive childlike dependency and immaturity that is mistaken for "femininity." Our society forces boys, insofar as it can, to grow up, to endure the pains of growth, to educate themselves to work, to move on. Why aren't girls forced to grow up—to achieve somehow the core of self that will end the unnecessary dilemma, the mistaken choice between femaleness and humanness that is implied in the feminine mystique?

It is time to stop exhorting mothers to "love" their children more, and face the paradox between the mystique's demand that women devote themselves completely to their home and their children, and the fact that most of the problems now being treated in child-guidance clinics are solved only when the mothers are helped to develop autonomous interests of their own, and no longer need to fill their emotional needs through their children. It is time to stop exhorting women to be more "feminine" when it breeds a passivity and dependence that depersonalizes sex and imposes an impossible burden on their husbands, a growing passivity in their sons.

It is not an exaggeration to call the stagnating state of millions of American housewives a sickness, a disease in the shape of a progressively weaker core of human self that is being handed down to their sons and daughters at a time when the dehumanizing aspects of modern mass culture make it necessary for men and women to have a strong core of self, strong enough to retain human individuality through the frightening, unpredictable pressures of our changing environment. The strength of women is not the cause, but the cure for this sickness. Only when women are permitted to use their full strength, to grow to their full capacities, can the feminine mystique be shattered and the progressive dehumanization of their children be stopped. And most women can no longer use their full strength, grow to their full human capacity, as housewives.

It is urgent to understand how the very condition of being a housewife can create a sense of emptiness, non-existence, nothingness, in women. There are aspects of the housewife role that make it almost impossible for a woman of adult intelligence to retain a sense of human identity, the firm core of self or "I" without which a human being, man or woman, is not truly alive. For women of ability, in America today, I am convinced there is something about the housewife state itself that is dangerous. In a sense that is not as far-fetched as it sounds, the women who "adjust" as housewives, who grow up wanting to be "just a housewife," are in as much danger as the millions who walked to their own death in the concentration camps—and the millions more who refused to believe that the concentration camps existed.

In fact, there is an uncanny, uncomfortable insight into why a woman can so easily lose her sense of self as a housewife in certain psychological observations made of the behavior of prisoners in Nazi concentration camps. In these settings, purposely contrived for the dehumanization of man, the prisoners literally became "walking corpses." Those who "adjusted" to the conditions of the camps surrendered their human identity and went almost indifferently to their deaths. Strangely enough, the conditions which destroyed the human identity of so many prisoners were not the torture and the brutality, but conditions similar to those which destroy the identity of the American housewife.

In the concentration camps the prisoners were forced to adopt childlike behavior, forced to give up their individuality and merge themselves into an amorphous mass. Their capacity for self-determination, their ability to predict the future and to prepare for it, was systematically destroyed. It was a gradual process which occurred in virtually imperceptible stages—but at the end, with the destruction of adult self-respect, of an adult frame of reference, the dehumanizing process was complete. This was the process as observed by Bruno Bettelheim, psychoanalyst and educational psychologist, when he was a prisoner at Dachau and Buchenwald in 1939.[1]

[1] Bruno Bettelheim, *The Informed Heart—Autonomy in a Mass Age,* The Free Press, Glencoe, Ill., 1960.

When they entered the concentration camp, prisoners were almost traumatically cut off from their past adult interests. This in itself was a major blow to their identity over and above their physical confinement. A few, though only a few, were able to work privately in some way that had interested them in the past. But to do this alone was difficult; even to talk about these larger adult interests, or to show some initiative in pursuing them, aroused the hostility of other prisoners. New prisoners tried to keep their old interests alive, but "old prisoners seemed mainly concerned with the problem of how to live as well as possible inside the camp."

To old prisoners, the world of the camp was the only reality.[2] They were reduced to childlike preoccupation with food, elimination, the satisfaction of primitive bodily needs; they had no privacy, and no stimulation from the outside world. But, above all, they were forced to spend their days in work which produced great fatigue—not because it was physically killing, but because it was monotonous, endless, required no mental concentration, gave no hope of advancement or recognition, was sometimes senseless and was controlled by the needs of others or the tempo of machines. It was work that did not emanate from the prisoner's own personality; it permitted no real initiative, no expression of the self, not even a real demarcation of time.

And the more the prisoners gave up their adult human identity, the more they were preoccupied with the fear that they were losing their sexual potency, and the more preoccupied they became with the simplest animal needs. It brought them comfort, at first, to surrender their individuality, and lose themselves in the anonymity of the mass—to feel that "everyone was in the same boat." But strangely enough, under these conditions, real friendships did not grow.[3] Even conversation, which was the prisoners' favorite pastime and did much to make life bearable, soon ceased to have any real meaning.[4] So rage mounted in them. But the rage of the millions

[2] *Ibid.,* pp. 162-169.
[3] *Ibid.,* pp. 231.
[4] *Ibid.,* pp. 233ff.

that could have knocked down the barbed wire fences and the SS guns was turned instead against themselves, and against the prisoners even weaker than they. Then they felt even more powerless than they were, and saw the SS and the fences as even more impregnable than they were.

It was said, finally, that not the SS but the prisoners themselves became their own worst enemy. Because they could not bear to see their situation as it really was—because they denied the very reality of their problem, and finally "adjusted" to the camp itself as if it were the only reality—they were caught in the prison of their own minds. The guns of the SS were not powerful enough to keep all those prisoners subdued. They were manipulated to trap themselves; they imprisoned themselves by making the concentration camp the whole world, by blinding themselves to the larger world of the past, their responsibility for the present, and their possibilities for the future. The ones who survived, who neither died nor were exterminated, were the ones who retained in some essential degree the adult values and interests which had been the essence of their past identity.

All this seems terribly remote from the easy life of the American suburban housewife. But is her house in reality a comfortable concentration camp? Have not women who live in the image of the feminine mystique trapped themselves within the narrow walls of their homes? They have learned to "adjust" to their biological role. They have become dependent, passive, childlike; they have given up their adult frame of reference to live at the lower human level of food and things. The work they do does not require adult capabilities; it is endless, montonous, unrewarding. American women are not, of course, being readied for mass extermination, but they are suffering a slow death of mind and spirit. Just as with the prisoners in the concentration camps, there are American women who have resisted that death, who have managed to retain a core of self, who have not lost touch with the outside world, who use their abilities to some creative purpose. They are women of spirit and intelligence who have refused to "adjust" as housewives.

It has been said time and time again that education has kept American women from "adjusting" to their role as housewives. But if education, which serves human growth, which distills what the human mind has discovered and created in the past, and gives man the ability to create his own future—if education has made more and more American women feel trapped, frustrated, guilty as housewives, surely this should be seen as a clear signal *that women have outgrown the housewife role.*

It is not possible to preserve one's identity by adjusting for any length of time to a frame of reference that is in itself destructive to it. It is very hard indeed for a human being to sustain such an "inner" split—comforting outwardly to one reality, while trying to maintain inwardly the values it denies. The comfortable concentration camp that American women have walked into, or have been talked into by others, is just such a reality, a frame of reference that denies woman's adult human identity. By adjusting to it, a woman stunts her intelligence to become childlike, turns away from individual identity to become an anonymous biological robot in a docile mass. She becomes less than human, preyed upon by outside pressures, and herself preying upon her husband and children. And the longer she conforms, the less she feels as if she really exists. She looks for her security in things, she hides the fear of losing her human potency by testing her sexual potency, she lives a vicarious life through mass daydreams or through her husband and children. She does not want to be reminded of the outside world; she becomes convinced there is nothing she can do about her own life or the world that would make a difference. But no matter how often she tries to tell herself that this giving up of personal identity is a necessary sacrifice for her children and husband, it serves no real purpose. So the aggressive energy she should be using in the world becomes instead the terrible anger that she dare not turn against her husband, is ashamed of turning against her children, and finally turns against herself, until she feels as if she does not exist. And yet in the comfortable concentration camp as in the real one, something very strong in a woman resists the death of herself.

Describing an unforgettable experience in a real concentration camp, Bettelheim tells of a group of naked prisoners—no longer human, merely docile robots—who were lined up to enter the gas chamber. The SS commanding officer, learning that one of the women prisoners had been a dancer, ordered her to dance for him. She did, and as she danced, she approached him, seized his gun and shot him down. She was immediately shot to death, but Bettelheim is moved to ask:

> Isn't it probable that despite the grotesque setting in which she danced, dancing made her once again a person. Dancing, she was singled out as an individual, asked to perform in what had once been her chosen vocation. No longer was she a number, a nameless depersonalized prisoner but the dancer she used to be. Transformed however momentarily, she responded like her old self, destroying the enemy bent on her destruction even if she had to die in the process.
>
> Despite the hundreds of thousands of living dead men who moved quietly to their graves, this one example shows that in an instant, the old personality can be regained, its destruction undone, once we decide on our own that we wish to cease being units in a system. Exercising the lost freedom that not even the concentration camp could take away—to decide how one wishes to think and feel about the conditions of one's life—this dancer threw off her real prison. This she could do because she was willing to risk her life to achieve autonomy once more.[5]

The suburban house is not a German concentration camp, nor are American housewives on their way to the gas chamber. But they are in a trap, and to escape they must, like the dancer, finally exercise their human freedom, and recapture their sense of self. They must refuse to be nameless, depersonalized, manipulated and live their own lives again according to a self-chosen purpose. They must begin to grow.

[5] *Ibid.,* p. 265.

Herbert Marcuse

Central to Marcuse's writings has been the attempt to expose the essentially repressive quality of capitalistic societies and to provide an alternative vision of a truly unrepressive socialist society. Marcuse sees the liberation of women and men, the establishment of a new relationship between the sexes, as vital to the emergence of a genuinely free community. In *Counterrevolution and Revolt* (1972), Marcuse argues that such a liberation needs a radical metamorphosis of needs and aspirations, whether cultural or material, an alteration of consciousness itself, and a transformation of work processes. More specifically, it would require abandonment of the masculine principle, the rule of which has been characterized by destructive productivity, and realization of the female principle, characterized by loving receptivity. While these distinctions are socially determined and mutilate the human personality, characteristics associated with women provide the model for future relations between the sexes, between generations, and between human beings and nature. They mark an end to the aggressiveness that typifies patriarchal culture and reaches its ultimate expression in capitalism. Marcuse argues that the liberation of women and establishment of equality between the sexes must not mean the absorption by women of the masculine nature. Rather, the female principle, created by paternal culture and representing as it does the negation of all associated with masculinity and capitalism, will finally destroy its creator. Ironically, although women and men have both been dehumanized by capitalist forces, women, who have historically been cut off from the work world and its destructive productivity, have been less brutalized and less cut off from their human sensibility. Unlike Montagu, Marcuse is not arguing that the female principle is equivalent to the matriarchal model, a view of woman that is itself repressive, since it defines the good for women in biological terms.

CAPITALISM AND WOMEN'S
LIBERATION *

It is not just in passing and out of exuberance that Marx speaks of the formation of the object world "in accordance with the laws of beauty" as a feature of free human practice. Aesthetic qualities are essentially nonviolent, nondomineering qualities which, in the domain of the arts, and in the repressive use of the term "aesthetic" as pertaining to the sublimated "higher culture" only, are divorced from the social reality and from "practice" as such. The revolution would undo this repression and recapture aesthetic needs as a subversive force, capable of counteracting the dominating aggressiveness which has shaped the social and natural universe. The faculty of being "receptive," "passive," is a precondition of freedom: it is the ability to see things in their own right, to experience the joy enclosed in them, the erotic energy of nature—an energy which is there to be liberated; nature, too, awaits the revolution! This receptivity is itself the soil of creation: it is opposed, not to productivity, but to destructive productivity.

* From Herbert Marcuse, *Counterrevolution and Revolt* (Boston: Beacon Press, 1972), Chap. 2, Sec. 4.

The latter has been the ever more conspicuous feature of male domination; inasmuch as the "male principle" has been the ruling mental and physical force, a free society would be the "definite negation" of this principle—it would be a female society. In this sense, it has nothing to do with matriarchy of any sort; the image of the woman as mother is itself repressive; it transforms a biological fact into an ethical and cultural value and thus it supports and justifies her social repression. At stake is rather the ascent of Eros over aggression, in men and women; and this means, in a male-dominated civilization, the "femalization" of the male. It would express the decisive change in the instinctual structure: the weakening of primary aggressiveness which, by a combination of biological and social factors, has governed the patriarchal culture.

In this transformation, the Women's Liberation Movement becomes a radical force to the degree to which it transcends the entire sphere of aggressive needs and performances, the entire social organization and division of functions. In other words, the movement becomes radical to the degree to which it aims, not only at equality *within* the job and value structure of the *established* society (which would be the equality of dehumanization) but rather at a change in the structure itself (the basic demands of equal opportunity, equal pay, and release from full-time household and child care are a prerequisite). Within the established structure, neither men nor women are free—and the dehumanization of men may well be greater than that of women since the former suffer not only the conveyor belt and assembly line but also the standards and "ethics" of the "business community."

And yet, the liberation of women would be more sweeping than that of men because the repression of women has been constantly fortified by the social use of their biological constitution. The bearing of children, being a mother, is supposed to be not only their natural function but also the fulfillment of their "nature"—and so is being a wife, since the reproduction of the species occurs within the framework of the monogamous patriarchal family. Outside this framework, the woman is still predominantly a plaything or a temporary outlet for sexual energy not consummated in marriage.

Marxian theory considers sexual exploitation as the primary, original exploitation, and the Women's Liberation Movement fights the degradation of the woman to a "sexual object." But it is difficult to overcome the feeling that here, repressive qualities characteristic of the bourgeois-capitalist organization of society enter into the fight against this organization. Historically, the image of the woman as sexual object, and her exchange value on the market, devalue the earlier repressive images of the woman as mother and wife. These earlier images were essential to the bourgeois ideology during a period of capitalist development now left behind: the period where some "inner-worldly asceticism" was still operative in the dynamic of the economy. In comparison, the present image of the woman as sexual object is a *desublimation* of bourgeois morality—characteristic of a "higher stage" of capitalist development. Here, too, the commodity form is universalized: it now invades formerly sanctified and protected realms. The (female) body, as seen and plastically idealized by *Playboy,* becomes desirable merchandise with a high exchange value. Disintegration of bourgeois morality, perhaps—but *cui bono?* To be sure, this new body image promotes sales, and the plastic beauty may not be the real thing, but they stimulate aesthetic-sensuous needs which, in their development, must become incompatible with the body as instrument of alienated labor. The male body, too, is made the object of sexual image creation—also plasticized and deodorized . . . clean exchange value. After secular- ization of religion, after the transformation of ethics into Orwellian hypocrisy—is the "socialization" of the body as sexual object perhaps one of the last decisive steps toward the completion of the exchange society: the completion which is the beginning of the end?

Still, the publicity with the body (at present, the female body) as object is dehumanizing, the more so since it plays up to the dominant male as the aggressive subject for whom the female is there, to be taken, to be laid. It is in the nature of sexual relationships that both, male and female, are object *and* subject at the same time; erotic and aggressive energy are fused in both. The surplus-aggression of the male is socially conditioned—as is the surplus-passivity of the female. But beneath the social factors which determine male aggressiveness and female receptivity, a *natural* contrast exists: it is the woman who "embodies," in a literal sense, the promise of peace, of joy, of the end of violence. Tenderness, receptivity, sensuousness have become features (or mutilated features) of her body—features of her (repressed) humanity. These female qualities may well be socially determined by the development of capitalism. The process is truly dialectical.[1] Although the reduction of the concrete individual faculties to abstract labor power established an abstract equality between men and women (equality before the machine), this abstraction was less complete in the case of women. They were employed in the material process of production to a lesser extent than men. Women were fully employed in the household, the family, which was supposed to be the sphere of realization for the bourgeois individual. However, this sphere was isolated from the productive process and thus contributed to the women's mutilation. And yet, this isolation (separation) from the alienated work world of capitalism enabled the woman to remain less brutalized by the Performance Principle, to remain closer to her sensibility: more human than men. That this image (and reality) of the woman has been determined by an aggressive, male-dominated society does not mean that this determination must be rejected, that the liberation of women must overcome the female "nature." This equalization of male and female would be regressive: it would be a new form of female acceptance of a male principle. Here too the historical process is dialectical: the patriarchal society has created a female image, a female counter-force, which may still become one of the gravediggers of patriarchal society. In this sense too, the woman holds the promise of liberation. It is the woman who, in Delacroix' painting, holding the flag of the revolution, leads

---

[1] This dialectic is the center of Angela Davis's paper *Marxism and Women's Liberation* (not yet published). Written in jail, this paper is the work of a great woman, militant, intellectual.

the people on the barricades. She wears no uniform; her breasts are bare, and her beautiful face shows no trace of violence. But she has a rifle in her hand—for the end of violence is still to be fought for . . .

United Nations

In 1967 the representatives of the peoples of the world unanimously adopted a Declaration of Women's Rights. In its sweeping mandates it addressed the most pressing cause for freedom in the twentieth century, a cause not restricted to a single group or a single nation, but one touching the lives of every man, woman, and child on earth. The significance of the United Nations Declaration lies in the legitimacy it lent to the women's liberation movement in every corner of the world, in its categorical affirmation that widespread discrimination against women violated the very Charter of that body. While lacking the power to enforce its Decree, the United Nations nonetheless publicly proclaimed its recognition that the cause of equal rights for women was one with the cause of human dignity, of familial and social welfare, of the economic and cultural progress of nations, and of peace itself. It spoke at a time when the status of women in male-dominated political structures varied from legalized inequality in the West, to near slavery in parts of the Middle East, to hypocritical acceptance in Russia. The

Declaration addresses not merely the question of formal legal rights for women, but also the roots of the issue, the question of attitudes and customs that conspire to preserve, in the face of evidence to the contrary, the idea that women are inferior to men. It is significant as a measure of what remains to be done that United Nations Covenants of particular application to women, which are legally binding (unlike its Declarations), are still not in force. Very few nations have signed these Covenants, completed in 1966. Ironically, the Declaration of Women's Rights, which nations unanimously signed, expressly calls for acceptance of all such international instruments.

UNITED NATIONS

DECLARATION OF WOMEN'S RIGHTS *

The General Assembly,

Considering that the peoples of the United Nations have, in the Charter, reaffirmed their faith in fundamental human rights, in the dignity and worth of the human person and in the equal rights of men and women,

Considering that the Universal Declaration of Human Rights asserts the principle of nondiscrimination and proclaims that all human beings are born free and equal in dignity and rights and that everyone is entitled to all the rights and freedoms set forth therein, without distinction of any kind, including any distinction as to sex,

Taking into account the resolutions, declarations, conventions and recommendations of the United Nations and the specialized agencies designed to eliminate all forms of discrimination and to promote equal rights for men and women,

* From Declaration on the elimination of discrimination against women, adopted by the General Assembly of the United Nations, Resolution 2263 (XXII), Nov. 7, 1967.

Concerned that, despite the Charter, the Universal Declaration of Human Rights, International Covenants on Human Rights and other instruments of the United Nations and the specialized agencies and despite the progress made in the matter of equality of rights, there continues to exist considerable discrimination against women,

Considering that discrimination against women is incompatible with human dignity, and with the welfare of the family and of society, prevents their participation on equal terms with men, in the political, social, economic and cultural life of their countries, and is an obstacle to the full development of the potentialities of women in the service of their countries and humanity,

Bearing in mind the great contribution made by women to social, political, economic and cultural life and the part they play in the family and particularly in the rearing of children,

Convinced that the full and complete development of a country, the welfare of the world and the cause of peace require the maximum participation of women as well as men in all fields,

Considering that it is necessary to insure the universal recognition in law and in fact of the principle of equality of men and women,

Solemnly proclaims this Declaration:

ARTICLE 1

Discrimination against women, denying or limiting as it does their equality of rights with men, is fundamentally unjust and constitutes an offense against human dignity.

ARTICLE 2

All appropriate measures shall be taken to abolish existing laws, customs, regulations and practices which are discriminatory against women, and to establish adequate legal protection for equal rights of men and women, in particular:

(a) The principle of equality of rights shall be embodied in the constitution or otherwise guaranteed by law;

(b) The international instruments of the United Nations and the specialized agencies relating to the elimination of discrimination against women shall be ratified or acceded to and fully implemented as soon as practicable.

ARTICLE 3

All appropriate measures shall be taken to educate public opinion and direct national aspirations toward the eradication of prejudice and the abolition of customary and all other practices which are based on the idea of the inferiority of women.

ARTICLE 4

All appropriate measures shall be taken to ensure to women on equal terms with men without any discrimination:

(a) The right to vote in all elections and be eligible for election to all publicly elected bodies;

(b) The right to vote in all public referenda;

(c) The right to hold public office and to exercise all public functions.

Such rights shall be guaranteed by legislation.

ARTICLE 5

Women shall have the same rights as men to acquire, change or retain their nationality. Marriage to an alien shall not automatically effect the nationality of the wife either by rendering her stateless or by forcing on her the nationality of her husband.

ARTICLE 6

1. Without prejudice to the safeguarding of the unity and the harmony of the family which remains the basic unit of any society, all appropriate measures, particularly legislative measures, shall be taken to insure to women, married or unmarried, equal rights with men in the field of civil law, and in particular:

(a) The right to acquire, administer and enjoy, dispose of and inherit property, including property acquired during the marriage;

(b) The right to equality in legal capacity and the exercise thereof;

(c) The same rights as men with regard to the law on the movement of persons.

2. All appropriate measures shall be taken to insure the principle of equality of status of the husband and wife, and in particular:

(a) Women shall have the same right as men to free choice of a spouse and to enter into marriage only with their free and full consent;

(b) Women shall have equal rights with men during marriage and at its dissolution. In all cases the interest of the child shall be paramount;

(c) Parents shall have equal rights and duties in matters relating to their children. In all cases the interest of the children shall be paramount.

3. Child marriage and the betrothal of young girls before puberty shall be prohibited, and effective action, including legislation, shall be taken to specify a minimum age for marriage and to make the registration of marriages in an official registry compulsory.

ARTICLE 7

All provisions of penal codes which constitute discrimination against women shall be repealed.

ARTICLE 8

All appropriate measures, including legislation, shall be taken to combat all forms of traffic in women and exploitation of prostitution of women.

ARTICLE 9

All appropriate measures shall be taken to insure to girls and women, married or unmarried, equal rights with men in education at all levels, and in particular:

(a) Equal conditions of access to, and study in, educational institutions of all types, including universities, vocational, technical and professional schools;

(b) The same choice of curricula, the same examinations, teaching staff with qualifications of the same standard, and school premises and equipment of the same quality, whether the institutions are coeducational or not;

(c) Equal opportunities to benefit from scholarships and other study grants;

(d) Equal opportunities for access to programs of continuing education, including adult literacy programs;

(e) Access to educational information to help in insuring the health and well-being of families.

ARTICLE 10

1. All appropriate measures shall be taken to insure to women, married or unmarried, equal rights with men in the field of economic and social life, and in particular:

(a) The right without discrimination on grounds of marital status or any other grounds, to receive vocational training, to work, to free choice of profession and employment, and to professional and vocational advancement;

(b) The right to equal remuneration with men and to equality of treatment in respect of work of equal value;

(c) The right to leave with pay, retirement privileges and provision for security in respect of unemployment, sickness, old age or other incapacity to work;

(d) The right to receive family allowances on equal terms with men.

2. In order to prevent discrimination against women on account of marriage or maternity and to insure their effective right to work, measures shall be taken to prevent their dismissal in the event of marriage or maternity and to provide paid maternity leave, and the guarantee of returning to former employment, and to provide the necessary social services, including childcare facilities.

3. Measures taken to protect women in certain types of work, for

reasons inherent in their physical nature, shall not be regarded as discriminatory.

ARTICLE 11

The principle of equality of rights of men and women demands implementation in all states in accordance with the principles of the United Nations Charter and of the Universal Declaration of Human Rights.

Governments, nongovernmental organizations and individuals are urged, therefore, to do all in their power to promote the implementation of the principles contained in this Declaration.

Biographical Notes

Thomas Aquinas (1225-1274) Thomas, the son of Theodora and Landolfo of Aquino, was born in Roccasecca, Italy. As a youngster he studied at the nearby Benedictine monastary in Montecassino. During his early teens he studied at the University of Naples. Having decided to become a Dominican priest, Thomas entered the order in 1244. He pursued his studies in philosophy and theology at Paris and later at Cologne, where he was a student of Albertus Magnus. During the years that followed he taught at various places including Paris, Bologna, Rome, and Naples. In 1268 he returned to Paris where he engaged in several theological controversies. He had already begun writing a systematic treatment of Catholic thought. Summoned back to Italy, Thomas taught at the University of Naples until ill health forced him to retire. While en route to France to attend the Council of Lyons under Pope Gregory X, he died at Fossanova, not far from his place of birth. Thomas wrote several voluminous theological treatises, philosophical disputations, and commentaries on many books.

Aristotle (384-322 B.C.) Aristotle was born in the city of Stagira in Macedon, the son of Nicomachus, who served as the personal physican of King Amyntas II. At the age of eighteen Aristotle was sent to Athens, where he became a student of Plato. He remained at the Academy for the next twenty years, studying and teaching. After Plato's death, when the Academy was taken over by Speusippus, Aristotle and a group of Platonists left Athens. Five years later the King of Macedon summoned Aristotle to tutor his son, Alexander, who later became known as Alexander the Great. He served in this capacity for a few years and finally, in 335 B.C., returned to Athens to establish a school, the Lyceum. In the bitter aftermath of Alexander's death in 323 B.C. Aristotle fled Athens and took up residence in Chalcis until his own death a year later. The surviving works of Aristotle cover virtually all the disciplines known in ancient Greece.

Augustine (354-430) Born in Tagaste, North Africa, Augustine was the son of Roman parents. His mother, Monica, was a Christian who over the years influenced her son greatly. While a teacher of Rhetoric, Augustine involved himself in theological and philosophical problems, eventually becoming a skeptic. Dissatisfied with his life, he was plunged into a prolonged period of personal turmoil which finally led to his conversion to Christianity in 387 in Milan. Within three years of his conversion and return to Tagaste, he was ordained a priest, and in 395 he became Bishop of Hippo in Africa, propagating his faith until his death. Augustine left behind many sermons, letters, formal treatises, and other writings.

Francis Bacon (1561-1626) Born into an influential family in London, Bacon had a less-than-consistent upbringing. His mother sought to inculcate in her son her own Puritan piety. His father, on the other hand, wanted worldly success for Francis and instructed him accordingly. After Bacon had studied at Cambridge for some years, his father died and he sought to improve his faded prospects by taking up the law. At age twenty-three he entered the House of

Commons. Bacon was appointed Lord Chancellor in 1618 and three years later he became Viscount St. Albans. His days in the courts of Elizabeth I and James I were not marked by moral integrity—he prosecuted a loyal friend who fell from favor, he assisted in torturing prisoners, and he was indicted on charges of accepting bribes. Stripped of his offices at Court, Bacon retired to write and pursue his lifelong interest in philosophy of science for which he is best remembered.

Simone de Beauvoir (1908-) De Beauvoir was born in Paris and educated at Catholic schools, finally entering the Sorbonne to study philosophy. Between 1931 and 1943 she taught. After the publication of a novel she left teaching and turned full time to writing. In 1945 she founded the controversial magazine *Les Temps Modernes* with Jean-Paul Sartre and in 1949 won the Goncourt prize for one of her novels. Her career in writing continued with a prolific outpouring of existentialist literature, both fiction and nonfiction, by which she became one of the most prominent literary persons of the twentieth century.

Charles Darwin (1809-1882) Born into an established family in Shrewsbury, England, Darwin entered the University of Edinburgh to study medicine, the family profession. Unsuited to this, he allowed his father's wishes to prevail and entered Cambridge to study theology. Eventually his continuing interest in collecting beetles led Darwin to study science. A five-year voyage aboard the *Beagle* as naturalist was decisive and culminated in Darwin's advocacy of the theory of evolution. With the appearance of his book *The Origin of the Species* an intellectual storm broke over Europe and America that revolutionized virtually every area of thought inside and outside the natural sciences. Much maligned and much honored, Darwin died of a heart attack and was buried in Westminister Abbey.

Ralph Waldo Emerson (1803-1882) A native of Boston, Emerson studied at Harvard University and taught for a period while working toward a theological degree. Dissatisfied with Unitarianism, he resigned his pastorate in 1831, the same year in which his young wife died. Troubled for a time by an intellectual crisis and failing health, he traveled to Europe, where he met Carlyle, Wordsworth, and Coleridge. Upon his return to America Emerson led the Transcendental Movement which established itself in Concord. His extensive writings, his wide travels, his numerous lectures, and his involvement in timely issues gave him an international reputation as America's most influential man of letters.

Friedrich Engels (1820-1895) Born in the German Rhineland, Engels moved to England to work in one of his father's textile mills. A versatile person, he pursued many interests as a linguist, soldier, scholar, writer, and businessman. In 1842 Engels met Karl Marx; their acquaintanceship culminated in a lifelong association in political causes and collaboration in writing. Throughout that association Engels contributed substantially to the philosophical aspects of Marxism, especially with his ideas on historical materialism and dialectics. In Marx's severe financial difficulties Engels contributed generously to the support of the Marx family. He outlived Marx by twelve years and witnessed the early growth of a worldwide political movement that, together with Marx, he had helped to initiate.

Sigmund Freud (1856-1939) At the age of four Freud moved from his hometown of Freiberg in Moravia to Vienna, where he lived most of his life. As a young student, Freud was attracted to science, history, and philosophy. Eventually he studied medicine, and although his interests were primarily in research, he practiced neurology for financial reasons. In 1885 he continued his neurological studies in Paris and began to turn decisively toward psychology. The following year Freud married Martha Bernays with whom he had six children. His influence grew over the years as his work progressed in the theoretical, technical, and clinical aspects of psychology. His investigations, especially in the area of childhood sexuality, were highly controversial and reaction was often abusive. Nonetheless his pioneering work in psychoanalysis was seminal in the development of psychology and in the impact it had on widely varying fields of study. In 1938 Freud fled to London as Nazi troops advanced into Austria. He died there the following year.

Betty Friedan (1921-) Born in Peoria, Illinois, Friedan was educated at Smith College, where she graduated summa cum laude in 1942. The following year she held a research fellowship at the University of California at Berkeley. Friedan married in 1947 and reared three children. During this period she wrote for several women's magazines and became aware of the profound dissatisfaction of women. Friedan published *The Feminine Mystique* in 1963 and was thereby thrust into national prominence. Since that time she has been a leader in the women's rights movement, founding the National Organization for Women in 1966 and organizing the National Women's Political Caucus in 1971. In 1972 she received the American Humanist Award. She has actively lectured on Feminism in Europe and America and has continued to write on the subject.

George Hegel (1770-1831) Born in Stuttgart, the son of a government official, Hegel studied philosophy and theology in the Protestant seminary at Tübingen. After tutoring in aristocratic families for a period, he went to Jena to teach philosophy in 1800. Only a year after being promoted to the rank of professor, he fled Jena when Napoleon's troops defeated the Prussians in 1806. For the next two years Hegel edited a newspaper in Bavaria and then directed the *Gymnasium* at Nuremberg for eight years. After a brief stint at the University of Heidelberg, he became a professor of philosophy at the University of Berlin in 1818. It was during this period that he achieved considerable fame and exerted much influence until his death of cholera. His extensive writings cover virtually all areas of philosophical concern.

Thomas Hobbes (1588-1679) A native of Malmesbury, England, Hobbes was the son of a vicar but he was raised by his uncle. Educated at Oxford, he became tutor to the son of William Cavendish, thereby traveling and meeting such prominent figures as Descartes and Galileo. Hobbes' interest in geometry and the principles of motion was eventually applied to the study of political theory. Caught in controversies because of his political writings, he finally fled to Paris in 1640 to pursue his philosophical writings. He returned to England in 1651, where he continued to produce numerous political works and periodically became embroiled in controversies. He died at the age of ninety-one, leaving behind some of the most influential writings ever produced in political theory.

Karen Horney (1885-1952) Born in Hamburg, Germany, Horney obtained a medical degree at Berlin and in 1913 began to practice medicine. By 1930 she had achieved prominence in the field of psychotherapy, and two years later she moved to Chicago as assistant director of the Institute for Psychoanalysis. In 1934 she joined the faculties of the New School for Social Research and the New York Medical College, teaching and working as a practicing analyst. She helped to establish the American Institute for Psycho-analysis. Horney's writings stress the importance of environment and social factors in establishing personality, marking a break with traditional Freudian views.

David Hume (1711-1776) Born in Edinburgh, Hume studied law at the prodding of his mother. Although he acquired an aversion for law, he sought to abide by his family's wishes and entered business. When that failed, he began a program of independent study and during his mid-twenties he wrote the *Treatise on Human Nature,* a seminal work that was largely ignored or ridiculed in his day. In 1752 Hume became a librarian at the University of Edinburgh and turned to historical writings which earned him a measure of success. He spent some years in Paris as Secretary to the British Embassy.

After returning to Edinburgh, he continued writing until his death from cancer. Hume's philosophical writings exercised a profound influence on subsequent thought in many areas.

Immanuel Kant (1724-1804) Raised in Königsberg in a religious family setting, Kant spent virtually all his life in his native city. After graduating from high school with honors, he studied philosophy, science, and math at the University of Königsberg. For several years he tutored the children of a number of families. After earning a master's degree in 1755, he took a position at the university as a lecturer in a variety of subjects in the natural sciences, philosophy, theology, geography, and anthropology. In 1770 he was finally appointed Professor of Logic and Metaphysics, a post he remained at until 1797, when he retired due to ill health. Kant's personal life is reputed to have been methodical and uneventful—he did not travel, never married, and took no interest in music or painting. Nonetheless, he was well-read, witty, and an interesting teacher who greatly enjoyed good conversation. Kant's many works in philosophy rank him as one of the most influential thinkers ever.

Søren Kierkegaard (1813-1855) Kierkegaard was brought up in a strict religious family in Copenhagen. He began studying at the University of Copenhagen in 1830 and fell into a period of melancholy that he sought to resolve by entering the Lutheran ministry. During this time he became engaged to Regine Olsen. However, he was unable to go through with his marriage and he could not abide the ministry, which he viewed as far removed from a genuine Christian life. The rest of his life was spent writing a prodigious number of works that expressed his existentialism and his contempt for anything systematic or conventional, be it traditional religion or philosophy or living in conformity to a static essence. Kierkegaard composed his own epitaph, which said only, "That Individual."

John Locke (1632-1704) A native of Somerset, England, Locke was reared in a liberal Puritan family involved in the struggle against Charles I. He studied at Oxford, although he was unhappy with the traditional medieval philosophy there. After lecturing in Greek for a period, he became interested in medicine and took training in that discipline. For many years Locke served the Earl of Shaftesbury as doctor and tutor, acquiring from him an abiding interest in politics. In 1679, during the political turmoil in England, Locke was suspected because of his association with Shaftesbury, who was tried for treason and fled to Holland. Locke followed him to Holland and remained there among influential scholars, writing and involving himself in politics. Locke was able to return to England in 1689 after William of Orange, whom he had advised, came to power. His philosophical writing continued until his death, amidst visits from prominent figures such as Isaac Newton and Samuel Clark.

Herbert Marcuse (1898-) Marcuse was educated at the University of Berlin in his hometown and later at the University of Freiburg, where he received his Ph.D. in philosophy in 1922. The following year he joined the Institute of Social Research in Frankfurt and began to write. When the Nazi presence forced the Institute to close, Marcuse moved to Geneva, where he reestablished it. A year later, in 1934, he moved to New York City and opened the Institute again, this time at Columbia University. An expert on Russian affairs, he worked for the State Department for a period. In 1954 Marcuse became Professor of Politics and Philosophy at Brandeis University; later he held this post at the University of California. Influenced by Hegel, Freud, and Marx, Marcuse became one of the theoretical spokesmen of the New Left Movement in the 1960s despite his criticism of its anti-intellectual bias. His many writings and lectures seek to articulate the vision of an unrepressive society.

John Stuart Mill (1806-1873) Mill was born in London. His father was an official in the East India Company and a writer on political and economic subjects. Mill never received a formal education but was tutored by his father, who imposed a rigorous discipline on his son, beginning with the classics at age three and moving to math, science, and philosophy. In 1823 Mill joined his father in the East India Company and remained there for thirty-five years in various capacities. Meanwhile his friendship with Harriet Taylor, whom Mill considered a genius, was a source of great inspiration to him. They married in 1851. He was elected to Parliament as a Liberal in 1865 and served for three years. His prolific writings on philosophical, political, and economic subjects exerted a great influence in his own day and also after his death.

Ashley Montagu (1905-) A native of London, Montagu studied at the University of London between 1922 and 1925, where he specialized in physical anthropology. After graduation Montagu took a position at the British Museum, but the following year he left to attend Columbia University in the United States. During this period he also worked at the American Museum of Natural History. After a year at the University of Florence and a year at Wellcome Historical Museum in London he returned to America. He taught at various places and received his Ph.D. in anthropology in 1937. His writings during this period established him as an authority on race. After Montagu resigned his teaching position at Rutgers University in 1955, he continued to write, producing an enormous number of works on anthropological and humanistic subjects.

Friedrich Nietzsche (1844-1900) A native of Röcken, Prussia, Nietzsche came from a family of Lutheran ministers on both his mother's and his father's side. When he was still a small child, his father became mentally ill and died soon after. One year later his younger brother died, and so he was raised among women—his mother, sister, grandmother, and aunts. In 1864 he entered the University of Bonn to study theology but soon abandoned it. Nietzsche was named Professor of Classical Philology at the University of Basel in 1869, an unprecedented appointment, since he did not yet hold the doctorate. He suffered almost constant ill health and his great consolation was his writing, although he never knew of the profound influence his books were to exert. In 1879 he resigned from the university and spent the rest of his life largely alone, sinking into insanity.

Paul (c. 10–c. 64) A native of Tarsus in Cilicia, Paul was a Hebrew who appears to have been a Roman citizen by birth. At an early age he left Tarsus and devoted himself to the persecution of Christians, a role he pursued so vigorously that his reputation spread. By his own account Paul's conversion to Christianity occurred on a trip to Damascus when Christ appeared to him. From that point on he devoted himself as vigorously to spreading the gospel as he had to crushing it. He traveled extensively, spreading the Christian word wherever he went. In addition he wrote many letters to the faithful, several of which have survived. Tradition holds that Paul was martyred by beheading in Rome.

Plato (427-347 B.C.) Perhaps one of the greatest of the ancient philosophers, Plato has exerted a profound influence on the history of Western thought. As the son of noble Athenian parents, he was provided an excellent education. At the age of twenty Plato came under the influence of Socrates, with whom he studied for eight years. After Socrates' execution on charges of impiety and corrupting the youth, Plato left Athens and, as tradition has it, traveled widely for some twelve years in Greece, Italy, Egypt, and Asia Minor. When he returned to Athens, he founded the Academy, a school in which he taught philosophy and mathematics until his death. Many of his philosophical dialogues and some of his letters have survived.

Plutarch (c. 46-120) Born in Chaeronea, Plutarch was descended from an ancient family in that Boeotian town. As a young man he studied at the Academy in Athens. Under the tutorship of Ammonius he studied Plato, Aristotle, and the rich heritage of Greek thought. Employed at an early age to represent Chaeronea on public business, Plutarch traveled to Alexandria, parts of Asia Minor, and Rome. While in Rome he lectured, visited libraries, and met many persons of official and academic repute. He later founded a school of philosophy in Chaeronea and for about twenty years served as a priest at Delphi, a position which he found more appealing than the offers he is said to have received from the emperors Trajan and Hadrian. Plutarch was a prolific writer; his extant works include biographies of famous Greeks and Romans as well as works on various moral themes.

Jean Jacques Rousseau (1712-1778) Rousseau lost his mother shortly after his birth in Geneva. A less than stable childhood followed with almost no formal education. After an unhappy period of apprenticeship in Geneva, Rousseau left the city. Soon thereafter he won the favor of Mme. de Warens, who supported him for about ten years. For the most part his life was quite unstable, including aimless travel, various attempts to establish himself, and several illegitimate children whom he abandoned to orphanages. In the midst of it all Rousseau wrote a number of important pieces which exerted considerable influence; such figures as Kant, Goethe, Schiller, and Herder were greatly affected by his thoughts. As he grew older his paranoia increased, causing, among other things, an irrational dispute with Hume, who had invited Rousseau to England in 1766. He finally returned to Paris and died there eight years later. His writings include philosophical works, essays, and novels.

Bertrand Russell (1872-1970) A native of Wales, the grandson of a prime minister of England, Russell led an unhappy childhood. Both of his parents died when he was very young and he was raised by his grandmother. Russell confessed that he constantly thought of suicide during his adolescence but his love of mathematics dissuaded him from killing himself. In 1890 he entered Cambridge University and studied math and philosophy. He began lecturing there in 1910 but was dismissed in 1916 because of his pacifist views. For the next two decades he wrote and lectured. In 1938 he moved to the United States, where he returned to teaching but was hampered by his reputation for political activism. After his return to England he unsuccessfully ran for political office and was jailed twice in connection with his pacifist activities. The influence of Russell as a philosopher, writer, and activist has been extensive in this century.

Arthur Schopenhauer (1788-1860) Schopenhauer was born in Danzig. His mother was a novelist and his father, a wealthy businessman. He was urged to enter business, and remained in business for some years to comply with the wishes of his father (who committed suicide), but finding this sort of life repulsive, he eventually abandoned it. His anxiety-filled youth and morbid sensitivity were intensified by his antagonism toward his mother. At the Universities of Göttingen and Berlin he turned increasingly to philosophy. When he took a post at Berlin lecturing, he deliberately scheduled his classes when the popular Hegel was teaching, in order, he said, to oppose the "windbag." He failed as a teacher, however, and in 1831 he retired, settling in Frankfurt to continue writing. In the years before his death Schopenhauer's fame and influence as a writer had already begun to grow, especially through his essays.

Mary Wollstonecraft (1759-1797) One of six children, Wollstonecraft was born in London, the daughter of a tyrannical father and a weak mother. In 1783, together with her sister Eliza Bishop (who had fled her brutal husband) and Fanny Blood, she established a school, a successful venture that became a center for liberal and dissenting thinkers. After almost a year of absence from the school Wollstonecraft returned in 1786 to find it in financial trouble. After it closed, she began to write in earnest and in the same year had already begun to publish. She achieved considerable notoriety for her outspoken views. After a period in Paris and an ill-fated liaison, Wollstonecraft returned to London in 1795, eventually married William Godwin, and died of complications after the birth of a daughter. Her writings are many and varied, including works in moral and political philosophy, history, and fiction.

HISTORY OF
IDEAS ON WOMAN